Praise for
THE ELEGANT SELF

"McNamara's clear and ground-breaking book is a quintessential example of a view that is 'translucent.' ... This book reminds us that we all are, at our best and at our happiest, evolutionary processes; we are works in progress. McNamara will teach you how to surf the waves of your own evolution."

~ Arjuna Ardagh, author of *Better than Sex*
& *The Translucent Revolution*,
founder of Awakening Coaching

"Clear, lucid and powerful! *The Elegant Self* is a must-read if you are interested in the further reaches of development."

~ Ken Wilber, author of *The Integral Vision*

"Probing, insightful and compassionate, *The Elegant Self* is a life-changing opportunity."

~ Diane Musho Hamilton, co-founder of Two Arrows Zen

"Innovative and insightful!"

~ Andrew Cohen, author of *Evolutionary Enlightenment*,
founder of EnlightenNext

"Rob McNamara has written a clear, passionate, integrated and intelligent book about human thriving. Practical, elegant and brimming with life."

~ Mariana Caplan, PhD, author of *Eyes Wide Open*
& *Halfway Up the Mountain*

"In *The Elegant Self*, Rob McNamara shares a host of thoughtful original insights into the nature of personal growth into the higher stages of adult development... If you coach or teach development, or even if you simply want to get a better feel for your own growth into the higher stages, you'll find a treasure trove of rich practical insights and metaphors in this book."

~ Terry Patten, author of *Integral Life Practice*

"Rob McNamara has written an informative, practical and immensely helpful guide to the crucial path of adult development. If you're on an inner journey, if you're seeking an integrated approach to self-cultivation, or if you're just wondering what your own next steps might be, *The Elegant Self* should be part of your toolbox."

~ Sally Kempton, author of *Meditation for the Love of It*
& *Awakening Shakti*

"This is applied evolution made flesh, ready to be lived and practiced!"
~ Ali Akalin, writer, faculty for Core Integral

"Robert McNamara's *The Elegant Self* is an essential guide for anyone on a serious path of self and spiritual development. Both advanced practitioners and newcomers alike will benefit from the profound wisdom, unique insights, and gentle guidance of this manual for enacting an embodied life... My admiration and appreciation for this volume is unbounded, as it speaks directly to people at all waves of human development, hence to all age groups. Indeed, I shall be sharing this book widely amongst friends, colleagues and students."
~ Michael Schwartz, PhD
professor of the history and philosophy of art, Georgia Regents University,
executive director, Integral Art and Media Center at MetaIntegral

"If you are intrigued with developing yourself to the fullest, willing to dig deep into confusion and not knowing, and wondering how to face the existential conundrums advanced development poses, this book *The Elegant Self* is for you. You will find many novel and important distinctions to ponder regarding adult development towards greater benevolence and wisdom... I highly recommend this book to individuals who want to know what it is like to live as an elegant self in a complex world."
~ Susanne Cook-Greuter PhD, author of *Postautonomous Ego Development*

"Rob McNamara has done for human development what Steve Jobs did for personal computing. With his new book, *The Elegant Self*, Rob effectively democratizes the entry point into human potential and makes it accessible... McNamara offers us this update by hacking our conventional self and shows us how to live a truly unconventional and elegant life. Welcome to your Elegant Self, 2.0!"
~ Claudius von Schroder, student, biohacker & entrepreneur

"*The Elegant Self* provides a compelling guide for personal evolution. It is certain to enhance facilitators' confidence in their journey of development and to orient the support they give to people in their groups."
~ Rebecca Colwell, co-founder, Integral Facilitator

"This book wonderfully explores the next step in human development we are all invited to... into the realm of who we already are... touching the intimacy of being what is and needs to be explored... right now! Challenging, inviting and inspiring!"
~ Leon Gras, CEO Venwoude,
Integral Practice Community
& Retreat Center in the Netherlands

THE
ELEGANT
SELF

A Radical Approach to Personal Evolution for Greater Influence in Life

ROBERT LUNDIN MCNAMARA

Revised Edition

PERFORMANCE
INTEGRAL

All Rights Reserved
Copyright © 2012 Robert Lundin McNamara

Performance Integral Edition
Copyright © 2013

Revised Edition
Copyright © 2016

No part of this book may be reproduced or transmitted in any form or by any means, electronic or mechanical, including photocopying, recording, or by any other information storage and retrieval system, without permission in writing from the copyright owner.

Published by Performance Integral, Boulder, Colorado.
www.PerformanceIntegral.com
www.TheElegantSelf.com

REVISED EDITION

Printed responsibly with the following sustainability certifications:
Sustainable Forest Initiative® SFI®
Endorsement of Forest Certification™ PEFC™
Forest Stewardship Council® FSC®

2 4 6 8 10 9 7 5 3 1

COVER ART DESIGN
BY
ALEXANDRU   MUSAT
WWW.ALEXMUSAT.COM

EDITORS: ROBIN QUINN ◆ ROSHANA ARIEL

LIBRARY OF CONGRESS CATALOGING-IN-PUBLICATION DATA

McNamara, Robert L.   1977 -
   The Elegant Self, A Radical Approach to Personal Evolution for Greater Influence in Life / Robert McNamara

ISBN-10: 0988768909
ISBN-13: 978-0-9887689-0-1

   Includes Bibliographical References (hardcover)

   1. Adulthood—Psychological aspects. 2. Developmental Psychology. 3. Self.
   4. Cognitive Psychology. 5. I.Title.

Library of Congress Control Number: 2012923998

For Love.

CONTENTS

ACKNOWLEDGEMENTS

To begin, I want to thank the many extraordinary people I have been privileged to work with over the years. Thank you for the opportunity to learn from and to be grown by your sincere interests, passions and struggles in life. Your curiosity to look precisely into how your present mind and my mind are limited inspires me. Your willingness to grow together has been and continues to be one of the most fulfilling dimensions of my professional life. Thank you for teaching me, articulating what matters most to you and for sharing your paths forward in life with me. I am convinced it is in these heartfelt exchanges that we evolve culture together and that we develop ourselves into more mature and capable human beings. Above all else, please accept my gratitude for the many opportunities you have gifted me to share my passion for development with you. In many ways, these gestures of my heart serve me beyond words.

Since the publication of the first edition of *The Elegant Self* I have been fortunate enough to be apart of an absolutely extraordinary team at Ten Directions. Rebecca Colwell, thank you for creating this important organization and for graciously supporting both my work around elegant leadership and our important work around maturing more capable leaders in our world. Diane Hamilton, thank you for growing me in countless ways and guiding our team though your elegance in our Integral Facilitator professional trainings. Cindy Lou Golin, thank you for our writing dates and for your love, passion and brilliance as we co-create our work together. Lauren Tenney, thank you for your unparalleled brilliance and for the many ways you shape and grow me every time we collaborate. Pete Strom and Gabe Wilson, thank you kindly for our growing friendships, mentorship and the many ways you support the mission of my life and work. And, I thank you both for welcoming me into the missions driving your lives. These gifts are treasures for me.

My business partner at Delta Developmental, colleague and close friend Trevor Tierney deserves my heartfelt gratitude and love. Trevor has been instrumental in shaping me into a more elegant human being for years now and as I have been immersed in edits for the revised edition you now hold. Trevor, thank you for our shared mission, your steadfast commitment to serve the many people you touch and your ability to help me find the simplicity beyond complexity. Not only are you one of the world's finest athletes, but you are an exemplary human being. Thank you for the work we are getting to do together and for modeling what it means to be a man living from a strong and bold integrity. More importantly though, thank you for our friendship. It means the world to me.

Our mutual friend and colleague Stuart Lord also deserves my heartfelt gratitude. Stuart, thank you for modeling a radical kindness, work ethic and leadership that is truly inspiring and, as I make sense of you, elegant. Thank you for the myriad of ways you support, grow and mature me into a more capable man. You've changed my life in many ways and the humanity you reveal to me has inspired much of what readers find within these pages. Thank you!

I'd like to thank Robert MacNaughton and Jeff Salzman for their invaluable and instrumental contributions in creating The Integral Center. While the content of this book has been working me for many years, both professionally in my coaching practice and privately in my alone moments late at night, many of the perspectives, orientations and exercises you are about to learn were first offered in my course on Human Elegance hosted at this center in Boulder Colorado. I would like to extend my gratitude to their leadership and to the many members who first dove into this curriculum with me.

Ken Wilber has inspired me for decades and he continues to be a beacon for examining the higher reaches of human development. In my many late nights, full days and surprisingly early mornings of intensive writing, I explored and was explored by some of the higher reaches of my intelligence. In the face of sleep deprivation, immense insight and inspiration, my sore hips as I typed from my meditation cushion, and what felt like malnutrition from long hours without food, I could feel Ken, his gift for writing and his probing of the human spirit for greater elegance. Ken, thank you for the many gifts that you are and how you have supported and encouraged me over the years.

I was fortunate to have one of the world's most gifted and talented runners as my professor as I began graduate school many years ago. Diane Israel holds world records running up mountains, she was considered one of the top runners in the world as a professional athlete, and she apparently had been developing her mind, emotions and subjectivity with a similar vigor as much as she was polishing her ability to run. Diane has supported me in ways I cannot find words for. Year in and year out, as we have taught together, she has sculpted me into a greater human being for serving our beautiful world. Her presence, passion and authenticity have been a weekly gift to me over the past decade and this book points toward the domains of vitality and sincerity Diane exudes every time I see her. Diane, thank you for who you are and what you give to me, our students and our world.

My second semester in graduate school, I was fortunate to encounter what I now call an elegant human being. My interactions with Bruce Tift in the class room, both as a student and inviting him in as a guest lecturer in my courses, as well as my work with him in retreats are still working me to this day. He is the most elegant psychotherapist I have had the opportunity and privilege to see at work. His clarity, power and responsibility have been instrumental in shaping me and the book you now hold. Bruce, thank you for cultivating yourself into the instrument of service that you are.

This book principally rests upon the research conducted by Robert Kegan and Susanne Cook-Greuter. I would like to extend my heartfelt gratitude for their pioneering work in adult development. They continue to be foundations for how I understand the human being and they inform my driving passion to investigate mature adult capacities personally and professionally. Furthermore, I want to thank Susanne for graciously reviewing this manuscript, providing ways to both simplify and clarify its message, and for warmly welcoming me into deeper conversation about the core challenges at the heart of life, adulthood and development.

Alex Musat has generously wrapped this book in his beautiful art. It means the world to me to have my writing encased and graced by his illuminating artwork. Alex, thank you for taking the time to read this book as a means of discovering what art most appropriately accompanies it. Thank you for helping me refine the title and subtitle as I approached publication. It is always a pleasure to work with you and I fondly appreciate you by my side in so many ways as my writing leaves the privacy of my mind and enters into broader culture and world. Thank you from the bottom of my heart, Alex.

My dear friend and beloved Zen teacher Diane Hamilton is one of the most important diamonds in life that continues to shape and polish me. Diane, thank you for your daily commitment to grow me. I am honored to share life with you and I bow to the elegance you show me year in and year out. Writing on the higher reaches of human functioning has been richly supported by your broad, open embrace and embodiment of humanity. Thank you for the myriad of ways you have shaped this book and the service I am able to bring into the world. Your lively authentic exemplar of elegance is an ongoing resource as I study development, help others and allow life to refine and polish what I am able to do for our world. Diane, thank you with all that I am.

My Wife Brooke McNamara has lived with a human being part in this world and part within the world of writing and being re-written by a mysterious yet elegant intelligence that appears to be both me and, in many ways, not me. My love, thank you for your undying support to create that which matters most to my heart and for being a clear beacon leading me toward a larger participation with elegance. Thank you for you the mother, writer, dancer, artist and Zen monk that is living you. You have helped shape this book in countless ways. I could not do this without you. And thank you for the countless times you brought me food and for dragging me to bed in the middle of the night and early hours of morning when I desperately needed sleep. Thank you for our marriage, our family and the many ways you grow and mature me. This book has been richly supported and refined by you in a myriad of ways. Thank you my love!

I would like to warmly thank some of my early readers. Rochelle Fairfield, Deb McNamara and Emily Biever all contributed critical insight and feedback to improve the book you now hold. Rochelle without fail can point toward, and in most cases directly at, my blind spots encouraging a broader perspective and approach. Rochelle, thank you for your profound clarity and for the generous gift you offered to improve this book. My sister Deb took many of the exercises following each chapter and qualitatively improved them with a rigor that undoubtedly improves what readers can take away from this book. Deb, thank you for sharing your guiding brilliance yet again on our journey through life together. It means the world to me to have you support and hone my love, passion and gift to our world. Emily helped polish and clarify much of the foundation of this book. Emily, thank you for the feedback and for continually challenging me to write with more elegance, not just about elegance. David McCallum was immensely helpful bringing his expertise, mastery and understanding of adult development. David, thank you for your clear direction and clarifying questions; these have shaped final edits and left important marks upon how I am approaching future books. However, and more importantly, thank you for the love and companionship we share every time we are together. You are truly an elegant man. Michael Schwartz articulates an insight and understanding of mature adult development that is both shockingly beautiful and pragmatically focused upon cultural transformation. Michael graciously helped formulate some of the graphics to better help elucidate some of the core concepts in this book. Thank you for the myriad of ways you have all helped craft this book. I want to thank my friend Saniel Bonder who was instrumental in supporting this book and my work. Saniel, thank you for the encouragement and support in making this revised edition a reality.

Thank you to my editors Robin Quinn of Brainstorm Editorial in Los Angeles and Roshana Ariel, both who brought clarity and refinement to this book in countless ways. Their instruction, challenge and invitation to simplify my writing has been important for me, as I aspire to not only write about elegance but to write more elegantly. Robin and Roshana, thank you kindly for the encouragement and guidance. You may not know it, but you work on me every day I write.

Thank you to John Eggen who helped expedite this book into your hands. What once took me years to accomplish took me weeks. John, thank you for your immense gift. My heart has been nurtured profoundly by pouring all of myself into my writing as you and your team have supported me.

Finally, thank you to the many readers, most of whom I may never meet. This is for you and what we can do in our precious world together.

INTRODUCTION

This book is about the development of *you*. We are set to explore how you can accelerate your evolution and how the larger capacities within elegance can generate powerful change in yourself, your life and our world. You are embarking on a journey that is likely to fundamentally change you and what you are capable of.

Whether you are aware of it or not, mental development determines the underlying context of your life. It determines what you can dream of, how you are motivated, what you are capable of seeing and feeling and, thus, what you can achieve. Development sets fundamental limitations on how you communicate with others, and it powerfully shapes the concepts you hold about the world you live in. Your mental development sets the stage for how you understand (and misunderstand) yourself, and it is interwoven with how you create meaning. It defines how you can accept, embrace and embody contentment with yourself and establishes how you struggle with and deny facets of yourself. Put succinctly, mental development has a far-reaching governing influence on what you are capable of accomplishing in countless ways in every area of your life.

We are about to step into the territory of human functioning that Harvard's developmental psychologist Robert Kegan calls *the "honors track"* of our culture's curriculum.[1] This is the advanced curriculum adults need to master in order to thrive in today's world. To be an authority, an expert, and to shape the fabric of discourse in today's world requires a careful and rigorous study of the higher reaches of the adult mind. Kegan's research is only one of our orientations, as this text also explores and draws on research into the further reaches of developmental maturity. So we are embarking on a journey in the honors track of development and beyond. This beyond is rooted in two different domains. The first is grounded in rigorous adult developmental research. The second rests on the author's own personal experience and perspective, as well as his work with clients embarking on transformations in this domain of maturity.

The perspective and vantage point inherent in elegance, as we are to explore it, is rare. Research shows less than 1 percent of the adult population is stably accessing this honors track. Another 6 to 7 percent are in the process of transitioning from a conventional adult stage of development to this higher echelon of functioning. Approximately 35 percent of the adult population functions at a conventional stage of development.2 We will define these stages, and others, in depth as we get into the book, but for now we can generically orient to these three groups. The first group we find operating from a conventional adult stage of development. Next is a group where adults are transitioning from conventional to postconventional stages. Finally, we have the adults who have stabilized the honors curriculum or postconventional stage and perhaps are exploring even higher, more refined forms of human functioning, what we will be calling postautonomous development.

This book is designed to serve and engage all three groups. Let's first look at what the top two might get out of it. Individuals in the top 1 percent of functioning will likely begin to see novel ways of refining their ongoing maturation process. They can also discover ways to clean up or fine-tune areas where they slide back into less functional behavior, thought, feeling and relating. Individuals in the process of bridging from conventional stages into the honors track and beyond can expect to enjoy an accelerated boost to their growth process that is already under way. This will be a useful road map of the often confusing transformation that is in process.

Finally, those who are stably functioning from a conventional stage have the most to gain. This book is likely to be a dramatic stimulus for accelerated evolution. The book you now hold is going to support and challenge you in significant ways. Dramatic change may be closer than you realize. Pay close attention. There are many approaches to change and growth out there. The vast majority are rooted in helping people get to a conventional adult stage of functioning and/or expanding this level into new spheres of functioning. While these can provide immense support growing out of what we may call the adolescent mind, or the early adult mind, they do not provide guidance in the territory where we are headed. It is fairly safe to assume only a small percentage of books, coaching and programs focused on development are aimed to explore the territory ahead of us. The vast majority are focused on establishing and reinforcing conventional functioning, which, in many cases, can inhibit your further development. As such, you are likely to find divergent recommendations when you contrast this book with other advice, perspectives and guidance. As you assess your life, the people, and the various programs supporting you an important question worth holding asks: *What stages of development are the supports and challenges I am receiving aimed at?* This book will guide you in refining your discernment in answering precisely this question.

WHY ELEGANCE?

As we are headed directly into a close study of some of the highest known expressions of adult maturity, you may be asking, *"Why?"* The reason is actually quite simple. Our human elegance is becoming a necessity. Each day, our larger developmental capacities become less a luxury that is nice to have and more a basic necessity. Elegance is not just a stage of functioning making you dramatically more efficient, capable, happy and fulfilled. You, the people your heart genuinely loves, and our world legitimately require more human elegance.

Many of us live in a post-modern informational techno-economic system that yields tremendous industrial and military power on a global scale. There are now more than 7 billion precious and unique human beings living on or around Earth's seven continents.[3] Much of the world's economy suffers from a global financial crisis closely interconnected to the financial problems in the United States and the eurozone.[4] Climate change continues to be a major issue.[5,6] Core questions around sustainable relationships between human beings and the environment stand to be adequately answered. Clean sustainable energy is a major global issue, especially for economic growth in impoverished countries.[7] At the time of this writing, approximately 21,000 children died around the world today.[8] Why? Poverty and other preventable causes explain most of the deaths. Sexism, racism, classism, sociocentrism and ethnocentrism fuel violence, exploitation, wars and terrorism across our planet. Addiction continues to kill unknown numbers of human beings each year. Tobacco use is the leading cause of preventable death with most deaths occurring in low- and middle-income countries. If current trends persist, tobacco will account for 8 million deaths annually by 2030.[9] Today, human beings still buy and sell other humans on our planet. Slavery is not just surviving in small pockets. As of 2010, there were more slaves than in any other point in recorded history.[10] The International Labor Office estimates nearly 21 million human beings are treated and exchanged as slaves in various forms of forced labor.[11]

As we tour the global issues that challenge our human community, as well as life as a whole on Earth, it appears that something novel is required. The conventional stages of adult maturity have pioneered significant advances in economics, medicine and human rights, to name just a few. Yet there is also a pervasive failure to adequately respond to the complexity and demands of our current global condition. Some may even suggest that it is precisely the conventional stages of adult development (and its even less complex adolescence and earlier stages) that have given rise to many of the major problems facing today's world. To understand, cope and skillfully respond to life's complex demands, a qualitative leap forward into the upper echelon of adult development seems to be a growing necessity.

Continue to tour the global challenges facing humanity today. Hold them and explore these issues as an astronaut may as she circles our beautiful blue orb floating in dark open space. Next, tour your own personal life unfolding in your small section of the planet. You are likely to see a life and world in which your greater, more mature, developmental capacities are required. Perhaps you need greater social awareness, a more robust wellness initiative to refine you and your family's health and well-being. Maybe you need a new techno-economic means to support yourself, and/or you require a novel approach to intimacy and contact while also respecting and preserving your need for personal autonomy and solitude. Perhaps, in some cases, these adaptations, among many others, are desperately needed.

So, ultimately, why are we focusing on elegance?

As human beings, we need to develop and evolve. There is a powerful and adaptive force moving toward the survival and further evolution of life. The more we participate with the unfolding of evolution, the greater our chances are of surviving and improving the condition of life on planet Earth. The more elegant you are, the more elegant we are together, the greater the likelihood of our survival.

We are all in this together. This is why.

So, just as you had some growing up to do in adolescence, we all have some growing up to do in adulthood as well. As it turns out, adulthood is not just one stage, as many wrongly assume. Instead, adulthood involves a series of transformations increasing our complexity, capacity and worldview. Each transformation brings novel sets of expectations, possibilities to live into, and expanded ways of functioning. You need it. Your family needs your elegance. The people you work with need it. And our world most desperately needs your elegance.

HOW TO READ THIS BOOK

This book is a focused reshaping of the very structure of the way you think, create meaning, make decisions, and engage and function in every facet of your life. The book you now hold will have its greatest impact upon you the more dedicated focus you give to it. You are encouraged to read this book, by itself, from cover to cover. If you are studying other personal growth literature, you are encouraged to do one of two things:

1. Set aside these other books and make a commitment to resume them *after* you have completed this book.

2. Finish reading the book or books you find absolutely essential to your life right now. Then begin this book, by itself.

The degree of focus you bring to this book determines the depth in which you can learn, absorb and ultimately grow. Clearing competing messages you are reading is an important first step. Most books focusing on personal development do not pick up the honors track curriculum, thus they will likely have divergent agendas. Ultimately the greater your focus, the greater the return you can yield from this book. So protect the focus you are bringing to your emergent elegance.

Next, commit to reading this book daily. Metabolizing parts of this book every day increases its ability to initiate changes inside of you. You may want to think of this book as a high-grade fuel that helps you function from a gear that has greater power, efficiency and fluidity than how you may typically function. Regular consumption yields greater adaptation when compared to picking up this book a few times a week, or worse, a few times per month.

For best results, *do not* skim or speed-read. Skimming and speed-reading are essential for quickly gaining information. This book provides a wealth of information, but this is not the essential purpose of the book you now hold. The purpose of this text is to reshape and restructure how you relate to all information and experience. Skimming and speed-reading will offer certain data points from this book but the existing structure of your mind holding this information is likely to remain unchanged. This misses the entire point of the book in your hands, as well as your elegance as a human being.

Instead, slow down and take your time. Re-read parts that are challenging and stretching you in new ways. Pause when needed. Actually stop reading when you are in the process of restructuring the way you make sense of yourself and your experience. Stop mid-sentence and turn toward what is restructuring within. Use the journal sections following each chapter to capture key insights for later reflection and integration. Once this organizational shift has settled, return back to the beginning of the paragraph in which you stopped and continue reading.

Readers are recommended to make a commitment to read two chapters each week. You will complete the book in just under six weeks. If you are more driven and have more time for reading, reflection and integrating your study of elegance, commit to reading three chapters each week. You will finish this book in just under a month if you choose this option. Regardless of which option you choose, I want to emphasize again slowing down and pausing. This allows for greater integration as your mind acclimatizes to new vantage points and more flexible ways of being.

Once you have finished this book, it can serve as a powerful reference guide. When you find yourself stuck in a less mature habit that is holding you back, revisiting specific chapters and their exercises (along with your notes) is likely to become a powerful tool. When needed, revisit sections of this text to shift, augment and open up your larger perspectives and capacities.

Finally, enjoy yourself. Development is a challenging process that almost always involves pain, dissonance and anxiety. Yet development also expands you. You grow into a larger space with greater freedom, more diversity of choice, and a greater fullness and richness of experience. This basic expansion of you becoming more is also immensely pleasurable. So enjoy!

Welcome, dear friend, to the part of you that unknowingly always leans toward an unknown mystery. Welcome to a gentle, curious, open leaning toward being and becoming more.

THE ELEGANCE TRILOGY

Finally, I want to situate this book amidst a broader conversation around intimacy and relationships, as well as leadership and your professional development. As the concept of elegance was shaping my thought and writing, it held what George Vaillant, MD, Harvard University's Director of Research for the Department of Psychiatry, refers to as the three major tasks of adulthood: identity, intimacy and generativity.[12] Elegance has important features to contribute to how you come to know yourself, how you cultivate and function in relationship, as well as how you function personally and professionally in giving back to the world. This book takes a deep dive on what we can call your *identity development*. The central focus of this book is to *reshape you*.

You can also expect this book to impact intimacy, relationships and your professional development. While we take brief tours of how elegance can influence your intimacy and leadership abilities, I have saved more exhaustive exploration of these topics for two subsequent books. The elegance trilogy thus lays out a robust exploration of the major demands placed upon adulthood investigated from more complex developmental vantage points.

1

THE DANGER OF THE ADULT PLATEAU

Distortions from adulthood that cost you
and everyone around you

Most adults have an intuitive understanding of the development of the mind when it comes to relating to babies, children and adolescents. We understand that there are about two decades of physical growth until you become, at least from a biological standpoint, an adult. We see children getting physically bigger throughout childhood and, as they do, we also notice different phases of life. New ways of communicating, playing and relating mark transitions and memories that we often recall from our own distant past. Yet, once adulthood arrives, many presume that the development of the mind ceases. It is as if once you are done growing physically you are also done growing psychologically.

The mind can be thought of as the embodied and relational faculty that regulates the flow of energy and information.[13] As an infant, we can think of the mind as being quite small. The brain is relatively undeveloped. Important neurological connections have yet to be established. Neurons themselves are still in formation. As infants we are therefore largely unable to regulate much energy on our own, and the infant's mind is also quite limited in terms of the types of information it can process. As such, an attuned mother, father and/or caregiver is required most of the time. As the baby grows, the mind expands. The brain matures and becomes more connected and efficient. With this growth comes the ability to manage new forms of energy and information. Where the infant once could not discern separate objects in the world, now the infant can actively seek that toy you are holding in front of her. By exercising her will she can grasp hold of the toy she is attracted to, and let go of it when she is done. If we look with greater curiosity at our growing baby and start to watch children and adolescents in new ways, we can see with more nuance that the mind's ability to manage and regulate more energy and information is undergoing significant changes.

The presumption that the adult mind does not also continue to grow, expand and increase in its ability to hold and manage complexity throughout adulthood is the adult plateau. The belief that adulthood is a single playing field where all adults, more or less, share the same capabilities in regulating energy and information flow is a major distortion that has far-reaching consequences. Before diving into our investigation of development, a useful starting point is to explore some of the dangers inherent in our world when adults do not see, understand and consider adult development more explicitly. What follows is not an exhaustive exploration of this problem. Instead, you find a brief survey of just a few of the major problems you are likely facing today and have been for much of your adult life.

THE DISTORTION OF MORE

As you will learn in detail, the development of your mind involves you being and becoming more. These are two of the major thrusts of evolution that show up and are reflected in the mind's growth. Who you are expands such that you are more than who you once were. Development brings with it a larger mind that is more capable, powerful and integrative.

The innate drive to grow gets distorted when adults fail to recognize how their own mind and other adult minds are in a developmental process and how their ongoing development is an essential facet of their overall well-being. This is because adult development is participatory in nature. It is not like the development found in the infant or child, where development unfolds largely without much conscious attention on or explicit understanding of development. Adult development progressively shifts toward you participating more consciously with the growth of your mind. So when you fail to actively participate, costly distortions become common features.

The first distortion misguides the internal drive to become more in an outward fashion. The self now takes up projects of having more in the external world. This focus on possessing more externally acts as a substitute. The danger is found in the preoccupation with having more externally—more money, a flashy car, a newer larger home, more distinctive clothes, more profitable investments, more influential and/or attractive partners and so on. There is nothing inherently wrong with valuing and striving for any of these external achievements. However, when the immensely powerful and unrelenting drive to grow your mind is channeled into external acquisitions, an imbalance and misdirected deployment of resources is often created. When the internal drive for more turns outward, you can never possess enough to satisfy the immense inner drive to become more. This preoccupation often forms into unexamined automated patterns where you get more, which fuels an even greater desire to have more. Ultimately, external possessions can not substitute and genuinely stand in as replacement for the mind's inherent gradient toward being and becoming more. This often unseen distortion costs many their happiness.

A second distortion is a substitution of psychological power with social power. As you will see in the next chapter, the development of the mind brings with it greater psychological power. The increasing scope of freedom, choice and thus capacity to exert power internally is something virtually every adult, knowingly or unknowingly, needs and desires.

When the adult mind fails to cultivate his or her own internal development, a compensation is often made. This is when the drive for more psychological power over one's inner life gets subverted into the drive to obtain, possess and retain various forms of social and relational power. Similarly to the drive for having more, there is nothing inherently wrong with social and relational power. However, when adults are using social power and control to attempt to compensate for missing power over their inner life, we find a potent recipe for the irresponsible use of power and the exploitation of relationship. Instead of a responsible and judicious use of power, we often find people manipulating and exploiting as a function of regulating their own internal preferences, needs and desires. Chances are you have lived in the wake of these misguided attempts for power and control as well as fallen prey to exploiting power unskillfully as a means of compensating for a constrained capacity to regulate your own energy and information flow.

If you have been living inside of this adult plateau, or happen to be surrounded by adults who are, you have likely felt the consequences of both of these forms of distortion. An intentional, ongoing focus on your own development of mind is a powerful remedy and necessity for your overall well-being.

THE LEARNING DISTORTION

Within the adult plateau, development and learning are commonly used as synonyms. Learning more information is equivalent to developing yourself. This is a massive confusion. Learning more information is not the same as development. Learning is a wonderful way to enrich, change and progress in your life; however, if you are trying to learn your way out of limitations inherent in a stage of development, you are likely setting yourself up to waste a lot of time, money and effort.

Learning does not necessarily grow the mind. Often, learning fills your current level of mental capacity with more information. Development grows the mind so that new kinds of information can be retained, not just more information. Additionally, development refines your ability to monitor and modify the flow of energy. One of the reasons I wrote Strength To Awaken was, in part, because many books on fitness simply give you information. More information about how to train is not needed for the vast majority of people who are struggling with their fitness goals. Instead of only providing more information, many require a new mental capacity that can manage and modify the flow of information and energy so that they are actually capable of consistently deploying effective strategies in their lives. Until this added mental capacity is achieved, more information will not likely initiate immediate or lasting changes in well-being. If we look into dieting, nutrition, weight management and various forms of professional development, leadership and management trainings, we find similar patterns. People are sharing information and not necessarily growing the capacity and complexity of the mind. Sadly, untold millions of dollars of trainings, seminars, books, retreats, coaching and so on simply teach more information because they are rooted in the adult plateau mindset: Give them more technical information and this will solve the problem.

Learning is essential and important, and adults in virtually every field need to be more nuanced in their understanding of what level of mind they are teaching to in students. Additionally they can augment and build programs and products that are vastly more effective if they take developmental considerations into their planning. A larger market can be accessed and more pragmatic results can likely be obtained if they provide effective information as well as proficient strategies to support and challenge the developmental processes of the mind. So learning will not initiate the changes you likely need in your life. Learning and genuinely adaptive changes to the capacity of your mind will.

THE EXPERIENCE DISTORTION

In the professional world, experience is often treated as king. When you are in an interview, there is often a gravity placed on how much experience you have. Do you have 18 months of experience or do you have two decades? If the company has the economic resources to pay for two decades, they are likely to do so. To be clear, experience is indeed an important feature, yet it is not nearly as fundamental as the level of development your mind will be bringing to work every day. Experience means you know how to do certain things, presumably efficiently and well. Yet, in the face of complex changes in demands, markets, cultural politics within the office and so on, we find a need for more complex minds, not just minds with years of assumptions about how things should or can be done.

Experience was adequate in the modern economic climate when markets and production lines were more predictable. The adult plateau was less of a problem 50 to 70 years ago. In today's post-modern, techno-informational economy, development is a massive blind spot costing human resource departments untold amounts of resources. Companies that are largely inside the adult plateau are likely bleeding billions of dollars each year as they try to get experience to yield something that only a qualitatively more complex mind can provide. The mission of any human resource department in a company looking to be the top in its market should read: Hiring for mental complexity.

We hold ourselves back when we as a human culture value experience without consideration of developmental complexity. Our human commerce and community require larger, more flexible, dynamic, complex and capable minds. Development, as you will soon see, likely plays an important role in improving creativity and innovation. Measures of critical thinking often grow as development increases. Mental flexibility, attunement to self and others, leadership performance and other important measures are all likely positively impacted by development. Even psychological well-being may be positively impacted by development.

Failure to understand and participate with adult development is a costly mistake that shows up in challenges in marriage, parenting, employment, education, leadership and the responsible use of material and techno-economic resources. These distortions and dangers are, in many cases, functioning on a global scale.

EXERCISES TO UNCOVER YOUR DISTORTIONS

The following series of questions is designed to help you identify where you may be suffering from the costly distortions identified above. Carefully reflect on these inquiries and capture your insights for future reflection.

The Distortion of More

Are you attempting to acquire more as a substitute for being and becoming more internally? If so, how? Consider your consumption habits. Do you buy what you fundamentally need or do you find yourself often looking to get more?

_____
_____
_____
_____
_____
_____
_____
_____

How might you be exploiting relational and/or political power as a means to regulate your own experience? When might you pressure others to change in order to alleviate and/or regulate yourself?

Relational power if either of two.
on occasion...
Judgy/Critical →→ go on the
Offensive to prove my point or
point out flaws in others approach
(eg silo'd thinking; reactive vs
creative solutions...)

↳ detach from destination
                    outcome
                    expectation

A cynic is just an idealist who's
dreams have been squashed.

Me rubbing up against the system

_____

_____

_____

_____

_____

_____

_____

_____

_____

_____

_____

_____

_____

_____

_____

_____

_____

_____

_____

_____

_____

_____

_____

_____

_____

_____

_____

_____

_____

_____

_____

_____

Do you find yourself yearning for more effective and mature strategies to get what you want in life? How so? What glimpses do you see about how you want to live and spend your time?

_____

_____

_____

_____

_____

_____

_____

_____

_____

_____

The Learning Distortion

What persistent problems are you trying to learn your way out of?

_____

_____

_____

_____

_____

_____

_____

_____

_____

_____

_____

_____

_____

_____

_____

_____

_____

How are you trying to get more information into the same mind?

_____

_____

_____

_____

_____

_____

_____

_____

_____

_____

_____

_____

_____

_____

_____

_____

How are you working to transform your mind as a whole so that new kinds of information can be held, considered and acted on?

The Experience Distortion

Do you reference how you have done similar tasks in the past when looking at a new project? How often? Why? While experience of course serves you, how can you bring a fresh perspective to each new task, less biased by past experiences?

invitation to start with a beginner
mindset

_____
_____
_____
_____
_____
_____
_____
_____
_____
_____
_____
_____
_____
_____
_____
_____
_____

Think of a time when a novel approach solved a problem at work or home. What were some of the qualities present? How can you imagine yourself embodying these qualities? How might these creative solutions involve less time and fewer resources yet yield greater returns?

"Go for it" - Opportunity ... then anxiety
Let go of need to get it right from
outset ... curiosity, collaboration,
creativity ... design, test, iterate.

Down regulate 'self' image; focus on
'other' ... trust in preparation, the
process + power of the group.

Given persistent demands in your life and/or business, how can you change and be changed by novel approaches to commonly recurring problems?

Rigory

For an eight minute related audio clip and to learn more about fortifying yourself from these distortions, and others, visit:

www.TheElegantSelf.com/Distortions

Personal Notes & Reflection

2
MENTAL DEVELOPMENT
I can see with a different lens

Evolving Maturity for Performance

Development is the underlying process through which you transcend previous limitations, create novelty, expand your faculties and generate greater integrative capacities.[14] When you develop, you become *psychologically larger*. There is more room inside of you. There is more space to take different perspectives. Development enables larger considerations which ultimately leads to new behaviors in your life. Transcending limitations means this new larger you can actually hold, relate to and manage the previous you. This is a process that psychologist and philosopher Jean Piaget, perhaps the most famous figure in Developmental Psychology, calls *decentration* and developmental psychologist Robert Kegan renames as *recentration*.[15] As a new self and a new orientation are discovered and inhabited, new choices are created. A greater diversity of possibilities emerge. This larger size of the psychological makeup and broader inclusion bring an increase in complexity. There is more psychological space in which to develop. With this expanded space comes more freedom and a greater possibility for inclusion. As you will see, development creates greater facilities that ultimately can support novel functioning and performance in your life.

For example, when you were in your first year of life, you were largely an impulsive being. When you had to pee, you just peed. You were limited by the impulse's urgency. When the pee impulse arose, you peed whether you were wearing a diaper or not. Fast-forward 12 to 18 months and you have likely undergone a developmental leap forward. While the old you simply acted out impulses, the new you controlled impulses. We could say that the earlier you *was* your impulses. Now you *have* your impulses. You transcended your previous limitations and, in the process, something new was created—in this case, the choice of when to pee, where to pee, how you want to pee and so on. You could still choose to pee in your diaper, but you could also choose to "make bubbles" in the toilet as my nephew now says. You have integrated the impulse to pee and now can manage, regulate and control your peeing. Again, this is a developmental move from *being* impulsive to *having* your impulses. In the process of taking this leap forward, you become psychologically bigger, more capable and more mature.

Becoming psychologically bigger is not always better, though. While a bigger self always brings greater capacities with which to function and perform in life, how these are used is a separate inquiry into what supports and/or detracts from goodness. To continue with our pee example, you could use your newly gained psychological size to save some diapers and act like a big girl or big boy. We might say this is a good thing. But these larger capacities can also be used for less noble drives. Perhaps at some point you were frustrated. So you might have used your newly gained ability to control your pee impulses and decided to pee on a younger sibling. Maybe you decided to pee on your mother's favorite photo album or on the wall next to your bedroom. A larger mind has more resources, but how these added capacities are used is again a separate inquiry.

So while development is always a movement toward larger capacities, we can not necessarily equate it with progress. This is an important distinction we will return to as it is of central importance in our exploration of *human elegance*. Elegance is both a function of refined adult developmental maturity and the responsible deployment of our larger resources as a human being. Our ultimate aim is to both stimulate greater adult developmental complexity and responsibly employ our larger, more flexible and dynamic ways of functioning in the world to serve greater truth, goodness and beauty. We must aspire and participate with these two facets together or elegance will elude us. And even more importantly, we cannot use higher developmental capacities to serve lesser responsible motives when we do work with both facets.

Prerequisites for Elegance

1. Refined Levels of Adult Development

2. Responsible Deployment of Capacities

As an example, we can turn our attention to the United States during its sub-prime housing market boom. The American psyche was (and perhaps, in many ways, still is) presumably infatuated with having bigger homes. Similar to a toddler wanting a bigger truck instead of the smaller one, many Americans wanted a bigger house as opposed to a smaller one. Why? Because bigger is often equated with better. *Quantitative judgment* is what governs the action logic or decision-making in toddlerhood. If an adult does not fully grow out of this stage of development, he or she will, at least from time to time, make decisions from these less complex levels of functioning.

A four- or five-year-old is fairly harmless making decisions around bigger and more-is-better reasoning. However, an adult holding nuanced long-term planning skills, access to global resources for manufacturing, and belonging to a corporate culture of sociocentric entitlement is a much different consideration. Let's say, one adult is financing a home for another who can not realistically afford it. Yet both are, at least in this moment in our example, reasoning with "bigger is better" logic. This is a massive problem. One wants to loan a larger sum to presumably generate more revenue, while the other wants a bigger home because, for similar reasons, bigger or more square footage is better. Multiply this over billions of dollars and millions of people, and suddenly a global financial crisis is in the making.

Obviously the sub-prime housing market in the United States is vastly more complex than our example above. However, you can see some of the problems inherent in higher capacities serving less mature reasoning. Bigger-is-better logic should never have access to global manufacturing infrastructure, processes and technologies. It is fairly obvious what is going to happen. Most of the world's resources will end up in a small portion of our human family's hands. And like our young toddler who will likely want a bigger toy truck as soon as he sees one, they will be presumably unhappy or frustrated with their home that is lacking in some way compared to what they have seen through the media, friend, boss or co-worker.

In another example, we do not want nuclear weapons—a product of refined mathematical, scientific and mechanical development—getting into the hands of terrorists whose actions stem from a simplistic "kill those who are different from me" reasoning. Having developmental capacities hijacked by earlier, less complex, motives almost always leads to problems and in many cases disasters. So as we explore human elegance together, it is essential that you closely watch and monitor your less evolved motives as we unlock and investigate your higher developmental capacities.

THE ARCHITECTURE OF DEVELOPMENT

Robert Kegan is the William and Miriam Meehan Professor in Adult Learning and Professional Development at Harvard University and the Educational Chair for the Institute for Management and Leadership in Education. In the field of Adult Developmental Psychology, Kegan is one of the leading contemporary voices of our day. His developmental model is one of the most brilliant, insightful and clear. Additionally, his model is supported by an impressive body of research spanning decades of data with solid cross-cultural validity.[16] As such, Kegan's model is the backbone of our exploration of developmental functioning.

Subject-Object Theory

Kegan's developmental model rests on his *Subject-Object Theory*, which proposes that each developmental stage is a balance between who is subject and what objects can be possessed.[17] In his masterpiece, *In Over Our Heads*, Kegan goes on to define what is subject and what is object. *Objects* are elements of our knowing or organizing of experience that we can reflect on, handle, look at, be responsible for, relate to, take control of, internalize and/or otherwise operate on. Recall our example of the toddler who gains the ability to control his or her pee. The impulse to pee is what becomes object once our toddler can take control of his or her bladder. He or she can now be responsible for and make decisions about when and where to pee.

Another example can be seen in the newly promoted manager who is now entrusted with greater responsibilities. Amongst many new tasks she is now responsible for leading and managing her team, not just belonging to the team. To be successful at this next level she will need to be able to have her professional interpersonal relationships as an object she reflects upon and manages within herself. She has to be able to operate on the loyalties she feels with a close co-worker. She is better prepared to lead if she can reflect on the mutualities she shares with the people she used to be peers with. She can handle these interpersonal relationships and their influences on her decision making. As a result, she is better able to leverage and operate on her professional relationships to achieve outcomes that serve a larger purpose beyond her team and their interpersonal relationships. The key point is that development defines what objects we are capable of holding and being responsible for.

That which are *subject* are elements of our knowing or organizing of experience that we are identified with, fused with, tied to or embedded in. Before our toddler is potty trained, he or she is subject to his or her impulses. In this case, he or she is subject to the impulse to pee. If our young manager could not hold her interpersonal relationships as object, then we might find her being subject to her interpersonal relationships. As a result she could not see, reflect on or make decisions about her previous interpersonal loyalties. She would have no choice but to manage with the implicit and unchallenged agenda to preserve her existing loyalties. As a result, her closer colleagues will have unexamined influences over her decision making. What she will do, without even considering it, is take care of these interpersonal relationships. This can persist even in the face of major costs to the broader organization.

So we have objects and we literally are the subjective facets of our experience. Interestingly, we are unable to responsibly manage the subjective dimensions of who we are, No one can be in control of, reflect on, or handle that which is subject. Facets of experience that are truly subject are absolute and immediate while objects are relative and mediated.

When development occurs, the subject that was identified and fused with becomes a new object in awareness. In this way, the subject that once held you can now be mediated and managed as it is now an object inside your awareness. Returning back to our example of the impulse to pee one last time, first you were your impulse to pee. When the impulse arose, you peed regardless of what the situation was. We could say that the impulse to pee *had you* or that the subject that had you was impulsive. Next, through development, you gain these impulses as an object in your awareness. Now you can control, choose and regulate your impulse to pee in novel ways.

In development abilities and responsibilities increase and expand with each stage. Prior subjects become new objects in experience. A larger, more capable you is established. You exist inside of a new stage of development or what Kegan refers to a subject-object balance. These constellations of subjects and objects are the underlying architecture for how you, and what appears to be all humans, organize experience. The subject-object structure of your thought, feelings and the organization of how you relate socially are all governed by the developmental stage you are in.

When we look at human functioning through this lens, we are placing our attention on what kinds of objects someone can see and what facets fundamentally cannot be seen, at least not yet. It is a common yet grave mistake to look at the content of thought, feeling and/or social relating to attempt to determine development. For example, we cannot look at only the content of someone's values to assess their development. They may value personal power, conformity or universal equality. By itself, this content is inadequate to assess development. We must get *more* curious about ourselves and one another in order to better understand these underlying relationships between subject and object, what Kegan calls "the deep structure in meaning-evolution."[18]

For example, let's take two individuals who both value universal equality. At a surface level, we may presume that they are at the same developmental stage. When we probe in the subject-object architecture with greater nuance, which you are learning to do right now, we may discover how one of the individuals is reflecting the cultural beliefs of his family of origin in an unexamined way. The other individual, however, is elucidating a value system that she has created and authored for herself in response to her life experience. They have the same surface features, yet these two individuals are reflecting two different developmental stages. The first is held by values established by outside of himself, while the latter is creating a value that is based on her own inner authority.

Assessments of development become more accurate as we practice attending to the subject-object architecture of your own and others' self-organization. Through this book, you will learn to go beneath the content or surface features of thought, feelings and social relating into the defining structure of what is subject and what is object. It is here, in the subject-object balance, where you will gain more accurate and pragmatically focused insights. Get lost in categorizing people based on content and you will undermine your own insight, performance and skillful means in the world.

Developmental Constructivism

A second important feature of Kegan's model, and central to the developmental theories of Jean Piaget and cultural-historical psychologist Lev Vygotsky, is *Developmental Constructivism*. This theory proposes that human beings do not encounter a single world or reality with varying degrees of accuracy. People are not organisms that simply react to the environment as the behaviorists often maintain. Instead, Developmental Constructivism sets forth a position where human beings co-construct *many realities*. We form and establish many constellations of objects. We actively seek out a diversity of experiences and engage in an ongoing experimentation with ourselves and our environments. Furthermore, we construct an interpretation about what this all means. Human beings construct their meaning and this meaning, along with the reality as they hold it to be true, in their minds is developmentally constrained.[19] For example, children are constructing realities that are different from the realities we find in adult minds. Children are not so much inaccurately perceiving the adult world, as if there is but one adult view. Instead, children are constructing a different world, in response to a partially shared environment and their developmental level.

Experience is co-constructed by your developmental capacities, which are influencing your perception of the surrounding internal and external environmental stimuli. The developmental architecture of your subject-object balance determines what objects you can and cannot see. For example, we could ask an adolescent about his or her personal needs, interests and desires and expect a fairly accurate account because these are now, or at least they should be, objects in attention. However, we are not wise to ask our adolescent about his or her personally tailored ideology. This, at least for most adolescents, is not yet an object in attention, nor is it even apart of themselves they have discovered yet. They may very well need another decade or two of experience before they even begin to understand the question.

This subject-object structure of meaning-making, how you make sense of your reality, powerfully influences perception and how you interpret stimuli. The stimuli reaching your attention always stem from the physiological, psychological, social and cultural facets of experience. And, all of these forms of stimuli are being influenced by your present stage of development.

To summarize, you are always actively shaping, constructing and forming a reality that fits within your developmental capability at any given moment. And how you are presently co-constructing these very sentences right now is largely invisible to you until you developmentally outgrow your current subject and move it into an object. This is a feature of what Integral theorist and philosopher Ken Wilber calls the embedded unconscious.[20] You cannot see the activity and processes of your subject because you are fused to, identified with, and embedded in the activity of your meaning-making.

As you will see in detail, each developmental stage's subject actively co-creates a reality all unto its own. The implications of the developmental constructive view are immense. The more obvious implication is that each stage discloses a new strata of reality, where more objects, nuance and complexity become known as the human being develops. The less obvious implications can be found in the dramatic changes in the subject.

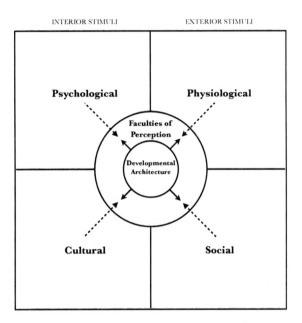

Daniel Siegel, clinical professor of psychiatry at the UCLA School of Medicine, identifies eight senses[21] that participate with the four domains of interior and exterior stimuli in the above diagram. (based on Integral philosopher Ken Wilber's 4 Quadrants[22]) The five senses (taste, touch, sound, sight and smell) largely participate with physiological and social external stimuli. The sixth and seventh senses leverage interoception (the sense of the physiological condition of the body) and mindsight (the sense of the functioning of the internal world) to sense the interior subjective psychological landscapes while the eighth sense provides an ability to sense relational and cultural stimuli.

Development changes *who you are*. When you stop identifying with impulses, the who that you become changes significantly. Changes in identity are just the beginning though. With development, *where you are* undergoes massive changes. You can be located in the same room of your house, yet when a developmental shift happens, you are inhabiting a

Aes Who, Where, What + How you are

different location. You are no longer located inside of your impulses. Instead, you stand somewhere else entirely, such that the impulses are now objects in your attention. So, while your physical location may not change, your interior or psychological location undergoes radical changes. Even *what you are* changes. The self that is impulsive is made up of a different interior substance than the self that is imperial in its insistence, reliance and allegiance to personal needs, desires and interests. As it turns out then, there is not just one type of human being. Human beings are made up of different interior substances based on their developmental complexity. Finally, *how you function* is shifted by development. Developmental Constructivism proposes the human being is actively co-constructing not only a reality "out there" but also a self or subject that qualitatively differs in identity, location, substance and function.

As you can see, if you are successful in leveraging this book to help yourself grow into your larger maturity, *everything in your life will change.* This is no exaggeration. The reality, or objects, that you constellate are going to be more distinct and nuanced. New objects appear. You naturally become more inclusive to the diversity of objects you create. How you function with these objects expands in flexibility and capability. The location of where you are within the immediacy of any moment expands. As you will see, you will discover more "roominess" or what we might call freedom. Even the substance of what you are is going to dramatically change in properties. As you grow, the substance of you becomes more expansive, creative, integrative and adaptive.

To highlight, development yields transformations in the following four domains:

1. **Identity**
2. **Location**
3. **Substance**
4. **Functionality**

All this leads to a simple pragmatism. Development makes you *more capable.* It brings forth your greater performance possibilities. You can become more functional. You can locate yourself into a larger space. The substance you are made up of, that which you are subjectively merged with, can expand to be much more integrative and liberated. Before we turn our attention to these larger capacities of your elegance, let's visit Kegan's most prominent adult stages of development.

Kegan's Stages of Development

Kegan's developmental model has five stages of development. The Three later stages are most relevant for the majority of adults. While some adults function from earlier, less complex stages, the vast majority of adults fall in or are transitioning between the third, fourth and fifth stages.

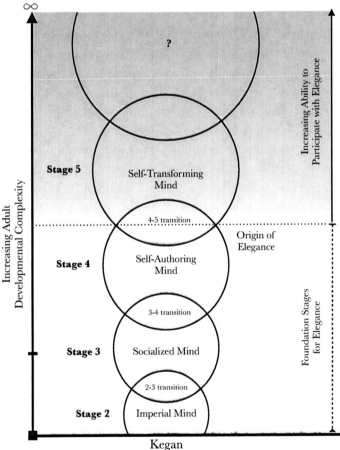

Kegan
Identity Development

The first two stages relevant for us to explore are Kegan's third stage or *the Socialized Mind* and the fourth stage *the Self-Authoring Mind*. Both are considered conventional stages of development. Research suggests that roughly 80 to 90 percent of the adult population falls in or between these two stages.[23] The highest stage in Kegan's model, *Self-Transforming Mind,* is a postconventional stage as referenced in the Introduction. Again, less than 1 percent of the adult population tests stably at this stage, while another 6 to 7 percent are transitioning out of the Self-Authoring Mind and in the Self-Transforming Mind stage.[24] In Chapter Three, we will take our first look at elegance in Kegan's highest stage of development. First, let's familiarize ourselves with where the vast majority of adults function from developmentally.

Socialized Mind

Development in the Socialized Mind stage begins as identity shifts out of a subject that is identified with personal needs, interests and desires to a self that identifies with interpersonal relationships and the cultural norms of the groups in which they are participating. When this stage emerges, your identity separates from being embedded inside of your personal needs, interests and desires. You are no longer stuck or entrenched in your own self-centrism. With this developmental distance, these needs, interests and desires can now be regulated, mediated and modified. In short you can make personal sacrifices so that a now larger identity and integrity can be nurtured. This larger identity is made by valued interpersonal relationships and mutuality. That is to say identity is now embedded in the social, interpersonal and cultural domains of relating.

To illustrate this transition, let's look at a common problem: infidelity in marriage. An individual operating in the stage preceding Socialized Mind may be asking him- or herself the following questions: "Can I get away with this without getting caught?" "What am I going to get out of this?" and "Can this person give me what I want?" As this person is asking these questions, they are reflecting his or her ultimate allegiance to his or her own sexual and/or emotional needs, interests and desires. This consideration is much different than the individual who is also contemplating infidelity yet is asking him- or herself, "How will this impact the trust and relationship with my spouse?" and "How is this relationship going to impact the person I might cheat with?" These questions reflect an identification with the relationships themselves, both the spouse and the person with whom they may begin to cheat. From the Socialized Mind stage, we may also find the question, "Can I get away with this?" but this is now only a part of the now larger consideration. With this development of the mind, getting caught is only one feature to consider. The larger, more significant inquiry circles around the damages this infidelity may inflict onto the relationships presently identified with. The individual in the Socialized Mind often experiences his or her own well-being and integrity as intrinsically connected to the well-being of his or her relationships. Furthermore, there is also likely to be a new loyalty to someone else who has interests, expectations and desires of which the Socialized Mind feels intimately a part.

As identity shifts from personal needs, interests and desires to mutual interpersonal relationships and the cultural expectations surrounding these relationships, the location of the self also changes. Instead of operating from inside of your own needs, interests and desires, you can now stand outside of these preferences and thus can see them as objects of your experience. What you now stand inside of a larger space of consideration that is inside of a socialized relational space. No longer is the world for or against just you. Instead, the world is now for or against us, most notably the relationships and culture the self identifies and participates with.

With changes in identity and location, we also find the substance of the self changing. Subjectively the self was made up of imperial domineering preferences. Now, in the Socialized Mind, the self can be thought of as being made up of relational loyalties. This socialized self is a constellation of loyalties to relationships and groups of all types. Because the self is held, organized and governed by its loyalties, individuals automatically defend and support these loyalties.

All these adaptations are a qualitative leap forward in how the self functions and performs. Perhaps the most pronounced is the subordination of self-interests on behalf of a loyalty to maintaining relational bonds, friendships, a group and/or team coherence and a broader cultural belongingness. As our exploration of infidelity demonstrated, the Socialized Mind is characterized by an orientation to the welfare of relationships, whereas earlier stages of development value relationships extrinsically or not as a basic part of self. When the mind grows to identify and merge with relational space, relationships become essentially valuable. Prior to this, relationship is only valued by how it can serve the imperially dominated orientation to the self's own needs, interests and desires.

With the subordination of self-interests to serve a larger relational context, operating from the Socialized Mind reflects a larger reliability on timing and commitments and an ability to hold up your own end of a relationship. At this stage of development, you can more easily get along with others, demonstrate respect, and are generally trustworthy as the activity of your subjectivity takes others into account beyond self-interest.

Individuals operating in the Socialized Mind Stage have a new landscape of objects to relate to, make meaning with, and begin to use to modify and mediate the unfolding of their life. Beyond seeing their own needs, interests and desires as objects that can be controlled and regulated, they are now able to see a complex internal psychological life in themselves and others. Enduring dispositions, ongoing needs, self-interests, a broad spectrum of preferences, abilities and inner motivations all emerge as objects to see, relate to and negotiate with. Additionally, internal emotional conflict is now an object that can be more readily acknowledged privately and shared within trusting and loyal relationships. These qualitative transformations of mind yield a more complex and capable human being than the earlier, smaller mind governed by the imperial, domineering self-interests, needs and desires.

And infidelity still happens in the Socialized Mind. This more mature stage is capable of qualitatively different capacities for empathy, relational connectedness and consideration, however this stage of functioning is still quite limited. One of the features making this stage confusing is that there are now presumably loyalties to both spouse and the possible new extra-marital relationship. And because the self is made up of these relational loyalties, and thus does not stand outside of them, physical and emotional proximity often determines which loyalty will be acted on in any one moment. To resolve this limitation, a qualitative growth of mind is needed.

Socialized Mind

1. **Identity:** Interpersonal relationships and the cultural norms of the group or groups participated with.
2. **Location:** Inside socialized relational space.
3. **Substance:** Relational loyalties.
4. **Functionality:** Subordination of self-interests to serve larger relational and cultural contexts.

Self-Authoring Mind

Stacey, a new client in her mid-twenties, explained to me in our first session that she was struggling with co-dependence in her intimate relationship. Her troubled blue eyes, tensed face and collapsed body language illustrated what she had learned from a handful of self-help books on relationships, as well as two therapists she had been working with over the past couple of years. Her dependency was perceived as a dysfunction. From her perspective, dependency was a pathology she wanted to get rid of. It was causing her great distress in her relationship as she could seemingly not find the ability to be herself around her partner. In particular, Stacey struggled to maintain her boundaries and take stands for what was ultimately important in her relationship. Thus she was not being treated the way she wanted and she was not creating the relationship her heart desired.

I waited for her to stop momentarily as she invited me into the world of her challenges. She paused, and I said something shocking to her: "Psychotherapy is likely not appropriate for you if this is the issue you want to work with." A puzzled look crossed Stacey's face. I continued to explain to her that this challenge was actually not pathological. "Quite the contrary, this is precisely the healthy struggle I would hope you would be having in your mid-twenties," I told her. "This is not reflective of something wrong; instead, this is happening in your relationships because things are going very well in terms of the growth of your mind." She looked at me with an inquisitive expression. I continued: "You are outgrowing a normal, healthy stage of development called the Socialized Mind and entering into a new, more adaptive and capable stage of adult development. Yes, we can look into the various emotional and psychological bumps and bruises in your biographical history, but none of that can get rid of the developmental unfolding you are in right now."

I recommended that we engage in performance coaching, instead of focusing on psychotherapy. The central thrust in her challenge was not pathological in nature. Instead, it was being able to perform and manage herself and her relationship in novel ways while in close proximity to her partner. Stacey's work ultimately required the *ongoing development of her mind*. So instead of focusing more on the reintegration and metabolization of unresolved experiences from her past, we focused on entirely new ways of orienting to herself and, as it turned out, many of her relationships, not just the one with her partner.

One of the major limitations of the Socialized Mind is where the authority resides. In this stage, authority is always located outside of the self. This is because the loyalties that make up the substance of the self are structuring, organizing and governing the self. Partners, parents, bosses, co-workers, siblings, cultural expectations, friends, other social circles or, as we touched on earlier, a seductive individual inviting infidelity all powerfully hold the authority "out there," and it is the Socialized Mind's job to conform and fit in.

While the Socialized Mind is a stable ground to operate in, it often fails to adequately address many of the complex demands of adult life. As Stacey was finding out, the healthy and appropriate relational co-dependence inherent in the Socialized Mind was not adequate to support her need to actually shape and direct a relationship that met her more genuine needs. As it turned out, Stacey was also in a graduate program where she felt challenged professionally around beginning to stand as an authority in her field and her area of expertise. No longer was it sufficient for her to point to other established figures in her field. Stacey had to now stand on her own two feet, so to speak. So, just as she was being challenged to take more judicious creative license professionally, her emerging larger mind was also demanding that she make this move in her intimate relationship as well.

The Self-Authoring Mind is the next stage of development in Kegan's model. It is precisely what Stacey was bridging or transitioning into, and she had good company. Research shows that anywhere between 32 to 47 percent of adults are bridging between the Socialized Mind and the Self-Authoring Mind.[25] Like many other adults, Stacey needed to move her unquestioned loyalties for her interpersonal relationships from subject to object. Here, she would be able to limit, regulate and manage her relationships and loyalties with greater nuance in connection to an authority residing inside of herself. In order for this to happen, though, she had to shift her identity and author herself from within. She needed to become the self that would sculpt her identity from the inside and cease to be the self that was reflected to her by the surrounding relational and cultural norms she participated in. Stacey's subjectivity needed to grow and expand so that she could become the mind's activity of authoring her own unique ideology, principles, and moral and philosophical orientations. She could then have, hold and manage her relational loyalties.

Stacey was in the process of outgrowing what psychologist and sex therapist David Schnarch calls the reflected self.[26] As Stacy began to self-author her identity from within her larger mind, she was be able to validate her own positions, thus creating a more solid, stable and flexible sense of self that was more internally regulated. This is as opposed to the other-validation and other-regulation found in the Socialized Mind stage.

As the identity grows out of the interpersonal mutuality in relationships, the Self-Authoring Mind subjectively fuses with the activity of authorship. Identity and ideology are generated from a larger subjectivity residing inside of the self. When this occurs, the self establishes a new location. No longer does the self reside inside of socialized relational space. Now the self steps into a larger interior sphere of consideration and capacity. Subjectivity is now located inside self-authorship, which can hold, consider and manage various interpersonal loyalties in new ways. This new location also brings forth a new substance. Instead of being made out of relational loyalties, the self is now made out of what we can call self-directing vision.

The capacity to become a larger, more liberated self who is able to envision, author, self-generate and create direction is an immense evolution of mind. Only about 34 to 35 percent of the adult population stably accesses this level of development.[27] This inner directed vision enables individuals to hold perspectives that dramatically reshape the functional capacities of the self. While our preceding stage of development was structured around the subordination of self-interests to serve a broader social, cultural and relational context, the Self-Authoring Mind stands as a powerful force reshaping social, cultural and relational contexts. Based on inner-driven guiding ideologies, uniquely authored expectations as well as creative intelligences (inherent to the self) can now effectively join with their intersubjective loyalties or take firm stands, as Stacey was learning to do.

The Self-Authoring mind is well-resourced for managing boundaries and setting limits in relationships. Instead of loyalties governing the self, the now larger self governs and manages the kinds of loyalties present and how they are leveraged. One way Stacey could grow was in her ability to choose between being more loyal to who her partner was or to be more loyal to the person he could become. The former provided support while the latter instilled challenge. With growth, Stacey would also be able to similarly give herself these different shades of support and challenge.

Stacey's emergent Self-Authoring capacities would enable her to simultaneously include and exclude facets of her partner and their relationship. As such, a few months into performance coaching brought with it Stacey's ability to embrace the relationship as it was while also being able to challenge and set limits on it. As our sessions progressed, Stacey's complaints began to taper off as she embraced more responsibility for her experiences. As a result, she began to make clear, direct requests based on her deeper aspirations for herself and her relationship. As she practiced this new level of communication with me, she gained confidence in her ability to negotiate the complex changes that were underway in her relationship. As she freed herself up from her own complaints, she began to exhibit other Self-Authoring traits—such as *multiperspectivism* (or the ability to hold multiple divergent perspectives). Instead of organizing her experience around complaints, Stacey began to open up her ability to hold many perspectives. She found greater flexibility within herself as she stopped identifying with her perspective as *the* perspective and began to relate to the orientations in her mind as one *possible* perspective.

The culturally defined roles no longer governed her functioning. Instead, she could manage roles, picking them up and putting them down at will. Additionally, Stacey was now able to create new roles as she functioned both privately with her partner and professionally in her graduate studies. After about six months of performance coaching, Stacey found a more reliable way to get closer to her partner, both physically and emotionally, while maintaining and refining the boundaries that fit her. The expectations were clear, both for herself and her partner, and she was beginning to enjoy new levels of intimacy and exploration. Where dissonance and difference once threatened her, her partner and their relationship, with Stacey challenging the relationship to grow, they were both now less anxious about differences. As Stacey told me, while it had been a rocky road at times, they both were starting to explore how differences in opinions, desires and needs actually began to bring them closer together in new ways.

Self-Authoring Mind

1. **Identity:** Ability to author, create and innovate from within.
2. **Location:** Inside of self-authorship.
3. **Substance:** Self-directing vision.
4. **Functionality:** Reshaping social, cultural and relational contexts by the inner driven intelligences inside the self.

DEVELOPMENT AND MATURITY

As you can see, development expands both the size of the self and the complexity that is able to be negotiated. The larger the developmental scope, the greater the possibilities for being and performing in more powerful and flexible ways. Remember, bigger is not always better though. Developmental capacity can be hijacked by less complex and refined motives. So, while greater developmental capacity comes with more possibilities for creating and participating in greater truth, beauty and goodness, it also opens up more risks for harm if less evolved motives leverage higher capacities.

One way we can refine our understanding of human development is to pick up the concept and application of *maturity*. Mark Forman, professor, psychotherapist and author of *A Guide to Integral Psychotherapy*, defines maturity as the ability of a person to apply his or her developmental "center of gravity" in an emotionally centered way across a broad spectrum of personal and public domains of human functioning.[28] Forman uses the analogy of developmental growth as the acquisition of height, whereas maturity is a function of width or girth. The broader the base, the more stable the functioning will be across divergent domains. Likewise, a narrower width or girth, along with more stress, demands in underdeveloped areas of the self, and other situational pressures, may knock off higher capacities altogether or support a psychological ecosystem where higher capacities are leveraged by less developed motives of the self.

Put simply, our investigation into development is not only interested in the higher reaches of complexity and functioning. It is also interested in the stability of the self's ability to perform over time and in different contexts. For Stacey, this meant not just myopically focusing on her intimate relationship but also broadening her ability to set limits, manage boundaries, and take stands for the many ways that could nourish and enrich her experience as a human being. As her developmental complexity emerged out of Socialized Mind and into Self-Authoring Mind, we could say she got developmentally taller and more capable as she explored new, more flexible ways to make meaning and carve forth new action in her intimate relationship. But Stacey was also practicing her larger developmental capacities in her educational training. And, as it turned out, her newfound ability to author and validate her experience showed up with friends and family and also in a newfound passion to write and publish two new articles in her field of expertise. As Stacey broadened the scope of her developmental functioning, she was also expanding her maturity. In addition, she was grooming her prerequisites for human elegance. She was refining her developmental facility and also expanding the responsible deployment of her new capacities. In the process, Stacey began to enjoy one of the central benefits of more development coupled with greater maturity: She became a more effective human being in more areas of her life personally and professionally.

EXERCISES TO REVEAL YOUR SOCIALIZED MIND AND SELF-AUTHORING MIND

The following questions help you identify where and how you may be functioning in these two important stages of development. Closely inspect your experience as you reflect on these inquiries and use the personal notes and reflection section to capture key insights.

The Socialized Mind

When do you find yourself being defined by the culture and or relationships surrounding you? For example, in what situations do you find yourself being influenced by peer pressure or peer opinions? Are there advertisements that have recently caught your attention? Reflect on what drives your consumer choices.

_____

_____

_____

_____

_____

_____

_____

_____

_____

How do social norms set limits and boundaries for you? Identify at least one social norm that sets a positive boundary for you as well as one social norm that may be limiting you unnecessarily. For example, do conventions of "being nice" keep you from greater honesty and transparency?

_____

_____

_____

_____

_____

_____

_____

_____

_____

_____

When are loyalties to others controlling you without much consideration? For example, do you keep yourself bound to a certain habit or behavior to maintain connection with a family member or close friend?

_____

_____

_____

_____

_____

_____

_____

_____

_____

_____

Paying close attention to the relationships that matter most to you, how are you and your behaviors pushed and pulled around by relationships? For example, do you conform to a set of behaviors in order to maintain a certain social personality?

Notice when you expect conformity and sameness in values, ideals, beliefs and behaviors from those around you. How and when do you complain in an attempt to get people around you to conform to your expectations? In particular, consider either a current or past intimate relationship.

The Self-Authoring Mind

Think of a time in your life when you were driven by an inner, yet fallible intelligence within yourself. What did it feel like? How did you act in relationship to others?

_____

_____

_____

_____

_____

_____

_____

_____

_____

_____

_____

_____

_____

_____

_____

_____

_____

_____

_____

Think of a time when you are able to be physically and emotionally close to someone important to you while also maintaining your distinctness. How would you describe your experience when you keep someone company without merging into and joining them in their experience?

_____

_____

_____

_____

_____

_____

_____

_____

_____

_____

_____

_____

Think of an example of when you create your own roles and manage your own boundaries. Reflect on one or two examples of how you set limits and take stands based on your own inner guided convictions.

_____

_____

_____

_____

_____

_____

_____

_____

_____

_____

_____

_____

_____

_____

Do you welcome diversity, both in the people you presume to be similar as well as those who presume are different? How?

_____

_____

_____

_____

_____

_____

_____

_____

_____

_____

_____

_____

_____

When and how do you support other people's plans, goals and aspirations independently from your own? Think of an example of how you have supported others while also supporting yourself.

_____

_____

_____

_____

_____

_____

_____

_____

_____

_____

_____

_____

_____

Consider an example of when you directly communicate wants and needs and make clear requests. How do you do this? What qualities of internal experience are present?

_____

_____

_____

_____

_____

How do you work with disappointment (both your own and others) while welcoming and encouraging the autonomy of others? For example, what is your internal response when others don't act as you wish they might or you do not conform to other people's expectations?

To learn more about the Socialized Mind and Self-Authoring Mind, visit:

www.TheElegantSelf.com/Kegan

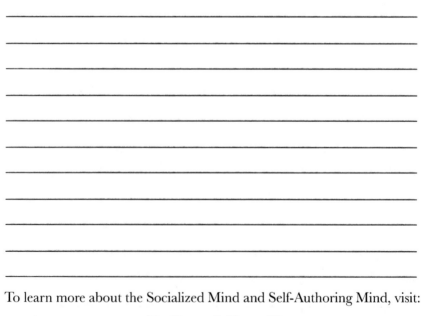

Personal Notes & Reflection

Review Videos

Jennifer Garvey Berger, - Table ?

Non-attachment as coach - how might this
benefit our clients?

3

GROWTH BEYOND AUTONOMY

The Self-Transforming Mind & The Birth of Elegance

Each developmental step forward brings forth greater capacities for functioning and performing in life and, at the same time, each stage introduces defining limitations. So, while growing into a new stage, an increase in freedom and possibility can often be felt. However, if you "fill out," or more or less leverage a stage's functional benefits as much as possible, you are likely to experience your stages' developmental constraints as a painful, confusing struggle. Just as Stacey was struggling with having her sense of self and boundaries regulated by parties outside of herself, individuals who are outgrowing a self-directed, internally guided autonomy demonstrated in Kegan's Self-Authoring Mind experience confusion, challenge and struggle as they bump up against the core limitations of their own autonomy.

LIMITATIONS OF AUTONOMY

The *growth beyond autonomy* as a reflection of a larger adult maturation can be found in William Perry's influential work. A well-known educational psychologist and professor at Harvard Graduate School of Education, Perry provided some of the initial pioneering research into growth stretching beyond the established autonomous conventions that many adults are intimately familiar with. His influential book published in 1970, *Forms of Intellectual and Ethical Development in the College Years*,[29] illustrated Perry's research, which influenced many of the early formulations of *post-formal*[30] stages of intellectual development. These post-formal ways of thinking stretch beyond conventional autonomous forms of thinking. In the late 1970s, Michael Basseches, professor, author and researcher in mature adult thought, developed an impressive body of literature spanning over three decades, published a seminal work titled *Dialectal Thinking and Adult Development,* operationalizing 24 forms of higher-order thinking[31] available in adulthood, facilitating better measurement and further research.[32] Also in the mid-1980s, Michael Commons and Francis Richards introduced a General Stage Model of development intended to unify the emerging field of post-formal psychology, which covered, in part, some postautonomous issues.[33,34] In the late 1980s and early 1990s, William Torbert proposed a developmental-constructive paradigm outlining growth for both individuals and organizations.[35,36] Torbert's eight-stage model includes two stages demonstrating features of postautonomous development.[37] Herb Koplowitz provided an important early synthesis of Eastern and Western perspectives on reality while formulating two postautonomous stages of adult development.[38] In the late 1990s, Susanne Cook-Greuter begins to provide us with more than 16 years of research supporting two postautonomous stages of ego development, refining and building on Jane Loevinger's developmental model.[39] Finally, Terri O'Fallon continues research in the further reaches of adult development.[40] Her current study, the Edge of Consciousness Research Project, explores Cook-Greuter's highest stages of development to uncover further clarity and insight into these stages and to document any further emergent stages of development yet to be studied.

This brief overview over the past 40 years is important as we are about to embark into a territory where the vast majority of adults have not ventured. These notable examples all lend evidence for the limitations and inherent weaknesses in autonomy and the larger developmental capacities in adulthood. While many of these grounding theorists propose different variations, insights and instruments for testing higher stages of adult development, one consistent pattern can be found. The conventional autonomous stage of adult development, often presumed to be the terminus of adult capacities, was in fact limited. Furthermore, there were indeed individuals who were accessing larger, more complex and less understood forms of cognition, meaning-making and self-identity.

Kegan's *Self-Transforming Mind* often emerges in response to the pain points inherent in the Self-Authoring Mind's highly differentiated autonomy. While this is certainly not always the case, it is common. Some transformations of mind appear to spontaneously show up, bringing with them profoundly relieving, ecstatic and enlivening experiences. However, these immensely pleasurable facets of growth are often couched in the loss of a self that once held meaning, worldview and purpose together in a coherent way. This structural and systemic loss of orientation inside the mind is often painful, confusing and layered with anxiety.

One of the gifts of developmental research is that we can begin to see the patterns showing up that are largely, if not entirely, invisible to the self making developmental transitions. These patterns can be useful guideposts as human beings traverse the abyss of unknown open space and larger undiscovered possibilities. And, as I teach my students who are seriously interested in growth, intentionally picking up more developmentally advanced struggles is a powerful way to accelerate the growth of your mind.

Central Struggles

Loneliness

One easily accessed limitation found in individuals living from the Self-Authoring Mind is the felt experience of loneliness. This pronounced aloneness, often born from years of hard-earned self-sufficient autonomy, stands in contrast to the Socialized Mind's challenge of not quite being able to get enough space from others so that he or she can inhabit his or her emerging internally directing identity. One feels constantly pulled on and pressed on by others while the highly differentiated autonomous individual often feels somewhat untouchable. This stems from knowing all too well the challenges of being overly influenced and connected to others. Yet, inside the defense of inner-authored identity is a profound yearning for a new way to make intimate contact with others and perhaps everything in life.

Individuals outgrowing the Self-Authoring identity often exhibit a different flavor of loneliness than earlier stages. In contrast, the Socialized Mind often shapes individuals to experience loneliness when they are alone and missing the defining authority and holding context that others provide. Another form of loneliness can be found in the individual who is just beginning to grow in his or her Socialized Mind. Here, a desire to fit in, connect and belong to a group is coupled with immature and under-practiced social skills. Not quite yet knowing how to belong to a group often creates experiences of being alone.

Loneliness, as an individual outgrowing the Self-Authoring stage, is not a function of needing someone to help define and regulate you. Nor is this loneliness rooted in lacking the social skills necessary to participate in the group. Self-Authoring individuals are, by and large, self-governing and often quite socially savvy. Yet, loneliness persists, even while in close contact with others.

This loneliness is a simple, pervasive consequence of consolidating an identity around being separate and autonomous. Feeling this texture of loneliness is not a symptom that something is necessarily wrong. Just as Stacey should have been struggling with her boundaries in her intimate relationship, many adults outgrowing the Self-Authoring Mind are encountering their own self-generated loneliness, and they are wise to struggle with this loneliness if they are interested in their further growth. This struggle is a demonstration of further development, not a pathology to treat, seek relief or in some way avoided.

Loneliness is an often misunderstood point in coaching and therapeutic practices. Only a rare few practitioners are able to see this rich and diverse phenomena as clear objects in their attention. Only the professionals who have themselves sufficiently outgrown the Self-Authoring Mind stage can see loneliness with this greater clarity.

For example, these practitioners can vividly see the kind of loneliness that is born from underdeveloped social skills and/or unsupportive cultural contexts. They can can see the type of loneliness that emerges as someone is outgrowing his or her present identified culture, valued interpersonal relationships and trusted communities. And, they can also recognize the kind of loneliness that is born from an existential separateness or highly developed autonomy. And, that in each type of loneliness different interventions are required.

Because very few professionals have possession of all of these different types of loneliness and understand how they are also developmentally constructed we find these experiences often worked with from earlier stages of development. Most attempt to resolve the experience of loneliness with greater social and relational contact that is governed by less complex forms of meaning-making and social functioning. This can stunt the growth process. It can leave many adults —research suggests 6 to 7 percent of adults[41]—lingering in the conventions of adulthood for decades while some sincerely desire to grown and others may be immersed in environments the require them to grow. Regardless, the honors track of adult development eludes many as well as their well-intending, coaches, therapists and other professionals supporting them.

Loneliness is a fuel for greater contact and intimacy; however, how this larger relatedness emerges is entirely invisible and unseen to earlier, less complex stages. To understand and genuinely leverage this loneliness for growth, we must not only engage relatedness in new ways but we are required to shed the autonomous self and inhabit an entirely novel construction of self. Loneliness is a fuel or dissonance that can be a powerful core process for outgrowing the constraints of autonomy.

The Refusal of Wholeness

One of the central features research has discovered about the Self-Transforming Mind is these individuals are suspicious of wholeness and distinctness.[42] In fact, it is common for these people to refuse to see anyone, themselves included, as a distinct, whole and complete self. The differentiated self-guiding autonomy, once the prized seat of their developmental achievements and subjective home for what was likely decades, has become a new object in awareness. And this new object is often colored with a healthy suspicion because this less complex construction of self confined subjectivity and identity in its autonomous grips for what many come to see as the vast majority of their adulthood.

People growing in the Self-Transforming Mind often do not want to get stuck in their earlier, less integrative selves.

The Self-Authoring Mind's distinctness, once an unmediated default that defined the self's subjectivity, can now be held as an object. This means the individual in the Self-Transforming Mind can now pick up and put down his or her inner guided autonomy. This fluidity involved in picking up and putting down autonomy is a function of stable maturity exhibited in this next stage of mental complexity. However, as individuals are initially growing in the Self-Transforming Mind, they often keep a safe distance from these recently out-grown facets of their subjectivity. Thus, they are, at the beginning, hesitant to pick up their highly differentiated, separate and distinct autonomy for there is often a risk of falling back into a collusion with the Self-Authoring Mind's now more limited meaning-making, worldview and way of being in the world. As such, this suspicion of their own and others' wholeness and distinctness facilitates the differentiation from an earlier identity and the reinforcement of the new one. As Kegan illustrates, individuals growing beyond autonomy and in the Self-Transforming Mind are also proud of precisely this suspicion.[43]

To give an example of this refusal of wholeness, let's consider the popularity of the enneagram personality typology (usually taught as nine interconnected personality types). A man functioning from the Self-Authoring Mind who encounters this classification system may enjoy identifying with one of the nine types. He may say to himself and his friend over lunch, "I'm a seven." He enjoys identifying with the distinct and separate number that most speaks to him, in this case his current best estimate is that he's an "Enthusiast." Unlike individuals in the Socialized Mind, he is not spending his money consulting with enneagram experts to find out his type, nor is he taking an online quiz (both forms of external authority). Instead, he is studying the model rigorously and he is making a decision as to his type based on his inner authority. This all feels quite good to him.

In contrast, his friend who he is in conversation with is a woman growing into the Self-Transforming Mind. She may be having an allergic reaction of sorts to the concept of identifying as a single type. The idea of simplifying herself into a singularity is a frightening idea for her. She may even feel some panic around identifying as just one number. Her investigation of the enneagram leaves her with the following position, which she articulates with her friend over lunch: "Sometimes I may present as a type six while other times I have a preference and tendency to act, think and feel as a two, eight and a nine. You would not believe how I can get into a nine dynamic with my partner. Ultimately, though, I can relate to all nine of the types as they all have legitimate life in me. Depending on the situation, different characteristic roles emerge." She is unwilling to identify as a singularity for herself. Similarly, when her friend is telling her that he is a seven, she is unwilling to simply classify him as a seven. Just as she will orient toward her own larger complexity, she will do the same with her friend. She refuses to collapse complexity into a simplified wholeness.

One important distinction to note here is that development does progressively, or incrementally, create larger, more integrative wholes. One stage's subjectivity transcends the prior stages in a larger inclusive coordination that itself is a larger whole. This innate wholeness of development is not the wholeness that is refused and skeptically held at a distance as the Self-Transforming Mind is psychologically grown into. Instead, the larger functional wholeness is the Self-Transforming Mind itself. This wholeness is being identified with and thus included. Yet, the larger developmental wholeness of the Self-Transforming Mind is now refusing to limit itself as only being the wholeness indicative in the self-governing autonomy found in the Self-Authoring stage.

As it turns out, development is an ongoing process where the prior stage's wholeness is rejected, refused and denied in service of the next stage's larger, more novel whole. For example, wholeness in the Socialized Mind is often attempted to be achieved interpersonally. One of the most vivid examples I use in the classroom is found in the movie *Jerry Maguire*. Tom Cruise, playing the lead character, confesses his love to the woman he so desperately desires. His personal love life and his now shaky professional life are both intertwined with his lover, Dorothy, played by actress Renee Zellweger. In his passionate confession in Dorothy's living room, he states a now famous line, "You complete me!" This is precisely the wholeness that is sought after in the Socialized Mind.

As I share this example, students in my classrooms almost always have a similar thematic response. The vast majority make repulsive sounds as they distance themselves from precisely the kinds of relationships they were trying to cultivate just a short time ago. Underneath the disgust, there is a quiet, unspoken longing saying something to the effect, "That would be nice ... if it worked." As many of my undergraduate students are traversing from their Socialized Minds into their Self-Authoring Minds, this response makes sense. They no longer trust trying to create the perfect pairing with their romantic partners. Similarly, many have already learned that getting into their preferred school, making an athletic team, getting a particular job, all as a means of attaining some larger sense of wholeness, does not work.

For many of the same underlying dynamics, the emerging interdependent and differentiated functioning of the Self-Transforming Mind no longer trusts the self-directed identity and functioning rooted in the now presumed whole and autonomous self. Creating a self-sufficient identity that is separate, distinct and complete is no longer trusted. This newly outgrown way of establishing who you are is no longer tenable; self-sufficient autonomy just does not entirely work.

The Opposition Inside Polarity

One of the major underlying processes governing the formation of identity, culminating in the Self-Authoring Mind, is the opposition inside of polarities. To define the self, you prefer one side of a polarity while simultaneously opposing the other side. You get to author, choose and direct which side of a polarity you identify with and, consequently, what side you are in conflict with. Are you conservative or liberal? Are you masculine or feminine? Do you move toward challenge or away from it? Do you trust or mistrust? Do you prefer connectedness or separateness? Do you privilege external objective achievements or internal subjective achievements?

At the height of the Self-Authoring Mind's autonomy, individuals are either establishing or working fiercely to establish what appears to them to be a whole, distinct and complete self. This self is positively identified with one constellation of polarities while simultaneously not identifying with the opposing qualities, attributes and/or functions. At its core, the opposition inside of polarity is some expression of "I am this and not that."

For the individual functioning in the Self-Authoring Mind, the self is distinctively *inside* of a broad spectrum of polarities. This is another facet of the location of the autonomous self. Moving on, it is the location of the self inside of the polarity that creates tension and struggle in the individual who is emerging into the Self-Transforming Mind. Being inside of polarities and being in a habituated conflict or struggle with one side no longer fits the emerging complexity of mind that is under way. Developmental research shows an interesting characteristic in people living in the honors curriculum of adult development. Instead of only being inside of polarities and thus in conflict with half of experience, we find individuals who are also able to be friendly to opposites. They are *open to contradiction.*[44]

This is a dramatic shift in identity from one that organizes around one pole inside of a polarity to an identity that embraces, holds and is friendly toward polarities. Instead of being disturbed by contradictory positions, unresolvable tensions, and oppositional agendas, the Self-Transforming Mind is spacious enough that a kind, welcoming embrace is not only possible but a defining feature of their mindset.

As an example, a man functioning from the Self-Transforming Mind would not answer the question, "Are you a liberal or a conservative?" in a simple either/or fashion. No longer does he perceive himself as being one and not the other. The Self-Transforming Mind does not collapse identity around being one while those other people are the other. In contrast, his more developed self sees how he can be liberal in some cases and conservative in others. Furthermore, he also sees how he can participate with both ideologies in the moment. As he peers into his complexity, he feels the irresolvability between these two positions inside of himself. He notices how many of his thoughts and feelings are conservative, but ultimately in this present situation his actions and moral understanding appear to be more liberal in orientation.

THE BIRTHPLACE OF ELEGANCE

Interpenetrating Subjectivity

Robert Kegan calls the subjectivity found in the Self-Transforming Mind "interpenetrability of self-systems" and "the interpenetration of self and other."[45] With my clients, I call this *the interpenetrating self*, although I am cautious to watch for my clients to begin to construct and interpret a distinct and separate self that is then interpenetrable, which commonly happens. However, this stage of development—the Self-Transforming Mind—does not reside in a self that is then interpenetrable. Please note the presupposition that the self is first and is then somehow being interpenetrable or doing interpenetrability. This is more of the way the Self-Authoring Mind likes to make sense of a landscape and a complexity it cannot quite grasp. We'll look at how interpenetrability works in the Self-Transforming Mind stage in the next section.

For now know that the interpenetrating self has a significant shift in orientation around the self and its formation. Earlier stages generally do not have insight into how the self takes form moment to moment. For example, a man in the Self-Authoring Mind stage makes sense of his formation of himself over time through accomplishing projects, gaining more experience, completing trainings and perhaps furthering his education. In doing so, he shapes his sense of self *over time*. What he is unable to experience is how he is being co-created by a vast network of relationships in the immediacy of any given moment. Yes, his autonomous directionality and intention has tremendous impact on the form of who he is; however, the immensely complex interpenetrating relationships are also in flux in the texture and momentum of this and every moment. In the Self-Authoring Mind, this facet of experience is invisible to our gentleman. While it is invisible to him, this is not to suggest that it does not influence him. Quite the contrary, he is changed, shaped and governed by forces he cannot yet see. However, when he grows out of his consolidated autonomy, he will start to experience this territory of relational flux and interpenetrability. And with it, a new world will be revealed to him. Let's talk a look at that new world now.

The Primacy of Relational Flux

Recently I was leading a section of a large annual conference through the developmental transition you are exploring right now. Most of the people in the room would have likely tested as stably accessing the Self-Authoring Mind stage, with some unfinished threads occasionally drawing them back into their earlier Socialized Minds. A much smaller group of people in the room probably would have tested as individuals who were outgrowing the Self-Authoring stage, yet had not found stable access to the Self-Transforming Mind.

I began by asking people to raise their hands if they felt their self preceded this moment. Everyone in the room raised their hand. The self was perceived to be prior to the immediacy of the moment. I continued, "Good, this is exactly the assumption we are going to work with this evening. It is partially true that you do, indeed, precede this moment. You, in part, are prior to this immediacy. You appear to be somehow separate and distinct from right now, thus you experience that you, in your separateness, are now entering into this moment, and... now this one. Correct?" Just about everyone was nodding their heads yes.

"Your next developmental leap forward is a step beyond the primacy of the self," I told them. The energy in the room got still, quiet alertness settled throughout, and I sensed we were resting in a pregnant space for the growth of mind. I continued, "What we find in the research into this stage of development is that the primacy of self shifts from subject to object. No longer is the self, in its distinctness, experienced as that which precedes immediacy. What emerges next is the experience of the primacy of interpenetrating relatedness. Your larger maturity is rooted in the growth, refinement and development of your nervous system such that you become plugged into immediacy, and out of this relational flux the self discovers itself." People were stretched; some had "lightbulbs turn on," as new insight flowed into clarity. Puzzled and inquisitive looks shaped many of the faces in the room, while a sense of delight and relief softened the faces and body postures of others.

The conference was an event dedicated to evolving spiritual practices for integrated development. I continued to discuss how injunctions to meditate, plan, prepare, self-regulate and so on, rooted in the presumption of the primacy of self, were all unable to illicit the further developmental growth many were hungry for. Sure, interesting states of consciousness and emotive exercises could be experienced; however, they all largely failed to elicit a shift beyond the primacy of the self. This was simply because probably 99 percent of all spiritual practice injunctions and self-development exercises are embedded in the primacy of the self. Thus, they are largely impotent to facilitating growth beyond the separate, distinct autonomous identity. Instead, injunctions stemming from a presumed primacy of selfhood often reinforce and further entrench autonomous functioning, instead of frustrating it in service of the next developmental move into the Self-Transforming Mind's interpenetrating self.

Kegan discusses this difference as whether the self identifies with the self-as-form, as found in the Self-Authoring Mind, or the self identifies with the *process of form creation*. One is subjectively fused with the form of the separate self, while the other can experience the formation of selfhood arising out of a larger relatedness to the broader social, cultural, psychological and physiological contexts. The all-important question is: *Do you take the self-as-form as subject or do you hold it as an object?* Being identified with the self-as-form often establishes the basis for the experience of being independent and self-authoring in encounters. Having the self-as-form as *an object* in your experience frees up greater subjective flexibility, so that the self now discovers itself being transformed by and through encounters. Thus we find Kegan's label for this stage: the Self-Transforming Mind. The self is transformed, changed and influenced by its larger relational immediacy, which includes, but is no longer limited to, the history of the separate and distinct self.

The interpenetrating self is *the holding environment* for human elegance. Elegance is a more direct, nuanced and proficient way of being and functioning in your life. Elegance is a simple yet ingenious expression of you. In order for elegance to even have a chance of coming into form, it requires the dramatic reorientation we have been discussing. You as a separate and distinct self that wants to then create something elegant and/or perhaps be elegant is often clumsy and unskillful because of its lack of connection with the immediacy of the present moment's larger relational flux. Elegance is elegant most directly because its intelligence is sourced from the larger relational interpenetrability responsible for more open information flow and greater dynamic responsiveness.

THE INTIMACY OF ELEGANCE

In Kegan's first book *The Evolving Self*, he highlights how the Self-Transforming Mind stage creates a "culture of intimacy."[46] This refinement of intimacy is born from this stage's greater ability for relating with immediacy more directly and consciously. Instead of only presupposing a self that is distinct from this moment, we find a self that can discover its truth and identity in response to and in relationship with an ongoing interpenetrating experiential flux. This capacity for co-creative discovery yields much more contact with the present moment.

This larger intimacy informs a self that is more flexible, dynamic, responsive and open to a broader, ongoing information flow. As a result, the relationship to boundaries is reorganized so that personal boundaries can be discovered and mediated in the present moment. The individual functioning in the Self-Authoring Mind creates fixed concepts about boundaries and expectations he or she is clear about, which are then imposed on the present situation and carried forth for the foreseeable future. This supports the separate, distinct and whole autonomy supporting the less attuned, less functional self found in the Self-Authoring Mind.

It is not that the individual functioning from the Self-Transforming Mind does not have formulated positions that clarify boundaries. Instead, these often well-thought-through positions are no longer exclusively identified with, thus they no longer govern the self and his or her various relationships. Pre-existing boundaries now serve a subservient role to a larger consideration that is embedded in the arising experiential flux inherent within immediacy.[47]

The immersion in and as an ongoing relational flux of moment-to-moment experience, when coupled with a self that is actually friendly to opposites, creates a grounded, wakeful presence and intelligence. As such, individuals with these facilities of mind do not habitually leap into organizing themselves against one side of a polarity prematurely. To do so often results in a de-evolution of mind. In contrast, individuals in the Self-Transforming Mind have a much larger capacity for self-regulation, discernment and tolerance for what we may call *experiential intensity*. What used to be defended against as an assault on the integrity of autonomy is now often experienced as a *creative exploration*, one that is a rich context for the further transformation of the self.

It is here in the co-creative discovery that boundaries arise when needed, and they fluidly dissolve when not required. Fixed positions and the boundaries that support them come into form as a function of exploration and discovery. The Self-Authoring Mind, in contrast, defends a more solid, fixed, inner valued position the self is identified with. The individual in the Self-Transforming Mind can create, defend and maintain a pronounced and nuanced boundary; however, her added development enables her to also readily drop the boundary in order to explore her experience with greater experiential intensity. This is due to at least two factors. First, she no longer needs to rigidly defend against an entirely foreign and alien other because she is capable of embracing, welcoming and being kind to polarities. Secondly, her larger maturity enables her to metabolize experiences that might have overwhelmed a less developed mind.

The result of dynamic, fluid boundaries, coupled with a subjectivity that is more unmediated and in contact with the relational flux of immediacy, is an intimacy and connectedness that can soothe and nourish the loneliness often experienced by individuals outgrowing their autonomy. Contact with one's own inner, cultural and relational life, as well as the surrounding social and physical environments, is increased dramatically. Thus, the ongoing and persistent desire for more intimacy exhibited in the Self-Authoring Mind's autonomous functioning softens and relaxes. The larger relational flux can be thought of as an intimacy with all facets of experience nourishing subjectivity in new ways.

Attunement, Conflict and Creativity

Dr. Daniel Siegel, professor of psychiatry at the UCLA School of Medicine, faculty of the Center for Culture, Brain, and Development and the founding co-director of the Mindful Awareness Research Center defines *attunement* as "the process by which separate elements are brought into a resonating whole"[48] While this definition rests upon a more autonomous world view, it nonetheless provides us with a sound starting point to explore attunement. We often think of this process as one person attuning with another person (or system) through which a larger synergy, coherence and resonance are established between the person doing the attuning and the other person (or system) being attuned to. This is often achieved by one person intentionally placing attention onto the other. Through effort and close examination a coherence and synergy build.

Attunement can also function on a new level. Instead of relying on the self placing attention onto some person (or system) through effort, this larger relational flux can now also be sourced by the Self-Transforming Mind. This enables you to be immensely attuned to what is happening within the experiential field that is co-creating you. One way it can be useful to think about this is to soften, open and relax into the immediacy that is emerging with tremendous amounts of information. While functioning in your life, billions of data points are almost always flowing through your nervous system. Thus attunement is less a matter of focusing on one part of experience to then get attuned to it. Relax and surrender to the immediacy that is already doing, working, informing and shaping you. Inherent in this larger information flow is a more natural, less mediated attuning process. Individuals in the Self-Transforming Mind thus enjoy, and can leverage, greater attunement and resonance because of the interpenetrating self.

Another defining feature Kegan identifies in the Self-Transforming Mind is *how individuals relate to conflict*. Your greater developmental capacities resides in a *larger trust* of conflict. The Self-Authoring Mind's autonomy and the Socialized Mind's need for sameness between self and other both lack this larger, trusting relationship with conflict. With the Self-Authoring Mind, conflict is experienced as a personal challenge to find workable resolutions for both sides of the conflict. Individuals functioning from this stage will work diligently to resolve conflict. The Socialized Mind, in contrast, is not challenged but, instead, threatened by conflict. This less resourced self needs greater social coherence and, as such, conflict is often experienced as a threat to one's survival and well-being. Respectively, enormous amounts of energy and resources are often expended in the attempts to find or create resolution to conflicts, as in the case of the Self-Authoring Mind, or to entirely get rid of conflict, as is commonly found in the Socialized Mind.

For individuals stably functioning from the Self-Transforming Mind, there is an underlying pre-existing conflicting relationship between two or more polar perspectives. These deeper, energetic and perspectival relational tensions are prior to the formation of the self. It is the relational discords that then create the selves or parties involved in the conflict.

There are two important implications from this larger orientation. First, the fantasy of resolution no longer governs the self's attempts for working with conflict. While working with clients, retreat and seminar participants, many individuals consumed by the Self-Authoring Mind's attempts to resolve conflict are often relieved to learn that the underlying conflicts they are tirelessly trying to figure out are likely not resolvable. The situation may indeed be able to find some relative resolution; however, the core dynamics of conflict are, perhaps, unresolvable. I have seen many initially fight this presupposition and then suddenly stop and release. Their body language softens and, oddly, by embracing the conflict and welcoming it more fully, they commonly experience less anxiety. They start to experience that perhaps the conflict is actually okay.

Secondly, the predominant approach to conflict within the Self-Transforming Mind is to allow the conflict to *solve you*. This is facilitated by a larger ability to regulate and tolerate ambiguity, not knowing, and the accompanying anxiety of trusting and even welcoming conflict. With the larger attunement to and intimacy with conflicting dynamics inherent in the relational flux of experience beyond autonomy, individuals functioning in our honors curriculum welcome being changed, transformed and organized in a larger functional coherence by a source of stress and challenge that is larger than themselves and in many ways outside of their control. In Kegan's own words:

The protracted nature of our conflict suggests not that the other side will not go away, but that it probably should not. The conflict is a likely consequence of one or both of us making prior, true, distinct, and whole our partial position. The conflict is potentially a reminder of our tendency to pretend to completeness when we are in fact incomplete. We may have this conflict because we need it to recover our truer complexity.[49]

Conflict is a way to recapture complexity. It can serve as a reminder that we have an engrained habituation to formulate positions and pretend for them to be complete. In the context of the larger complexity that development can reveal to us, we come to discover how we are in fact quite open, dependent and in a more unmediated intimate relationship with more than we are often aware.

Kegan's 4 guidelines for working with conflict with more complexity:

1. Conflict is a signal that you and your opposition have likely become embedded in the oppositional poles inherent in the conflict.

2. The conflict you find yourself in is an expression of your own incompleteness taken as completeness.

3. Value the conflict as an opportunity for you to live out your larger complexity.

4. Focus on ways to allow the conflict to transform the people and parties involved, rather than on the people and parties attempting to resolve the conflict from their presumed distinctness.[50]

The novel abilities inherent in intimacy and attunement, in addition to a larger capacity to welcome conflict often exhibited in individuals functioning from the Self-Transforming Mind, are likely to result in favorable advantages in creativity and innovation. The Self-Authoring Mind largely focuses on problem-solving, which can often limit creative output. The presumed distinct and autonomous self is focused on negotiating and establishing a means of getting rid of the problem. This is likely to yield a less creative response than the Self-Transforming Mind, which is capable of not just problem-solving but problem- finding. Once the autonomous distinct self is confronted with a problem, vast amounts of resources are often myopically deployed to solve it. Whatever the fastest, most economically feasible option will likely be their first choice. This may or may not be the most skillful approach. And perhaps there are more creative options available that are often unseen to the Self-Authoring Mind.

In contrast, the Self-Transforming Mind will continue to look for problems, as well as possibly deeper, more systemically entrenched problems rooted in the broader, more influential interrelated contexts. A surface-level problem rarely consumes an individual's focus and attention when functioning in this higher developmental complexity. They may very well take note, and perhaps take decisive action; however, the individual with this greater development is embedded in a process of openly experiencing, searching and discovering more in the immediacy of unfoldment.

This, coupled with the more complex and refined approach to conflict, often yields entirely different scales of creativity. The autonomous and presumably distinct self works diligently at a creative resolution while he or she remains in many ways, unchanged, while the interpenetrating self, at the next level, is ensconced in something quite different. Problems, often being symptoms of a lack of complexity, are a creative potentiality. The systems, processes, people and perspectives are all interrelated. The problem or problems are something that ought not to be solved with an autonomous response. To do so would be to cover up a greater systemic challenge and creative opportunity to the network of systems, processes, people and perspectives involved. Take note, the people in the system are just as much in consideration for creative transformation as the system itself. This includes the people implementing and managing the change process to work with the problem.

Additionally, the Self-Transforming Mind, being larger than and more friendly toward polarities, can actually attune to the creative tension and dissonance happening on larger scales. Instead of only creating a response from a presumed separateness and distinct autonomy, individuals in the honors track of adult development can also allow the problem(s) to co-create and co-construct systemic transformations that are in an ongoing creative dialogue with the underlying tensions. The results often reflect greater creative opportunities.

For example, let's pick up a perennial challenge in education: *student engagement in the undergraduate and graduate-level classroom.* The persistent problem is that students lack in classroom engagement. This issue spans from students checking their email and visiting websites during class, nonchalantly browsing their classmates for potential romantic partners, to paying attention but passively taking notes. From the perspective of the Self-Authoring Mind, we have a clear problem and we need to get rid of it. One popular response is to initiate a systemic overhaul to create "smart" classrooms throughout the educational departments. By infusing a classroom with technology, multimedia capacities and creative ways to test the recall of students through push-button remotes, an improvement in student engagement is likely to be yielded. This is one scope of creativity that is a genuinely good innovation; however, as we will see, it is also quite limited.

Once the Self-Authoring Mind has reached this point in its own mind, the problem has been adequately addressed and thus the attention moves to what else is in need of resolution. A highly self-directing achiever may say something to the effect of "What other challenges are we facing? I can give you a competent, well-thought-out, coherent strategy to solve it by next Monday." And she means it. What is missing is how this challenge can be leveraged to transform our self-directing achiever who is presumably responsible for solving the problem. Because of her collusion with her own autonomy and distinctness, she presumes to be separate from what is going on in the classrooms. When the classrooms are changed and the human resources directing our educational institution are left in stasis, creative possibilities have been lost. With this loss, we are likely to find a correlating loss in impact on our ongoing problem of student engagement.

Additionally, what is missed is an attunement to the larger irresolvability that is entrenched inside of the persistent challenge to harness the attention of youth. The line of thought "How do we, in the role of a guiding generation, inspire and harness more attention and engagement in our youths to further the quality and impact of their education? How is the challenge of our students' engagement in our classrooms challenging our own culture to grow in new ways? This keeps persisting. There is something here; I'm not sure what, but I sense we are missing something. How are students and our professors co-creating this challenge? What are we as faculty and administrators not wanting to experience?" Much of this never gets considered because these inquiries turn into the larger problems, heighten the experiential dissonance and, most importantly, look into how they themselves are on the transformational stage along with the students and likely the professors.

Systemic change to the technological infrastructure may still indeed be needed, but we are no longer limited to this solution. We are now seeing new possibilities for doing education. Perhaps changes in the way we relate to information as a whole are being asked for. The Self-Transforming Mind may peer into how our students are dulled by fixed static notions of learning. So we may need to educate our professors, perhaps grow their minds and their skillfulness in teaching methods to highlight and uncover alive, co-creative explorations into territories of knowledge claims. In order to do this, the administration is required to look at the process of education quite differently. Perhaps we need to cease to be limited by the notion of providing access to information and also include access to more dynamic ways to hold and relate to information, as well as how to educate students to generate new knowledge claims.

If you are starting to feel overwhelmed by the vastness of these inquiries, you are likely starting to get a taste of why a continual rediscovery of complexity is required. Also, a need for divergent perspectives and values from a spectrum of individuals connected to this problem is an essential resource. From student input to faculty training and the administration's support, all these provide dynamic perspectives on a problem that is itself changing from moment to moment and student to student. The distinct and autonomous mind plays in a landscape that is much simpler. Yet to yield the larger creativity available, our professors and administrators require a mind that is rooted in an interpenetrating subjectivity. This problem, if it is to be worked with and not simply solved, requires an ongoing initiative to genuinely pick up this problem in the classroom and allow this dissonance to develop the systems, processes, people and perspectives involved. To do so might yield an elegant approach and may lead to a greater creative response serving more elegance in education and our growing youth.

In summary, the Self-Transforming Mind has an identity and subjectivity that is interpenetrating. This seat of the self is located outside of polarities. We will explore this in greater detail later; however, an additional perspective on the location of this self is that when you inhabit the Self-Transforming Mind you are inside of an immensely unitive or integrative space. The substance of you can be thought of as a dialectical, co-creative relatedness. At this stage, you are a human being that embraces polarity, is co-creative as well as internally creative, and you are made up of a substance that is highly relational. In terms of functionality, we have covered an impressive scope. The Self-Transforming Mind yields a larger culture of intimacy in response to the loneliness that often anticipates this growth of mind. There is an active and conscious refusal to consolidate a self that is whole, complete and distinct. The self is larger than many polarities, regularly growing beyond dichotomies, often as soon as they are identified. As such, this self resists formulating a self that is inside of polarity creating an oppositional stance toward one. The primacy of relational flux, as we discussed, yields a new set of skills for exploring co-creative, flexible and dynamic boundaries. Finally, we find greater attunement, greater skillfulness working with conflict and a greater scope of creativity. All this points toward the central organizing thesis of this book. *Our higher stages of complexity can yield greater elegance in the world.*

Self-Transforming Mind

Identity: The interpenetrating self or interpenetrability of self-systems.

Location: Outside of polarity, inside of unitive/integrative space.

Substance: Dialectical co-creative relatedness

Functionality: Enhanced intimacy, dynamic co-creative boundaries, spontaneous attunement, conflict trust and broader scopes of creativity.

EXERCISES TO REVEAL YOUR SELF-TRANSFORMING MIND

The following questions help you reveal emergent and already established areas of functioning from the Self-Transforming Mind stage of development. Closely inspect your experience as you reflect on these inquiries and use the personal notes and reflection section to capture key insights.

The Self-Transforming Mind

DISCOVERY PRACTICE

Practice re-discovering who you are in the present moment (rather than relying on your self-perception as something 'fixed' and historically defined) in your interactions today including your work tasks.

Consider whether you are more interested in discovering who you are in the present moment rather than knowing yourself as a separate, fixed self that is historically defined. How does this practice of discovery impact the vividness of your experience, moment-to-moment? What did you notice when undertaking this exercise?

_____
_____
_____
_____
_____
_____
_____
_____
_____
_____
_____
_____
_____
_____
_____
_____
_____
_____
_____

If you habitually define yourself based on historical events and 'facts' about yourself and your experience, what are those traits and qualities? Reflect on why you may or may not be attached to a particular form of self-identity.

_____
_____
_____
_____
_____
_____

_____

_____

_____

_____

_____

_____

_____

_____

_____

_____

_____

_____

_____

_____

_____

_____

_____

_____

Consider a time when you allowed yourself to be formed, without the need for control, by the ongoing flux of experience. How would you describe this experience?

_____

_____

_____

_____

_____

_____

_____

_____

_____

_____

_____

_____

_____

_____

_____

_____

_____

_____

_____

_____

_____

Consider your relationship to conflict. Identify a time when you were in conflict and were able to inherently trust the process of conflict rather than attempting to 'fix' something. How do you or can you allow yourself to be transformed by conflict instead of solving the conflict from your autonomy?

_____

_____

_____

_____

_____

_____

_____

_____

_____

_____

_____

_____

_____

_____

_____

To learn more about the Self-Transforming Mind and how to cultivate this stage of development visit:

www.TheElegantSelf.com/Kegan

CONFLICT PRACTICE

In your next conflict, allow conflict to transform and change you. Practice trusting conflict as a gesture of growth for all parties involved and pay close attention to the experience.

Personal Notes & Reflection

Polanties p. 81 , + Jennifer Garvey-Berger
"How could the opposite be true?
How might I be wrong."

" If we can detect it, it's not there."

The 10,000 things .... + the value of a
teacher to validate you are all
of it ...

Jill Bolty Taylor - Stroke of Insight

4

THE ORIGIN OF INADEQUACY

Biographical and Existential Considerations

Inadequacy is one of the core organizing obstacles for most adults who are desiring to outgrow their autonomy and inhabit their larger complexity and maturity as human beings. As such, we are going to dive into this subject matter now that you have gone through a fairly exhaustive exploration of how the autonomous stage of development takes shape and some of the territory that resides beyond the separate and distinct self. This chapter is likely to save you thousands of dollars on psychotherapy, coaching and/or personal and professional trainings of many types, so perk up. If you have been pouring resources into trying to resolve your own sense of inadequacy in life, maybe even debilitating inadequacy, this chapter is especially tailored for you. However, if you have managed to distance yourself and negotiate around feeling inadequate with relative success, also pay close attention to this chapter because it is designed for you in mind as well. As you will learn, understanding inadequacy is often an important feature for your larger elegance showing up in and as your life. But first, let's begin with a pivotal session with a client.

I was sitting across from a client in my office, legs crossed with my hands folded together resting on my lap.. Sam was wearing a clean tan button-down dress shirt and jet black slacks. He was on a break from work and he looked good. He was clean and crisp in his appearance. His top button was unbuttoned, which added just enough of a hint of casualness to accent his otherwise lean, powerful appearance. He sat, alert, on the couch. On this day we were exploring his felt experience of being inadequate, despite his competence and relative mastery in the private and public spheres of his life. I kept prodding him to turn the clock backward as we explored his past together. "What is the origin?" I asked again.

The room fell silent. He was searching inside himself, looking before some of his earliest memories surrounding his felt inadequacy. His inquiry inside appeared to become more quiet. He felt more still to me, and simultaneously I sensed his uncertainty was growing. The inquiry that I gave to him was working me as well. Despite my years of training graduate students who are in the process of becoming therapists, I had just done what I frequently instruct them not to do. "Do not split your own transformation from the growth of your clients," I said. "When you change, they change. When you grow, they grow. When you split yourself from your clients' work, you often remain fixed. When you are fixed, your client now has his or her own obstacles to work with, as well as the ones you are failing to work with." By asking "What is the origin?" I had presented a question for Sam to work on and as I offered this inquiry it was purely for him. I had separated myself from his process. Fortunately, a more evolved facet of myself swept through as I spontaneously picked up and began exploring my own inquiry with him.

In the quiet introspective space, I suddenly had an "oh, my god!" moment. I thought I knew where I was headed with Sam; now I realized I had been deluding myself and my clients for years. My hands released one another as I reached for the arms of my chair. I slowly pressed my hands in the leather and lifted myself in a more upright position. My whole narrative around inadequacy was reshaping and recontextualizing itself before my mind's eye. It was dramatic and fast, maybe two or three seconds in clock time, but by the end of that second or third tick I was fundamentally a different human being.

Interestingly, Sam looked up at me and started to describe some of my own recently emerged insight. "I can't find anything else before this," he told me. "I'm looking for what memory precedes me at three or four years old, but now I just come up with this empty, open black space."

I responded, "This empty, open black space does appear to be something, though, don't you think?"

Sam was looking into his own facets of what I had also experienced as the interrelated flux of experience working me just moments ago. He just had not connected two important dots yet. Sam nodded his head yes.

I posed another question for Sam. "This open space, as you call it, are there any boundaries or limitations?"

Sam's attention turned inward. The office became immensely still. It was so profoundly still it was almost deafening in its silence. I was now inside of the answer to my own question, while also staying attuned to Sam. Sam's breathing was slow. The pauses between breaths were long and appeared to be unmoving in some sense. After a short pause that felt as though time stood still, Sam looked up at me, straight in my eyes and calmly stated, "No." His presence was powerfully piercing.

Next, I found myself asking a question I had literally never before asked, let alone considered. Yet right now it made complete sense. "Does this empty, open black space come before your conception?"

Without missing a beat, Sam responded, "Yes."

I continued, "Coming from being unlimited, perhaps without any boundaries, into form, where you are a finite, limited being in a tenuous world, how would that make you feel?"

Sam burst out in laughter. I joined him in the hilarity of our shared insight. I was laughing for his realization as well as my own. I was laughing so hard my eyes were tearing up and I was doubling over in my chair. Soon after, we began to collect ourselves and returned to our conversation.

Sam said, "Inadequate; how else could I feel?" And Sam said this with a totally different affect. He now spoke of his inadequacy with a smile on his face and what felt to be in his heart as well.

Necessity of Biographical History and Ontological Origin

Until Sam and I explored the origins of inadequacy, I had fallen prey to believing that inadequacy was rooted in our biographical histories. By revisiting the experiential intensity of these historical events, you can metabolize and make sense of them in new ways. This often frees you up to function more freely. As it turns out, though, only part of your experiences around inadequacy are due to your biographical history. None of these historical events are the origin. It is not in your mother saying something to you or your dad doing this or not that. Inadequacy's origin is not in a sibling giving you some early experience, and it is not, at its center, due to birth trauma. Reintegrating your memories around your biographical stories and historical experience can bring more insight and some greater resolution to your historical experiences. In fact, creating a more coherent narrative of these facets of your history does appear to be good for your brain and nervous system, as well as your overall well-being.[51] However, the experience of inadequacy is likely to continue throughout your lifespan.

Why?

You are fundamentally inadequate.

If you are like most adults functioning in or around the Self-Authoring Mind, you have likely formulated and consolidated a position for yourself inside of the polarity "I am okay" or "I am not okay." Regardless of which side you have chosen (or rather which side has chosen you), your more conventional self is identified with one and is likely consumed in an attempt to fortify your position of either being okay or not being okay and inhabiting an ongoing struggle with the opposing position.

"I am okay"  **"I am not okay"**

When I write, "You are fundamentally inadequate," I am not offering this assertion in response to any biographical narrative. A larger truth that embraces a more experiential scope is found in the existential, or more specifically the ontological, origins of inadequacy. Ontology is the philosophical study of the nature being or existence.[52] This form of science attempts to observe what appears to be the essential fabrics of reality. By identifying an existential or ontological origin of inadequacy we are welcoming the possibility that parts of our experiences of inadequacy are rooted in the very fabric of existence itself. And, these forms of inadequacy, perhaps these unresolvable expressions of inadequacy, are not dependent on any historical narratives or your more relative experiences.

To understand this, you must first grasp that there are parts of human experience that are limited, finite, bound in time and always changing. And there are also facets of human experience that are unlimited, infinite, boundless, changeless and eternal or outside of time. We could say that our relative experiences have everything to do with the facets of our historically unfolding life, while boundless experiences have everything to do with the facets of our experience that are unconditioned.

Prior to your conception, you—or some facet of you—was likely embedded in and identified with the unconditioned, boundless and formless dimensions of experience, even if you presume that prior to your birth you were nothing. What if this nothing also had subjectivity? If so, you might describe this nothing similar to Sam's description: "it's empty, open black space." When you transition from being boundless into a human form that is bounded to an immensely limited form, you are likely to feel both a profound and pervasive sense of inadequacy and an ecstatic desire to return back to and once again taste, know and be that which is unbounded, free from constraints, and unconditioned in the fullest sense of these terms. This transition or contrast between that which is infinite and that which is finite is the existential or ontological origin of inadequacy. You changing from that which is, as Sam put it, "empty, open black space," which has no limits, to something, most notably a small, vulnerable human being, is going to leave a pronounced experiential texture of you now not being enough.

The unfolding of your life—the growth of you through infancy, childhood, adolescence and throughout adulthood—has been a journey of finding out the myriad of ways in which you are inadequate in response to some demand or demands in your life. And this journey has also been a process of discovering how you can grow and thus meet or exceed the demands life is presenting. Falling short, so to speak, is painful and often instills an experience of being inadequate in some sense. The expansion or growth of you and your capabilities, in contrast, is often pleasurable. So, while the inadequacy of limitation is often painful, the growth process where you outgrow limitations, expand yourself and what you are capable of, often yields tremendous pleasure and joy.

At some point in the development beyond your self-directing autonomy, you will outgrow your biographical narrative, which we will explore at length later in Chapters Nine and Ten. When you do step beyond your historically governed narrative, you will see that many of the experiences surrounding inadequacy are in response to your personal history and can function somewhat independently from your historical conditioning. A more direct energetic experience of inadequacy can be accessed, which we are referring to as your ontological inadequacy. This larger experiential intensity and flavor of inadequacy resides beneath, or prior to, most, if not all, of your more personal narratives around being good enough or inadequate at various parts of life.

Finding a reference point for what is being discussed within your own experience can be a challenge here. So, you are not alone if you happen to be struggling here. The vast majority of adults have not, in an enduring way, outgrown their biographical and chronological narratives. As such, all experiences are attributed to some facet of their history. If this is you, take this into consideration. Your parents were likely struggling with the energy of inadequacy, in their own unique ways, prior to your conception. Your grandparents had their own energetic relationship with the pleasure of overcoming limitations, along with the guilt of falling short in various ways. Human beings have likely been struggling with inadequacy and its polar experience indefinitely. When you die, your unique expression of this tension will dissolve, but the underlying dynamic around inadequacy, both its ontological forms and biographical expressions, will presumably continue to persist. Some facets of inadequacy are simply much larger than your historical experience and the narratives that surround these experiences.

Here are two of the essential points relevant for our exploration of inadequacy. First, if you happen to consolidate an identity around not being okay, which is in the habit of forming a covert or explicit conflict with being okay, you are likely avoiding and inhibiting how you can grow and perhaps exceed the various demands of life. In contrast, if you happen to consolidate an identity around being okay, you are likely acting out a covert or explicit habit of keeping yourself from experiencing yourself as inadequate.

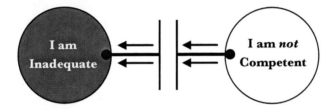

The shaded circles represent which side of the polarity the self is consolidating around and identifying with. The arrows represent the movement away from one polarity and toward another. The above diagram illustrates the subjective experience closing down from the experience of feeling and being competent while identifying with experiences of inadequacy.

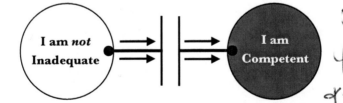

In the second diagram, subjective experience collapses away from feeling inadequate and identifies with being and feeling competent.

In both cases, the self organizes itself inside of the opposition of polarity. Both forms are conventional forms of struggle with inadequacy, although their surface features and appearances are quite different. One

(handwritten margin note: Stepping outside of the polarity + trusting I am enough / my not enoughness)

appears immensely confident, while the other appears quite stuck in inadequacy. Both of these oppositional postures toward the other polarity contract your contact with an ongoing experiential flux capable of creating a more complex, developed you. By consolidating a separate and autonomous self distinct from this moment, which is also in a chronic conflict with one side of this polarity, you forfeit your larger, more developed self that is embracing the dichotomous and polar dynamics already occurring in a larger experiential context.

Inside this larger context, beneath the more habituated constructions of self, there is an ongoing, perhaps unresolvable energetic exchange occurring. On one side of this experiential flux, we find an ever-present inadequacy born from the ontological status of being an expression of limited form, which commingles with your biographical narrative at times. On the other side, we find the radical okay-ness inherent as the unconditioned, limitless and formless facet of experience, which appears to be continually drawing form into greater, more complex and competent expressions of form, or perhaps inspiring form to exceed the constraints and limitations of any position.

THE FUNCTION OF ELEGANCE

Inadequacy and the drive to grow, to exceed and go beyond are, we might say, not two. The experience of inadequacy is not separate from the drive for growth and development. Human elegance joins these two poles together. Your elegance turns toward your inadequacies, welcomes them in their full experiential intensity and, in so doing, connects this vital energy into a powerful drive to develop. Similarly, the drive to develop is not something to leverage as a means to get out of inadequacy, as the autonomous self often attempts to do. Elegance grows not as an attempt to get out of inadequacy but instead as a function of magnifying and celebrating your limitedness. And, let's be clear here. Your limitedness is inextricably connected to your uniqueness.

Elegance enables you to be *both* inadequate and competent as an inherent movement toward becoming more. This is a function of the dignity of elegance. Additionally, elegance is a function of an inclusion of precisely that which is unconditioned. This embrace of the eternal, or infinite, enables elegance to also rest as inadequacy and not habitually need to become anything else or more. This is one of the unique features of elegance; it is not necessarily invested in getting rid of any facet of experience that is already present. Elegance often functions as an ingenious and simple functional integration of polarity that creatively responds to and as immediacy again and again.

For example, in my coaching I often find myself searching for what my clients' most need in a specific situation. In one moment, I can peer into my client and find a profound uncertainty about the direction we should go. It is here where I often experience an uncomfortable sense of inadequacy. Yet, ten seconds later or ten minutes later I may discover myself captured by an apprehension of my clients' process and an insight that is precisely what will serve my client in this moment. In these experiences I am filled with a vivid sense of my competence.

The more autonomous dimensions of myself like to grab hold of these insights. Less evolved parts of myself want to hold onto, own and control these coaching interventions. By doing so the more conventional parts of my identity attempt to solidify my experience of being competent. Perhaps you too can relate. The ingenuity of our past selves are used to erect strong, competent and confident selves right now.

Yet, these tactics fail in the end. If I allow the autonomous facets of myself to secure my sense of competence as a coach I invariably start to supply my clients with prefabricated tools. Instead of birthing tailored innovations uniquely hugging the specific contours of my client's challenges I sell a lesser product. Coaching no longer genuinely belongs to my client, myself and who we are together in the present moment. It belongs to someone else's coaching session. And, because elegance has hold of me, invariably the re-deployment of an excellent intervention belonging to the past feels inadequate. There are at least two betrayals. I betray myself and my own ongoing process of self-transformation. And I also betray my client.

Elegance participates with the fluid and unmediated movements between our inadequacies and our larger competencies. Inadequacies are married to the ongoing re-formation of what it means to be competent to match the present demands. And inadequacy is already and perhaps always married to your present competencies. This of course serves the stripping away of accomplishments of all types in service of a more focused and tailored contribution to this moment's specific uniqueness.

In closing, the conventional attempts to consolidate a separate, self-governing autonomous self can entrench you, your life and your unique purpose into a pervasive mediocrity. When you consolidate yourself into a presumably "highly achieving" and competent autonomous self (judged from the reference point of your own and other, similarly autonomous selves), this self is likely shackled to a conditioning that avoids experiencing the direct embodied energy of inadequacy. Alternatively, you might happen to construct a project of defining yourself as being inadequate (again, in reference to yourself or other conventional selves), and in doing so, avoid the more unmediated experiential intensity of your greatness. In either case, the options are mediocrity or more mediocrity, both of which are governed by autonomy's constraints.

Two ingredients are essential for going beyond the inherent mediocrity of your autonomous self. The first is *courage*. Can you participate with an inherent courage to go beyond the commonly habituated struggle that opposes one side of this polarity? Structuring a self on a pervasive and systemic avoidance of one side of a polarity often creates the need for courage. Can you step into the experiential intensity and consciously welcome the anxiety and dysregulation when you do the counterinstinctual move of going toward what you have been fundamentally organized around avoiding? To do so, you must risk that which you could call home to your sense of identity. Can you do this? The answer for many functioning from the Self-Authoring Mind is yes. However, will you step into this challenge and begin to integrate the experiential intensity of stepping outside of your comfort zone?

Most autonomous functioning adults fail here. The risk is often too much from their limited perspectives. As such, we often find the separate autonomous self creating a culture amongst other like-minded individuals. They often collude with one another, many times nonverbally and unknowingly, about what forms of achievements are to be praised, celebrated and cultivated and which ones are to be collectively unchallenged. The Self-Authoring Mind establishes its own gradation of perceived value. Yet, from the larger vantage point of the honors curriculum of adult development, the autonomous self is functionally confined to a mediocrity. Yes, some mediocrity is better than others; however, the defining features of average are just that—average.

A Perspective on the Elegant Self

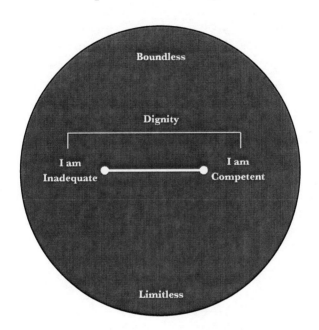

The dignity inherent in the elegant self fluidly embraces the polarity of being competent and being inadequate in its scope. Furthermore, inside of the elegant self—represented as a now much larger shaded circle—paradoxically experiential facets of limitlessness and boundlessness are also included inside of the embrace and function of elegance.

If developmental testing is any indication, it does appear that most presumably distinct autonomous functioning adults fail to embrace the courage to participate in these larger movements of the developing mind. This is, in part, caused by an ignorance of any further developmental complexity beyond autonomy. Courage is, however, one of the few actions your autonomous functioning does have as an option. And it is likely the easier of the two identified here. The second ingredient is *surrender.*

Surrender, as elucidated in my book *Strength To Awaken*, is not a form of "giving up." It is a relinquishment of your often unexamined fixation in and compulsion to autonomous control. However, surrender paradoxically *increases* your functional capacities for control. Surrender can be thought of as a letting go. This letting go is something you, your autonomous self, participates with and is also something that the immediacy of the present moment does to you. It is the latter part of this equation that is perhaps most essential, as it reflects a larger, more mature trust in immediacy. Surrendering your separate and distinct position is something your separateness cannot ultimately do, as this would only heighten and accent your already differentiated autonomy. Surrender involves, at least in part, a welcoming of an experiential flux that is profoundly embedded in an interpenetrating relatedness to and as immediacy. This is the fertile ground of human elegance.

EXERCISES TO INVESTIGATE INADEQUACY ANEW

1. Explore your biographical stories of inadequacy.

What are your most influential historical experiences that have created a sense of being inadequate?

_____

_____

_____

_____

_____

_____

_____

_____

_____

_____

_____

_____

_____

_____

_____

_____

_____

_____

_____

_____

_____

_____

How have these experiences influenced the identity largely given to you through the Socialized Mind?

_____

_____

_____

_____

_____

_____

_____

_____

_____

_____

_____

_____

_____

_____

_____

_____

_____

_____

_____

_____

_____

_____

_____

_____

_____

How do these experiences impact the identity you author and activity you construct in the Self-Authoring Mind?

_____

_____

_____

_____

_____

_____

2) Investigate the ontological presence of inadequacy. Sense into how, perhaps, there is always more.

This week, where are you falling short in your life? Scanning your present life, how are you being challenged to grow, right now, in this moment?

Self-Care
Contribution → How & Where am I
energized and called
to Contribute?

_____

_____

_____

_____

_____

_____

_____

_____

_____

_____

In the area(s) where you have the most amount of competence, what are the limitations you feel must be exceeded?

_____

_____

_____

_____

_____

_____

_____

_____

_____

_____

_____

_____

_____

_____

For additional resources on cultivating courage and participating with the movement of surrender as well as embracing inadequacy, including a 16 minute audio recording, please visit:

www.TheElegantSelf.com/Inadequacy

Personal Notes & Reflection

5

THE TRAP OF COMPLETENESS

Moving Beyond Completeness & Your Embrace of Incompleteness

I was 23 when I started my graduate program in psychology. A few months after beginning, I stumbled across a dim but disturbing realization. At the time, I was in my bedroom surrounded by stacks of books, notes spread across the bed, as a laptop glowed from my desk in the dimly lit room. A document was open ready for writing. This was all, more or less, normal, until you looked at the 50 or more sheets of paper lining my walls with notes, outlines and ideas to learn, hold, consider and integrate. Walking into my room was intense if you were not prepared for it. On this quiet evening, I was sitting on my bed feeling into the dissonance between reading, writing and studying more and the seemingly polar commitment to sit and meditate. Daily meditation practice was a requisite in my graduate program; however, I was in limbo. I resisted meditation while simultaneously suspending my intense drive to learn more.

In this suspension of activity, I could for the first time see and feel what was working me. Virtually my entire life had been largely governed by a massive drive to grow and evolve. Finally, I could see a powerful drive that had owned me for most of my life. I was always on the search for more information, knowledge and insight that would somehow bring a larger sense of wholeness and completeness to my sense of self. As I saw into this facet of myself, I began to feel into some of the meditative injunctions I had been practicing. These all appeared to be organized around the radical acceptance of the self, along with everything else, just as it is. In a flash, something became painfully obvious. My fierce drive to develop myself was, in some ways, a betrayal of the simple and open acceptance of who I already am, right here and now in the present moment.

This was a tectonic shift for me. I could see that for me to continue to grow and evolve I had to somehow embrace what appeared to be an unresolvable tension. I needed to continue to develop and, simultaneously, my further evolution now also challenged me to embrace a radical acceptance of everything. This involved me embracing precisely who I was right then, flaws, imperfections and limitations included. As I made sense of this insight, I realized I needed to include a cessation of sorts. To grow further required me to stop habitually striving for more growth. Growth had now become a paradox. On the one hand, it offered me a path forward, moving toward a larger sense of completeness or perhaps perfection. I thought to myself, "If I could just get one step further, then..." Simultaneously, growth was demanding I stop habitually taking that next step.

As this realization and contradiction poured through me, I started to feel something immensely uncomfortable. I was incomplete. My stomach gave me a gut response that something was fundamentally wrong. In juxtaposition of potential and future possibility, I felt profoundly inadequate. My drive to develop, this seemingly noble movement, was more a denial and betrayal of myself in that moment. Perplexed, I sat on my bed as the constellation of my inner life reshaped and reformed almost entirely. Slowly I felt my passionate drive to become more, to develop and evolve, beginning to align with something else. My undying drive to grow was drawing away from and ceasing to feed my inner denial and beginning to serve something much more precious. My inspiration to develop had not ceased, but this drive had begun to find a new master.

Fast-forward about a decade; this time I was in the classroom in front of about 25 graduate students who were all, just like I had done, bringing their robust drives to develop and grow in their academic lives, intimate relationships, and personal selves. It was the first class of the fall semester and these were first-year graduate students starting their second semester of graduate school. Invitingly, I said to the class, "Raise your hand if you are working hard to develop, grow and become more of a whole and complete human being." Every single person raised their hand and a soft warm glow filled the relational space throughout the classroom. Just about everyone smiled and looked around the room at each other. There was a bonding happening amongst the students. Most of them were used to being out in an adult world where the drive for personal development was often clouded and/or forgotten within the various facets of life that stand as false substitutions for genuine development. Now they were in a potent culture where just about everyone around them was focused on one central aim: growing and developing themselves such that they could be the very best psychotherapists possible.

I paused briefly, enjoying the unique cultural texture present, and then I continued. "Becoming more can be, and often is, a habituated betrayal to the unconditioned seat of being." The energy in the room dramatically changed. "Your habituated drive to grow is often a disloyalty to *this* immediacy. The persistent movement toward growth and development is good, it is true, and it is immensely beautiful. However, at some point, your further development requires you to paradoxically cease this drive so that you can access a territory of experience that is beyond your habituated movements to get from one place to the next in pursuit of development. Right now, development is calling you forward and—in what is perhaps an unresolvable tension—development is now calling you to simply be, right here and now. The project of focusing on getting somewhere else, which is likely running you, severs you from the larger maturity as a human being we are to explore in this course."

The energy in the group had shifted from the warm, light uplifting energy to that of a dropping or settling in an open stillness. These bright students got it. The sober appraisal on their faces and body language appeared to both shake them up and wake them up, even if for just a brief moment. I think to myself, "The semester is now under way."

THE COMPLETION PROJECT

The completion project is the unexamined drive to become more whole and complete. It is characterized by a strong and often pervasive drive for the acquisition of more. Depending on a broad diversity of values and sociocultural conditioning, the completion project organizes around divergent expressions of being and/or becoming more. The acquisition of more is perceived to bring you closer to being more whole and complete.

If you happen to create a completion project similar to how I did, as well as many of my graduate students, you might be interested in psychological development offering more and more psychological power. However, you could be organized around acquiring professional training to secure more confidence at work. Perhaps it is more money securing greater economic power, or it may be more intimacy enhancing connectedness. You may be consumed by a drive for more social power. As such, effort and attention often go into political maneuvering within your chosen organization and/or community. Regardless of what kind of *more* you are likely after, there is an underlying presumption that getting it will bring you closer to, and perhaps one day into, wholeness and completeness. This is the completeness project at work.

It is a pervasive and immense driving force that structures the type of selves we often find in Kegan's Socialized Mind and the next stage, the Self-Authoring Mind. While the completion project is a healthy and natural expression of these stages of development, we are going to investigate its limitations as a means of generating greater dissonance. This challenge can be a powerful developmental incentive to outgrow an unexamined and unquestioned relationship with the completion project that is likely running parts of, if not vast reaches of, you and your life.

The Socialized Mind's completion project is the same fundamental process of attempting to become more whole and complete; however, the complexity and features are quite different from those found in the Self-Authoring Mind. The central organizing distinction is individuals in the Socialized Mind attempt to complete themselves through joining with and by being regulated by others. Whether this other is a person, group and/or organization, the Socialized Mind is searching for an external source of structure and cohesion.

For example, the Socialized Mind often looks for and attempts to create a feeling of completeness through joining with and being regulated by an intimate partner. By sharing the same mind (from the vantage point of this stage) where interests, values and worldview are all presumably the same, these individuals can experience joining with and merging in a larger whole that includes their intimate partner. Furthermore, because this stage depends on people having others to help regulate, define and manage themselves, intimate partners often covertly "hire" each other to fill a broad spectrum of needs.

One of the most pervasive patterns happening in this stage's completion projects involves partners hiring each other to play out one side of the polarity between separateness and connectedness. Generically, for our example, we can treat these as masculine and feminine roles. The masculine partner hires the feminine partner to represent, act out and behave in ways that reflect the connected relational facets of being human. Meanwhile, the feminine partner has also hired the masculine partner to represent, embody and maintain the more separate and distinct energies of being human. Both partners are hiring each other to take on facets of experience they are simultaneously organized against in themselves, yet are also simultaneously attracted to themselves. Finding a partner that plays out the other side of a polarity that is less comfortable for you, in which they are more skilled in negotiating, is one common expression of the completion project found in the Socialized Mind. When this happens, individuals often experience a relaxing sense of completeness or wholeness when they are close to each other. It is more challenging to find a clear and distinct "I" in these relationships. Instead, the completeness project at this stage presses personal considerations into the realm of what "we" think, feel, do, believe and so on.

The completion project within individuals functioning from the Self-Authoring Mind is decisively different. The co-dependency inherent to the prior stage has now been replaced by a more genuine, differentiated autonomy. As such, completion is not so much looked for in merging with a person or organization "out there," as it is now looked for inside of his or her—now more self-directing and inner-defining—self. While the self still looks for resources, accomplishments, organizations and relationships "out there," he or she is no longer as interested in an ongoing relational dependence where a connection to other provides a sense of completeness. In contrast, one form of the completion project commonly found in the Self-Authoring Mind is the search for more experiences, systems of information, trainings and/or relationships that can be integrated in his or her ever-growing ability to be more whole and complete as he or she navigates his or her world. If you happen to be in this form of a completion project, learning more, mastering more and achieving more all lure you further, with each additional step presumably bringing you one step closer to that sense of wholeness and completeness where you can, at last, relax. Inside of this meaning-making, you might say something similar to "That person who I have a tremendous amount of respect for, and who has much of what I ultimately value, he or she has 'made it.' Someday, I too will get there. But right now, I first need to do..." This autonomous, self-directing drive for more is a prized resource. Or, more accurately, we could say it is *the* prized resource, as this is the subjective seat or functional identity of the Self-Authoring Mind.

Following our earlier example of masculine and feminine, or separateness and connectedness, the completion project at this next stage of the Self-Authoring Mind has at least two basic types or flavors. Growth in the autonomous Self-Authoring Mind does not necessarily mean individuals suddenly, by and large, inhabit the separate or masculine pole. The Self-Authoring Mind functions with individuals inhabiting either separateness or connectedness in their own specific, now more autonomous ways, similarly to how the Socialized Mind has individuals who tend to organize themselves around the masculine or feminine poles of being separate or connected.[53]

The underlying developmental architecture of autonomy emphasizes separateness; however, the self-directing intelligence can then author or create a self that is more superficially organized around being more separate or more connected. Put another way, the subjective seat of the self, as we explored in Chapter Two, is unmediated, unseen and uncontrolled. At the Self-Authoring stage, the underlying autonomy does not come with a choice. However, in terms of the objects that are seen, mediated, chosen and controllable, they can be more masculine or feminine in orientation and expression.

Put more simply, we might say that both masculine and feminine autonomy is highly self-directed. This autonomous functioning is the seat of subjectivity for the Self-Authoring Mind. Thus, the inner-guiding self is not a choice; rather, this form of subjectivity is a given. What this autonomy then does possess is the opportunity for immense diversity of choice. An individual who privileges being connected, what we could call a feminine autonomy, may consciously direct his or her attention, energy and action into creating more experiences where he or she is more connected with others. Similarly, someone who prefers being separate, what we may call a masculine autonomy, may intentionally direct his or her attention, energy and action toward experiences that create more separateness.

These orientations often color or flavor the completeness projects created from the Self-Authoring Mind. The more feminine completion project feels more whole and complete by progressively gaining, integrating and accessing more connectedness. And it follows that the better the skills, the more pronounced the experience of staying in and being in an ongoing connectedness. In contrast, the masculine completion project is organized around progressively insulating the experience of being separate.

Your completion project has likely been a powerful incentive to grow into and mature yourself in both the Socialized Mind and the Self-Authoring Mind stages of psychological development. However, at some point, the completion project often acts as an inhibiting force to the growth of your mind beyond autonomy. Creating wholeness and completeness is often dependent on organizing a sense of self in opposition to a polar facet of experience. As we explored in Chapter Four, the development of mind beyond autonomy involves outgrowing and becoming larger than polarities. As it turns out, the inadequacy and competence polarity is just one of what is perhaps an undefined number of polarities that the evolution of mind requires us to outgrow. The completion project, and our experiences of incompleteness, represents another polarity to be outgrown.

Resistance to Critiques on Completeness

Oftentimes, when I launch a critique on completeness and wholeness, it is met by my clients, students and course participants with a healthy dose of defending that which is sacred to them. If you are experiencing this, excellent. You are likely more identified with the hard-fought, earned and won autonomy that is a result of decades of development. As such, you absolutely should be defending your achievements. This autonomy likely provides most, if not all, meaning and coherence in your life. If you are not experiencing this defense, you likely have already run into the limitations of your autonomy and are ready to explore other possibilities for yourself.

Part of this defense, I have found, is also semantic. Let's begin by looking at the terms *whole* and *complete*. The image that is often most readily available when we think of something that is whole and complete is the circle. The line presumably starts in one location and finishes its movement at the same point. In contrast the arch of a circle is uniform. The circle is immensely beautiful in its symmetry and completeness, and many of us, myself included, often are attracted to the concept of becoming a larger whole, a more complete self. Yet the circle's intrinsic completeness offers some insight into why completeness is also limited.

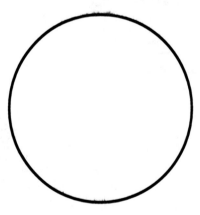

A circle can be defined as a line forming a closed loop where every point of the line is a fixed distance from the center point. By definition, a circle is closed, and, because it is circling a fixed location, it is not directed or going anywhere.

One of the most powerful examples is how a circle is *closed*. As such, completeness is often restrictive. The mind, as you may recall from Chapter One, is defined as an embodied and relational process regulating the flow of energy and information.[54] A mind that is attempting to become complete is a mind that is also, indirectly and unknowingly, trying to close itself off from larger, more diverse and complex energetic and information flows. This costs the conventional self in its ability to perform in countless ways. When I ask people who are defending their drive for wholeness and completeness the question, "Do you want to be more closed?" often most people start to touch into their skepticism of their own completeness. Virtually everyone I ask this clarifying question answers, "No." Pushing further, questions such as "Do you want to exclude and cut yourself off from others?" "Do you want to restrict yourself from other ways of thinking and processing information?" and "Are you interested in closing down from more flexible ways of being?" often yield a natural skepticism and wariness of the completeness project.

A second feature of completeness that is mirrored in the circle is that *neither is headed anywhere*. Completeness, by definition, possesses all the necessary or appropriate parts. We can think of this wholeness as an identity that is full, finished or perhaps even perfect. This would likely result in an immobility or stillness. Completeness may then result in no need for movement. Now, few individuals engaged in the completion project will propose that a perfection has been attained; however, this is one of the central risks. We may find some adequate and comfortable level of completeness. When this happens, people often do stall in their lives. Yet when I ask people, "Are you interested in not going anywhere else? Would you like to get to a point where you no longer are going, striving or moving anywhere else?" most can again access an immediate suspicion of what completeness offers.

Wholeness and completeness can be dethroned from one of the central driving forces governing yourself. As such, completeness can be placed in a more accurate and pragmatically focused position within your mind. Wholeness and completeness can provide stability and what we will explore later as *cohesive integrity*; however, this integrity also needs the open, directional facets of experience that incompleteness is tailored to provide.

EXERCISES TO EXPLORE YOUR COMPLETION PROJECTS

Curiosity is a powerful tool for discovering where completion projects may be operating in your life. Below you will find *four domains* which often house various expressions of these conventional constructions of adult identity.

Intrapersonal Completion Projects:

1)   What self-help, personal-growth programs or spiritual practices and/or retreats are you engaging in with the attempt to become more complete?

2) Consider how long have you been consumed by these books, programs and/or retreats. Reflecting on your experiences, what facets have been most useful in your learning and growth process, and where are the major limitations of these approaches for you today?

_____

_____

_____

_____

_____

_____

_____

_____

_____

_____

_____

_____

_____

_____

_____

_____

_____

_____

_____

_____

_____

_____

3)   How are you often holding yourself with a familiar theme and/ or perspective? Identify how you might become more diverse in the ways you relate to yourself privately.

Interpersonal Completion Projects:

1) How might you be attempting to complete yourself in and/or through relationships? How might you be consolidating a sense of self around social power, control and/or influence? Explore where you might consolidate relationships around certain feeling tones while avoiding others.

_____

_____

_____

_____

_____

_____

_____

_____

_____

_____

_____

_____

_____

_____

_____

_____

_____

_____

_____

_____

_____

_____

_____

_____
_____
_____
_____
_____
_____
_____
_____
_____
_____
_____

2)   Where in your life are you most comforted by being defined and held by your surrounding social roles and norms? Explore how you become more limited when you identify exclusively with the socially defined facets of yourself.

_____
_____
_____
_____
_____
_____
_____
_____
_____
_____

_____

_____

_____

_____

_____

_____

_____

_____

_____

_____

_____

_____

_____

_____

Physical Completion Projects:

1) Physically, how might you be striving to achieve a desired end in which you then would be happy and/or content?

_____

_____

_____

_____

_____

_____

_____

_____

_____

_____

_____

_____

_____

_____

_____

_____

_____

_____

_____

_____

_____

2) How might you be attempting to change and/or fortify your body image as a means of reifying a more complete self? Explore what it would be like to bring a larger sphere of inclusion to your physical appearance.

_____

_____

_____

_____

_____

_____

_____

_____

_____

_____

Social and Economic Completion Projects:

1) How might you be attempting to create a greater feeling of completeness through purchasing various forms of property? Explore how money, income, investments and savings (in abundance or scarcity) may play a role in creating a sense of completeness.

For additional written and audio resources on working with completeness projects visit:

www.TheElegantSelf.com/Completeness

Personal Notes & Reflection

6
THE CENTRALITY OF INCOMPLETENESS
An Unexpected Resource for Leadership

Regardless of what variation the completion project has, it is organized around denying one core experience: *incompleteness.* Your self is likely organized around and committed to not feeling incomplete. As such, your completeness project is likely invested in learning, mastering and/or acquiring more such that a sense of completeness is gained, refined and perhaps even defended. If so, you are likely standing inside of the polarity of completeness and incompleteness, with an opposition toward experiencing incompleteness while investing energy into getting more complete.

You may be driving yourself to develop as I was or how my graduate students often are. Alternatively, you could be driving yourself to become more proficient professionally by furthering your education or training. Gaining these additional skills may fill out your ability to function independently as a professional in your field. Perhaps you are working hard at becoming more responsible for your feelings in your intimate relationship so that you can be less co-dependent and thus more complete in your autonomy. Or maybe you are a meditation practitioner who is investing countless hours on your cushion attempting to achieve and/or stabilize a unitive consciousness providing you with experiences of wholeness and completeness. Regardless, the completion project is a function of conventional stages of development that must be outgrown if you are to know the honors track of adult development and the kind of elegance you are capable of participating with. While the completeness project can yield solid returns within the conventional adult mind and its relative sphere of influence in the world, it is limited and functionally incapable of yielding the next-level performance and influence inherent in elegance as we are exploring it. To enjoy these, you must develop your mind so that the polarity of completeness and incompleteness is embraced inside of you.

There are at least two core reasons the completeness project must be outgrown for your larger abilities to flourish. As eluded to earlier, there is the risk that the completion project is actually successful. When this happens, you will likely create *a stagnant lifestyle* that has achieved some relative sense of completeness you are comfortable with. Mediocrity settles into your habits, and life takes on a routine quality of maintaining the status quo. Decades of hard-earned developmental capacity largely become a servant to whatever comfortable lifestyle you have settled for. Your drive for more is lost and the self is relegated to "rinse and repeat," as I often refer to it with clients.

The second reason this project needs to be outgrown is because your *larger capacities for performance and influence* inherent in elegance require it. The dynamic tension between completeness and incompleteness or certainty and approximation can catalyze a larger creativity the world likely needs. As we touched on in the Introduction, there are massive pressing problems facing humanity, both on a global scale as well as on a personal scale. The completion project often stands squarely in opposition to working more skillfully with the demands of your life. What the completion project reveals is that every human being who has achieved conventional stages of maturity in his or her development possesses a habituated, unexamined point at which he or she will settle. Once this point has been found, adults can easily—without much thought or consideration—switch from aspirations and drive to playing it safe and maintaining. Ultimately, both are required. Again, you want to embrace this polarity between aspiration and maintenance, which requires a rigorous investigation into how your personal comfort functions as an obstacle to the emergence of your larger capacities to influence, change and perhaps transform our world.

Elegance is not always comfortable. In fact, elegance is a larger exchange of more diverse, powerful and divergent energies and information. Sometimes it may be immensely comfortable, even pleasurable, while other times the creative exchange between polarities will challenge many of the beliefs your separate, autonomous self holds around what it is capable of experiencing and participating with. By going beyond the completion project, you can grow, expand and broaden the energetic and informational circuit you are able to participate with, negotiate and metabolize. Encapsulated autonomy is traded in for a more open, dynamic and flexible self that is, as we first discussed in Chapter Three, interpenetrating.

Meanwhile, a useful injunction that can help you outgrow your identification with or embeddedness in autonomy is what I call *the centrality of incompleteness*. To help you separate yourself from the collusion with completeness, this exercise rests on an intentional skepticism of wholeness and completeness. As Kegan puts it, the Self-Transforming Mind "both values and is wary about any one stance, analysis, or agenda."[55] While it is true that this higher stage of development both values and is wary or skeptical of completeness in all its forms and expressions, to help counter the overvaluation that is characteristic within many completion projects, we are explicitly picking up the skepticism, wariness and mistrust of any one perspective, agenda, insight, feeling, analysis, relationship or self that is, in any way, presenting to be complete.

It is important to note that this practice is not to be turned into a fixed position. This would only be another form of the completeness project playing itself out, but with incompleteness this time. Done properly, this is a powerful way to begin to value and experience part of the power incompleteness holds. Your work with inadequacy is an essential first step, as inadequacy is an emotionally charged layer of incompleteness. Now you will bring your mistrust and wariness of wholeness and completeness to yourself and the objects and systems in your life. To help you understand how this practice may impact your life, let's take a look at one way in which the centrality of incompleteness helped transform an executive taking on greater leadership responsibilities in his organization.

INCOMPLETENESS AND LEADERSHIP DEVELOPMENT

Jim was an executive working with a midsize technology company. Stakeholders and the senior executive team had recently identified how the company's acquisition of new technologies over the past two decades had left the company more stagnant in innovation within the organization. Jim had accepted an invitation to lead a team assigned to establish and implement a plan for increasing the company's ability for organic, or "in house," innovation. Although Jim's calendar was full with responsibilities, he felt excited and had a tremendous amount of new ideas, insights and possibilities for implementing what he called a "cultural change" within the organization. Jim delegated responsibilities lower on his priority list and opened up the space to take on this project. Jim was crystal-clear about his goal. He was going to bring his excellence to his team and inspire excellence in others, and he was committed to delivering the tangible results his organization needed in the next 18 months.

Like many accomplished managers and leaders functioning from the Self-Authoring Mind, Jim cleared part of his calendar, worked at home late at night after his family was in bed, positioned himself politically with key talent throughout the organization, and produced a well-thought-out, inspiring strategic position and a powerful vision for his team. As you might have guessed, he had positioned himself with these pieces in place before he called the first meeting two weeks after accepting the responsibility. Jim was focused, on task and crisply executing on the tangibles needed to move himself forward. After two meetings, his charisma, decades of strategic thinking, and polished political intelligence, along with a spectrum of gifts, talents and drive, yielded a cohesive team positioned for sparking the needed organizational change they had all now signed onto for the company.

About a year into his initiative, Jim was again crystal-clear, although this time the flavor was different. Two pieces were now certain. First, his plan—course corrections included—was not working. Changes in innovation were not taking hold and the bottom line tangibles were reflecting just that. Organic innovation remained a significant organizational weakness. After nearly four quarters, critical measures were indicating that he and his team were failing. This was, at that point, no surprise to Jim, as he had been regularly tracking his progress, or lack thereof. Course corrections, plus additional pressure on himself, his team and key players in the organization, yielded negligible impact. Jim was also now done analyzing his plan and the people he enrolled. The problem was no longer thought to be "out there." Instead, Jim was now convinced the problem originated with him. Jim was an adept learner, and he had executed many, if not all, of his time-tested reliable skills to achieve results. Yet something was still missing. Late at night while looking in the mirror and brushing his teeth, Jim was not thinking about his wife or kids. Instead, he was searching inside himself and asking, "What am I missing?"

Jim was considered by most in his organization as one of the stars. He out-performed, out-maneuvered and out-excelled most. Under pressure he typically performed at his best. Reshaping corporate culture was a massive undertaking, one that involved sparking greater creativity and innovation in employees. As it turns out, Jim's more conventional approach, regardless of how well formulated and executed, was doomed to fail, for his strategic planning, clearly defined measurable goals, diligence, approach to teamwork, leadership and attuned managerial skills all were necessary but not sufficient to create the complex changes needed in his organization. Unknowingly, Jim was running into the limitations of his autonomous self.

Turning back the calendar about a year, let's look at what went wrong. Not knowing it, Jim was inside his completeness project. For decades, Jim's highly nuanced and capable completion project was successful time and time again. He was driven to possess more competence than the man or woman next to him. And it worked most of the time. However, the effectiveness of his completion project changed when he picked up this innovation project. He recalled, for the first time, being overly stressed and anxious with his consistent inability to figure out why he and his team were failing. His typical smooth social and managerial skills, at times, eroded into more blunt pressure on people reporting directly to him. Instead of feeling on top of things as he was accustomed, he was losing sleep at night feeling that he was in over his head.

As my work with Jim revealed, the problem stemmed in the first moments of being asked to head up this new initiative. Jim's mind turned toward his current workload and scanned for opportunities for delegation. This involved a brief tour of two people directly reporting to him who would also likely need additional mentoring to be successful. His mind then saw a feasible new strategic priority in his workflow. Suddenly, he got excited. Jim was looking to have more influence in his organization and this was an excellent opportunity. A few creative ideas began to flow through his mind. He looked up from the desk toward his CEO, scanned the eyes of a few on the senior management team, and confidently said, "I can do it. It would be a pleasure to take on this initiative."

In this seemingly innocent moment, many mistakes were made that cost this company nearly a year of time and uncounted economic costs. The most relevant for our discussion lies in the self that Jim referenced when he said, "I can do it." In Jim's mind, he was tasked with the leadership role of framing the problems, casting forth the overarching approaches, and managing the methodologies and processes required from start to finish. In this moment, Jim failed to look at innovation at the next level. He was overly confident in his ability *to do the same actions* that got him sitting in front of the senior executive team. He was resolute in his belief that he could change the organization without ever considering that the need for a culture change around innovation might have to start with his own culture of mind. Instead, like many executives struggling with complex initiatives, Jim saw himself as separate. He was somehow complete in his position and it was those other people, they were supposed to change. When he walked in his first meeting, within the first few minutes Jim had set the precedent that he was going to conduct himself in his usual manner and he was in turn making similar demands on his team. He entered with his usual commanding vision, inspiring emotional leverage and politically savvy positioning with clear and measurable outcomes and well-differentiated responsibilities for delegation. In doing so, he kept any experience that he or his approach were also immensely limited and incomplete about out of his own mind as well as his teammates' minds. After two weeks, the team had quickly entrenched themselves in similar relationships, practices and processes, ones they had used for nearly a decade yet were deploying in a new area —innovation.

Jim needed what I call *performance coaching.* He was ripe to develop himself and he was in desperate need to perform at the next level. Jim was hot on the trail, had exhausted much of his expertise and most of his seen options, and had already sought out consulting and second opinions. Yet nothing over the course of the year had helped to shift the culture and brought the innovation he sought. Something inside him intuitively grasped the root of the problem was within him. He was largely correct. Many persistent ongoing problems are reflections of *developmentally defined constraints.*

The centrality of incompleteness was an easy sell to Jim because he was already directly running into his own self-generated limitations and he was already suspicious of himself. Picking up a more intentional skepticism of anything that was whole, complete and distinct helped Jim to continue to expand beyond his own autonomy, and, in turn, many facets of his life started to change. In the end, he did help initiate some dramatic shifts in organic innovation. His results, while they unfolded on a much longer time table, exceeded the expectations of most of his superiors and the company's stakeholders. Here are a few notable changes that did have tangible impacts.

First, Jim grew beyond his completion project and expanded the energetic and informational exchanges he was able to work with. Instead of unknowingly pushing away any sense of incompleteness, he started to welcome and embrace the energy of incompleteness. Here is what this change looked like in the office. Initially, Jim's drive for completeness governed and held him. As such, his actions largely presumed he possessed, or could create, the vision, strategy and skills needed to create culture change around innovation. You may recall, this led him to do a lot of work on his own creating and positioning his strategy prior to the first meeting with his team. Most of his activity was serving the drive to have a whole and complete position from which he could lead his team. Jim's next approach was decisively different. Instead of filling his mind with strategies, relationships and critical levers to influence as he used to, Jim now could quietly investigate his own uncertainty. He could see how all his skills, talents and experience had been used to get him out of experiencing this particular flavor of incompleteness. At his center, while he had many intelligent ideas and well-thought-out strategies, he noticed he actually was uncertain about how to truly get his company to be more innovative.

As Jim's mind became more complex, his energetic and informational circuit grew beyond the polarity of incompleteness and completeness. Given his growing skepticism of whole, complete and distinct positions, he naturally began to spend more time in his not-knowingness. Eventually, Jim no longer needed to defend himself from these types of experiences. As incompleteness moved his inner world, Jim saw a diversity of new questions all highlighting different, yet often related perspectives on creative possibilities. His blocks of focus time in the office were now no longer uniformly filled with focused action from one priority to the next in his already established strategy. Periods of stillness spontaneously showed up. From the outside, it may have looked as though he was not working; however, inside, Jim was participating with a culture change inside his own mind, one that turned out to be one of the missing critical levers. Inside Jim's mind was a growing and expanding circuit of incompleteness and completeness. The further his experience pulled him into not knowing, uncertainty and curiosity, the greater his access to creative novelty and diverse, yet integrated, ways to possibly move forward.

Jim was taking essential interior steps to becoming more innovative himself. The organizational initiative was now starting inside his own culture of mind. Fortunately, Jim's work around incompleteness was taking hold and also starting to show up in how he related and conducted himself in the organization. His coaching work helped him make sense of the transition he was in, and he became committed to functioning professionally beyond his often rugged, highly accomplished and capable autonomy. As he grew and continued to practice the centrality of incompleteness, he became increasingly skeptical of what he was capable of accomplishing from within his autonomy.

Jim called a special meeting with his team about six weeks before their deadline. He was mostly successful in negotiating one of the most challenging leadership moves: He stopped exclusively leading from his highly polished autonomy and he started leading from a larger, open, incomplete and interrelated orientation. Jim was clear about how his own inner work was generating much more creativity. Plus, fortunately, he also understood that his team not only needed more of his innovative thinking, but also more of each other's creative input. Jim could see his tendency to, once again, create a robust innovative strategy around his own, now more innovative mind. However, with his ongoing practice of the centrality of incompleteness, Jim could also see clearly how placing his team as an operational vehicle for his own autonomous strategy would, once again, command a less creative, less innovative team. He now had a strong sense of just how incomplete and limited his more or less isolated autonomous creativity was.

The hard work, discipline, effort and rigorous autonomous drive of Jim, along with his many personal, social and political gifts, were now, in many critical ways, positioned to serve a larger co-creative capacity of his more developed interpenetrating self. He was now more interested in inspiring the kind of innovation his company needed in his own team, himself included. This was a broader strategy taking shape in his mind, as he was beginning to think about the means necessary to shift the broader organizational culture and practices.

Jim opened his meeting with a few questions, starting with *"How do we get more creative ourselves, as a team?"* While Jim had received sound coaching throughout much his transformation thus far, this was really his first time leading from this new orientation. He was uncomfortable, anxious and uncertain about how to negotiate leadership without leading, as he had the past couple of decades. The room was silent in response to his first question. He continued: "Better yet, *how do we allow this challenge to shape us in new ways so we are more creative as a team?"* Jim paused briefly and then continued, "The ideas we come up with together need to be more innovative, as does our processes for initiating, managing and executing an organizational strategy to develop our company's innovation. We know that if we lead the same way—think and plan in the same ways— our organization is simply not going to make the change we are

nara ✛ The Elegant Self

nsible for. We already tried this, and it doesn't work. One of the questions for us to negotiate now is *How do we lead and manage in a way that models the very culture change we need throughout the organization?"* A few people looked down at notes, shuffled around anxiously, and sat back in their chairs still waiting for Jim to take the lead as they expected. Jim anxiously paused and then asked another question: "I'm also curious, *how has my leadership style over the past fourteen or fifteen months limited your creative input into this project?"*

At this point, Jim sat back and waited. He had insights and his own answers to each of these questions, but he also felt what appeared to be his larger uncertainty. So he held back. Instead of striving to lead his team, shape the energy in the room, catalyze his team around his own strategies, he sat attentively in his chair carefully watching what was happening in his meeting. The entire room was filling with tension. Jim shared how he could feel everyone in the room wanting to just go back to the way they usually operated. He felt it in himself, and he knew his team wanted him to command the space as he typically did. He could see it in their eyes and in their body language. Part of Jim was struggling with not filling the space with his confidence, cunning thought and usual brilliant mastery of strategy. Part of him felt he was born to do precisely that, but he remained quiet waiting for this tension to create something that belonged ultimately to no one and yet everyone.

Jim was commanding a much more subtle and fertile space amongst his team and within himself. He was unwavering in his commitment to leverage the team to serve a larger creativity that belonged to the team, not any one person. This co-creative position was indeed a stand; it just felt dramatically different from the kind of stands Jim put forth for others to follow in the past. Teammates were handed a larger responsibility to listen to everyone on the team in new, fresh ways and to also turn toward their own inner authorities to share their creative insights. As the team settled in this new groove, being right or correct was no longer a central focus. *Being creative* was. This proved to be one of the significant shifts in the culture at large as the team made its way forward. In the past, the group had discovered that being right and/or correct was valued more than being creative in the organizational culture that had taken hold of much of the employees, themselves and the executive team as a whole. As

150

Jim freed himself from this unexamined commitment, he opened up room for others to do the same.

Innovation had to be bold. Jim and his team discovered that they needed to stand in a courage that enabled them to traverse the highs of creative success and the lows of creative attempts that resulted in failures. Jim encouraged his team to work from a courage that was larger than success and failure. As such, they found new ways to support taking strategic risks and they also began to encourage finding failure fast.

This was no easy, simple linear path for Jim and his team, though. Initially, two of his teammates complained that Jim was failing to lead them. One mocked Jim as trying to lead through popular opinion, saying to Jim and the team, "I need a leader who can make the tough judgment calls and weather the storm. Yes, we've fallen short, but that means you need to revise our strategy. I don't want to waste any more time as you poll us because you are at a loss on where to go." Jim heard this from both his teammate and two of his senior executives who had received feedback about his presumed leadership failure. Yet Jim's leadership stand was stronger, more pragmatically focused and, over the long haul, significantly more effective. And it was not able to be seen and fully understood by the more conventional, autonomously functioning teammates who expected more traditional forms of leadership.

What Jim's example shows us is how the completeness project can be used to reinforce some accepted level of achievement. Jim had been largely successful in his completion project *until* he took on the daunting task of organizational change around innovation. Jim had stagnated in what David Bradford, Director of the Executive Program in Leadership at Stanford Graduate School of Business, and Allan Cohen, professor of management at Babson University, might call *heroic leadership*.[56] His attempts to perform at the next level failed despite his "rinse and repeat" efforts that governed much of his first year working on organic innovation. While many would not characterize Jim as mediocre given his accomplished stature, he nonetheless was exhibiting average stages of developmental complexity until he began to outgrow his own identification with autonomy.

We also saw how Jim opened up his mind to becoming more integrative of opposing energies and perspectives. This made him more creative and capable as a leader. For example, not knowing complemented his keen and nimble conceptual clarity and became a multifaceted asset. Expanding his ability to participate with not knowing helped keep Jim from prematurely committing to a strategy on his own, regardless how creative it was. Furthermore, Jim learned to turn "not knowing" into a leadership asset. By not leading with his own ideas, Jim invited greater personal and collaborative engagement from his team. Additionally, Jim invited his team, and eventually the broader organizational culture, to get beyond the polarity of the success of innovation and the downfall of failed attempts at innovation. But most importantly, Jim learned how including his own change process is often an essential tool for transforming broader organizational systems, culture and practices. He now had a healthy suspicion of "change management," as many of his peers were calling it, that involved changing the various systems and people "out there" while remaining distinct himself. He had shifted from a heroic leadership style to a *post-heroic leadership* style.[57]

Allowing the more full spectrum of incompleteness in its many facets —what we are calling the *centrality of incompleteness*—to co-create your experience often yields stronger, more nuanced and refined aspirations to become more competent in life. Simultaneously and paradoxically, when your separate, autonomous self can soften, release, turn toward and let go as incompleteness, a peacefulness with incompleteness, in its multifaceted expressions, enables you to be precisely where you are and how you are. You have now graduated from autonomy and can thus participate with a freedom from being pressed forward by an unexamined drive to get somewhere else. It is here that we find our next critical step into human elegance.

EXERCISES FOR RELATIONAL ELEGANCE

We spent quite a bit of time exploring Jim in his professional setting, primarily because it is essential that your efforts for personal development are not insulated from how you show up professionally and relationally. One of the fastest ways you likely freeze development beyond autonomy is to consolidate your functioning around largely *known ways of being*. This is most common in relationships—intimate and/or social in nature—and in how you conduct yourself professionally. While stability and consistency are highly valued assets, both in the professional currency you offer and in the social currency you provide, for most autonomously functioning adults, this homeostasis must be outgrown, just as we peered into Jim's journey beyond his otherwise highly accomplished autonomy.

The Centrality of Incompleteness

First, identify where in your life you might best be served by a skepticism, wariness and mistrust of various forms of wholeness and completeness. What perspectives, agendas, insights, feelings, analysis and/or relationships do you habitually collude and join with? How might you be simplifying yourself by attaching to and identifying with these forms of wholeness and completeness? You can review and use the forms of completion projects you identified in Chapter Five's exercises as a starting point.

Next, for each form of wholeness and completeness, investigate both its strengths and its limitations. This helps include the valuable and beneficial facets while also facilitating insights into how to set important limits to these forms of wholeness and completeness.

Finally, explore setting strong and clear boundaries for the functioning of each form of wholeness and completeness. Cultivate a clear skepticism, wariness and mistrust of the parts of you that have a habit of colluding, joining and merging with these expressions of wholeness and completeness. Describe where and how you intend to set limits.

_____

_____

_____

_____

_____

_____

_____

_____

_____

_____

_____

_____

Risk Taking

Your further growth and development is likely a path that will not come to fruition *without risk*. Adult development often involves a conscious decision to conduct oneself in the world in new, unknown ways of functioning. This is often experienced as a risk. Discerning when to take risks and when to fall back on more known ways of functioning is a perennial question for many adults growing beyond the conventions of their society and social circles. Regardless, if you are interested in elegance, you will need to take risks, two of which are especially helpful.

Calculated Risks

Identify two to three areas in your life where you can take risks. This should be areas in which you are able to preemptively plan and strategize around how and when you can "try on" or explore new ways of functioning. I call these *calculated risks*.

What are the two or three main recurring current situations in your life offering opportunities to take calculated risks? Briefly describe how you typically function in each situation.

Next, describe in detail the behavior that is perhaps needed and new to you in each situation. What actions do you see yourself doing? What is your body posture like? What does it feel like as you imagine yourself taking these calculated risks? Anticipate the kind of thoughts and emotions that may arise. Note mental and emotional cues that can support you in exercising these calculated risks.

_____

_____

_____

_____

_____

_____

_____

_____

_____

_____

_____

_____

_____

_____

_____

_____

_____

_____

_____

_____

_____

Forced Risks

Jim gave us a look into what I call *forced risks*, which are much more challenging, significantly less controllable and thus more powerful in their ability to develop you if you can successfully navigate the terrain. Forced risks are created by mismatches between your own mental complexity and the demands of your life. For example, Jim's mental complexity was not sufficiently developed to take on this new challenge of innovation within his organization. About a year into his valiant attempts, he was forced into dramatically new ways of functioning. Forced risks are often more pervasive and they are initiated by the environments you find yourself immersed in. When you find yourself in forced risks, life is demanding you to become more *right now.*

You likely will make many mistakes along the way of discovering the resolution to the complexity of life that is working you. And you will unearth or co-create novel adaptations bringing greater partial resolutions.[58] Once a new level of complexity has been co-created, you may be able to then leverage more calculated risks as a means of stabilizing your newfound functioning.

Please note, forced risks are immensely challenging and they are often not successfully negotiated. This is largely because of the adult plateau discussed in Chapter One. Forced risks require *development.* Attempting to solve them without adaptive growth largely, if not universally, fails. As such, developmentally informed coaching, consulting, mentorship and/or psychotherapy can be immensely helpful and in many cases critical in the successful negotiation of this form of risk.

Take a moment and reflect on any forced risks you may be immersed in right now. Below you will find a handful of questions to help you identify where forced risks are operating in your life.

What pervasive challenges are you confronted with in your life right now? Where are you consistently falling short even in the face of your best efforts? Where do you notice yourself getting confused, anxious and perhaps overwhelmed? What areas of your life do you heavily rely on your strengths and gifts at all times?

What developmental transition(s) do you suspect may be needed? Imagine a few divergent developmental responses that may be required in these areas of your life. Dialogue with a few trusted individuals who may provide insight, divergent perspectives and relevant strategies. Describe the thoughts, feelings and behaviors you may need to embody in the face of forced risk(s).

_____

_____

_____

_____

_____

_____

_____

_____

_____

_____

_____

_____

_____

_____

_____

_____

_____

_____

_____

_____

_____

_____

_____

_____

For an hour interview and additional resources on participating with incompleteness and working with forced risks and calculated risks, visit:

www.TheElegantSelf.com/Incompleteness

Personal Notes & Reflection

7
THE PARADOX OF COMPLETENESS
The Recontextualization of a Limitation

One defining feature of form appears to be its *incompleteness*. All form is limited and conditioned. In addition, form is never entirely static. It undergoes a continual, unending, persistent process of change and movement. Ken Wilber, one of the most widely read contemporary philosophers, rests his entire approach on one simple axiom: *No one perspective is 100 percent wrong.* He maintains that no one is capable of being *completely* wrong. To do so would necessitate grasping what is completely right, accurate or correct. This, for Wilber, is an impossibility. Every perspective, orientation and position—all different facets of form—are incomplete. They are all approximations. This is the foundation of Wilber's Integral Philosophy. Everyone is bringing important partial truths that need to be included and inherent limitations or distortions that need to be clarified. A second feature of Wilber's philosophy supporting an essential incompleteness has to do with his position on the fundamental building blocks of reality. For Wilber, the core foundations are not ideas as the idealists maintain, nor are the fundamental building blocks of reality matter as the materialists propose; rather, reality is composed of perspectives[59] that are *holons*.[60] A holon is a whole that is *simultaneously* also a part of a larger whole. We could say a holon is a "whole/part." As Wilber sees it, nothing is in and of itself a whole, nor is anything merely a part. Wholes and parts arise together and co-create one another. The series of nesting whole/parts that reality is composed of has no ultimate limits in terms of the diversity and scope of what holons can come into form. It is open and incomplete. Once again, we find incompleteness as a defining feature of Wilber's thought.

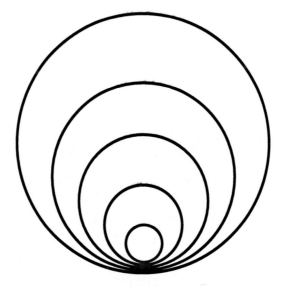

Each circle, representing a holon, is a whole/part. Each circle stands on its own as a separate and discrete circle and at the same time is part of a larger, more inclusive circle. By visualizing smaller and smaller circles cascading inwardly and progressively larger circles always emerging, we can grasp how holons have no ultimate limit.

French phenomenologist and professor of contemporary philosophy Renaud Barbaras maintains there is "a fundamental incompleteness at the heart of the living being."[61] Similar to Hegel's philosophy, essential to Barbaras' position is movement. According to Barbaras, movement is ontological irreducible. In other words, movement is essential to the fabric of existence. Similar to our earlier exploration of the primacy of relationship, Barbaras sets forth a position suggesting that "movement necessarily engages the essence of the subject."[62] Movement then is not a property, mode or attribute stemming from a presumed separate pre-existing self (or object). You do not have or possess movement, rather you are movement and movement is co-constructing you. Perhaps we could say *movement has you* and you have movement; however, according to

Barbaras, the prior is more fundamental. Movement is essential, not secondary as many stages of meaning-making presume. And movement is a function of incompleteness. As Barbaras puts it, "Life is from the start in touch with things other than itself."[63] Form is always incomplete and open, thus participating with a continual movement, touch and/or exchange with that which is outside of itself.

Turning our attention toward mathematics, we again find an essential feature of incompleteness. Kurt Godel, a close friend of Einstein and philosopher of mathematics, was an immensely influential logician whose significance is perhaps on par with the contributions of Aristotle. He is considered by many to be the greatest mathematical logician to date. His most famous and influential contribution is known as Godel's Incompleteness Theorem of 1931. This theorem maintains that within any consistent system there is a part that is neither provable nor refutable. Either the arithmetic is inconsistent or there is at least one of its truths that arithmetic cannot prove. Godel demonstrates absolute limits to what we can achieve by reasoning within a formal system. All consistent systems (form included) are inherently incomplete. *The Oxford Companion to Philosophy* calls his Incompleteness Theorem "a high point not only for logic but also for twentieth-century culture"[64] as his math demonstrated a novel scope of logical reasoning, which also turned out to be immensely influential for the invention of digital computers. Again, incompleteness can be a root source of immense creativity.

THE TWO TASTES OF COMPLETENESS

We can see incompleteness rooted in philosophy. Incompleteness can be found in the close inspection of subjective experience, as in Barbaras' phenomenology, as well as in some of the greatest discoveries in mathematics. We can continue our survey in physics beyond phenomenology if we look to the work of Werner Heisenberg, Nobel Prize recipient and one of the key pioneers of Quantum Mechanics. His famous Uncertainty Principle reveals an intrinsic incompleteness to what we can know about subatomic phenomena. If we were to tour other fields of study, such as economics, neuroscience or semantics, we may also reveal a core incompleteness. Presumably many, if not all, human endeavors reveal incompleteness as a central feature, if we bring a sufficient level of developmental complexity to a subject matter.

So while we might say incompleteness is at the core of who and what you are, this does not mean all completeness is merely a function of the conventional self's projects of driving toward more homeostasis, autonomy and/or separateness as exhibited in the Self-Authoring Mind. Nor can completeness be entirely relegated to the self's desire to merge with another, whether this is a lover, leader, friend and/or group, as we often find in the Socialized Mind. These are but one facet or one taste of completeness. The drive for cohesive integrity in the various facets of your relative life all can, and do, yield varying degrees of experiencing wholeness and completeness. Your innate movement toward a coherent narrative of the memories and events of your life are one example of the cohesive integrity of your self's integration. The basic pursuit of trust in relationship is another. The natural shaping of social space such that the shared connection of "we" feels good and allows our respective nervous systems to relax is another. Even the integration and coordination of the right half of your body with the left half is a function of your self's cohesive integrity, providing you with relative experiences of wholeness and completeness. Yet these are only one taste of completeness.

When we turn our attention to the second taste of completeness, it also appears to be at the very core of who and what we are, just as incompleteness is. The second taste of completeness stems from, or is rooted in, the formless dimension of you, which we first encountered as we peered in Sam's session in Chapter Four. Sam's inadequacy was related to both his biographical relationship with the relative experiences of falling short in some ways, and the ontological transition of being "empty, open black space," which had no limitation and is without form, to becoming a small, vulnerable being that is incredibly limited in form. Whether you are aware of it or not, it appears that perhaps you, too, possess a part of you that has no parts. Here you hold no conditioning. You are fundamentally not moving. This part of you remains unmoved regardless of your relative experience. You have no limitation and no location. One way you may refer to this facet of experience is through the concept and experience of *Big Mind*, or "Big Mind Big Heart" as Zen teacher Diane Musho Hamilton calls it.[65] We can speak of this taste of completeness as you, a profound mystery, holding nothing and thus being completely empty. This facet of you is without form and thus without any of the limitations of partiality and incompleteness. This facility of you is limitless and timeless. Your formlessness appears to be all-pervading and inaccessible, or, put another way, unavoidable. This unifying formlessness creates the second taste of completeness.

Returning back to our topic of the elegant self, while contradictory, it appears that it is the embrace, inhabitation and movement of an unresolvable contradiction and tension. The inclusion of completeness and incompleteness does appear to be one important facet of elegance. So while you may suspend parts of the cohesive integrity of your more conventional self, thus pausing the completion project's activity (the first taste of completeness) and functioning in the world, elegance often participates with a larger, more pervasive completeness (the second taste of completeness) in a more ongoing way.

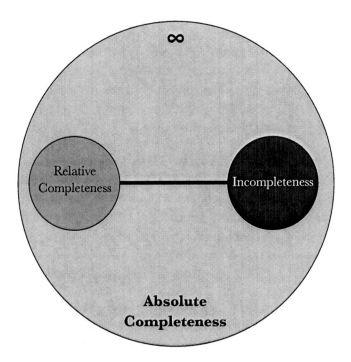

THE CENTER OF SUBJECTIVITY

Subjectivity can be thought of as having two basic facets. We can look at the first as being *a lens* that you look through. Or we can think of this as a *filter* through which life experience passes through. This lens or filter has properties and thus it colors, shapes and co-creates the objects of your experience. In addition to the objects and world you live in, this lens or filter also establishes the subject you identify with or your sense of self.

For instance, the lens of the Socialized Mind creates and colors or forms experience so that the authority ultimately resides outside of the self in the expert, the parent, a boss and/or a trusted group. A world is co-created in this mind where conformity is incredibly important. Similarly, the lens of the Self-Authoring Mind shapes the objects in experience, although now differently and with greater complexity. Authority has more nuance to it now. Sometimes the authority resides "out there" and sometimes the authority can be experienced within. This lens colors experience such that conformity still matters, yet so does standing apart from the group. These features of the form of the lens are initially unseen facets of experience; however, through development—as explored in Chapter Two—the subject becomes the object. Your lenses increasingly shift from subject and become objects that can be related to, managed and more intentionally negotiated.

The second facet of subjectivity is much more mysterious. Perhaps you have had the experience of sensing a *mystery* when looking deeply into the eye of a lover, or maybe when you were up late at night washing your face and all of a sudden you caught yourself in the mirror. In that moment, you were taken in by curiosity, as you peered into the very center of an eye and connected with the mysterious aspects of life. "Who are you?" or "Who am I?" are two of the recurring perennial questions.

So, at the center of subjectivity, there is a *mystery*. The subject, by definition, can never truly see itself. You have actually never seen, nor presumably will ever see, the source of your subjectivity. You will likely never see the very *essence* of you. Similarly, the source of your lover's subjectivity, the center of who and what he or she is, perhaps, equally unknowable.

This second facet of subjectivity appears to be the source of the second taste of completeness. The experience of mystery is one of the most basic responses to the part of you with no form, no limitation and ultimately no definition. The subjective ground, or mystery, is always already separate, complete and distinct from the objects of experience. This brings forth what is likely, again, to be an unresolvable tension within you. One facet is incomplete, interpenetrable and in a dynamic relationship with an ongoing experiential flux, while another is complete, untouchable and in an unchanging unconditioned relationship with the entire display of the ever-blooming experiential flux of phenomena. The parts of you having form are always incomplete, while the part of you that is without form remains simultaneously complete. We can think of these two selves as the *self-as-form* and the *self-without-form*. However, it is important to return to the understanding that these two types of self are ultimately one larger more capable self.

Elegance requires an open, participatory relationship with *both dimensions* of yourself. These contradictory positions can at times appear to be conflictual, yet they are also cooperative. It is the dynamic tension and creative cooperation between these underlying dimensions of you that is required for your participation with elegance. It appears that the ability to open into the immediacy of your experience, without many of the habituated closures of your conventional self, rests on a grounding as your unconditioned completeness that is, in part, separate from the changing manifold of experience in form.

This separation can often be experienced as a type of liberation or transcendence of form. It is important to note here that this is where our exploration of elegance takes a departure from many forms of spiritual and religious practices aimed at a transcendence of the world. This facet of liberation serves a larger engagement with and as the world of form. Elegance brings with it a broader or fuller participation with both the immediacy of your relative life as well as the overarching devotion to the rich arch of your life from birth to death.

To give a brief example, in the case of facilitation, we can find the elegant facilitator unwilling to exclusively consolidate a conventional self around her self-as-form. As she rests quietly in the self-without-form, she is better able to use of her self-as-form as an instrument. Most notably, her ability to listen, attune and resonate with specific individuals and the group as a whole is rooted in her ability to be open and receptive. The self-without-form excels here. In contrast, her ability to intervene and direct is found in her self-as-form and its unique set of skills. The elegant facilitator embodies an open participatory relationship with both facets. Listening and directing are often contradictory to one another. Most adults do one or the other. However, they can be trained and refined as found in the Integral Facilitation trainings conducted by facilitation experts Diane Hamilton and Rebecca Colwell (and supported by Dr. Cindy Lou Golin and myself who serve as faculty and coaches).[66] Here our facilitator learned to cooperate in her larger maturity so that the intervening and direction given is simultaneously an instrument to listen more carefully. And the quality of her listening itself is also part of the intervention. It is here that we can find the elegant facilitator broadening her participation with her life while simultaneously not being limited by the forms and scenarios life takes on.

Elegance leverages your unconditioned completeness to weather the often turbulent, chaotic and dysregulating experiences in life that appear to be largely unavoidable over time. One way I like to talk about second taste of completeness—the formless completeness—and its usefulness is to use an analogy of an insurance policy. Regardless of how developed your self's cohesive integrity is, the ongoing complexity of life's demands are likely to exceed your ability to maintain homeostasis. The stability or maturity of your relative self is always limited and incomplete. While you might not prefer the anxiety, discomfort and dysregulation inherent in being pressed beyond your comfort zones, these turbulent times can be, and often are, a potent source for development if the disturbance is within a workable range. Embracing the part of you with accesses to an unconditioned seat of completeness dramatically shifts what you can embody, transmute and negotiate skillfully.

While it is wise to continue to expand the relative maturity of you as we discussed in Chapter Two, I also recommend an insurance policy to back up and support your more relative completeness and stability. Do not place all of your assets on one form or taste of completeness. The relative integrity of your more conventional self is, in the big picture, fairly unstable when compared to a completeness and stability that is unconditioned, unmoving and unlimited.

Two facets are important to explore with regard to the insurance policy unconditioned completeness can provide. *Recognition* of the unconditioned or formless completeness is the first facet and your *participation* with the formless is the second. Many adults function with mainly their relative, somewhat tenuous completeness, resting on the cohesive integrity of their conventional selves. As such, the self often consolidates in opposition to some polarity, as we have already explored at length. This constricts functionality and performance in the world. Cutting yourself off from an energetic or experiential quality that is already present is an active severance from the larger possibilities of embrace and skillful negotiation. This polar organization of the self, where you are protecting against a foreign polar experience, establishes a situation where presumably only half of the full range of experience is safe. Elegance is simply not possible with this split governing the self's conduct in the world. Let's look at two different ways to sign on and leverage this larger, unconditioned insurance plan.

Turning toward Subjectivity: Accessing the Unconditioned

The first step toward reinforcing the self's ability to skillfully negotiate the complex demands of life is to access and/or recognize the formless, unconditioned stability of what we could call the essential heart of subjectivity. Turn your attention and perspective toward the center or source of your subjectivity. Steer the focus of your experience toward what is doing the experiencing. Inquire into who is the one experiencing this moment.

As you focus your attention and perspective here, you may notice a number of objects beginning to arise. Regardless of what inner objects surface, such as deeply engrained habits of mind, ongoing narrations of experience and the exercising of imagination, continue to direct your attention and perspective into the unmoving and unknowable mystery at the center of subjectivity. Many people find this to be calming and cooling to their nervous systems. Even in the midst of some of the most intense and dissonant experiences, this center point is always available.

I have seen this simple gesture of turning toward one's own subjective center calm, relax and open people in the face of some of the most challenging demands life has to offer. For example, a man telling his wife that he is going to file for a divorce, a woman facing her terminal cancer diagnosis, an individual losing his or her job and then home, the death of a child, or the loss of one's life's work in the face of a corporate takeover. The list could go on. Regardless of what stressful events life hands us, our relative self's cohesive integrity is often rocked by the larger waves of life. Opening to a larger integrity, stability and unmoving presence enables your larger maturity to make peace with the immediacy of life, even in the most challenging of contexts, war and violence included.

Making peace with the loss of our relative comfort is at the center of our discussion. Your relative stability will likely be knocked around again, regardless of your strategies and positioning. Avoiding this disturbance is, in part, the growth of your maturity. And our avoidance of the more discordant parts of life can also be a strategy to avoid the full spectrum of your experiential aliveness. At some point this avoidance stunts your larger postconventional maturity.

Our developing executive Jim, whom we visited in Chapter Six, illustrated this insurance policy when he met with his team and began to take the first steps to lead from his incompleteness. The anxiety, uncertainty and his desire to revert back into his more comfortable and known leadership style were negotiated from his ability to separate himself out of his conditioning. Jim was not only beginning to participate with a larger current of information flow within himself and his team, he was also participating with a larger seat of completeness as he was able to simultaneously take space from the powerful desire to collapse back into the leadership habits of his past.

Turning toward the Experiential Flux: Formless Embodied Participation

The second exercise is a participation with the less bounded, or perhaps unbounded, experiential flux in and as *immediacy*. While our first exercise involved a turning toward the heart of your subjectivity, the second involves allowing a counterinstinctual move to occur. This shift in orientation involves you getting closer to the experiential intensity most responsible for disturbing your relative self's homeostatic comfort. This can occur by developing your *embodiment*.

Embodiment can be thought of as having at least three central processes. These three processes of embodiment are *embracing*, *inhabiting* and *moving*. Lose one and your embodiment erodes. This causes your ability to participate with the immediacy of life to shrink. These three processes have been hierarchically arranged for our discussion; however, in the complexity inherent in and as the moment, a much more complex and nonlinear exchange is likely at play connecting these three processes. That said, let's begin with embrace.

The process of *embracing* means to cast out or reach outward, thus enabling you to encompass or envelop some facet of experience. In this case, your counterinstinctual move is to embrace the most provocative and disturbing facets of experience. This gesture involves an encircling or including. For example, when your mind considers a novel perspective, it opens and expands as it reaches out and includes this novelty. This is an expression of embracing just as your arms reach out and extend to embrace a loved one in a hug.

The second process is *inhabiting*. When you inhabit something, you are on the inside. To give you an example, let's consider the scenario where you are looking at your anger. You are noticing sharp judgements in your mind. You see the imagery in your mind's eye as you replay the triggering event. Or perhaps you are rehearsing what to say, how to say it, what to do and when. You can see the powerful energy coursing through your body. As you are readying to mobilize into swift action, or perhaps as you hold yourself back from foolish action, you attempt to hide your hands as they jitter in the face of this injustice.

While these physical, emotional and mental facets of anger may be vividly seen you are not yet inhabiting much of your anger. While you may very well being embracing your anger, at this point you are only looking at anger. To inhabit anger you must guide your attention, energy and presence into the inside of anger. This is a much more intense yet intimate experience.

You must step into, not merely look at, your judgements. To inhabit this anger you must locate the seat of awareness on the inside of the imagery and the visceral sensations coursing through your body. You cannot be looking at the heat and power conducting through your physical and emotional experience. You, the heart of you, must be on the inside of these experiences. It is here, when you are actually inside of your anger, that you can say you are inhabiting anger.

The more perception originating from the inside of your first person experience, the greater your embodiment is. The location, or root, of perception is the differentiating criteria. Just as I can ask you if you are perceiving your anger from the inside or the outside, a useful inquiry to ask yourself is "Am I perceiving facets of experience from the inside or the outside?" To inhabit requires resting the faculty of perception into an intimacy with the inside of the various dimensions of experience.

So while we are inhabiting many different things—our homes, cultures, relationships, towns and so on—inhabiting the full range of your first person experience physically, emotionally and mentally is an essential facet of embodiment. An important implication here, one that very few embodiment experts acknowledge, is that embodiment is not only invested in physical and emotional dimensions of experience. Elegant embodiment is invested in how mental phenomena of all types are embraced, inhabited and embodied. And, of course, it includes the physical, somatic and emotional facets of experience.

Finally, embodiment expands in important ways when you allow the already ever-present *movement* or flux of phenomena to move, shape and influence you in more full, less constrained ways. By turning toward the experiential flux through softening distinctness, releasing separateness, and embodying more of the immediacy of experience, you are likely to discover an interesting, often unexpected response. By making the counterinstinctual move of turning toward and opening to the most provocative, challenging and intense facets of experience, you can heighten your ability to participate with the unconditioned completeness and formless unmoving stability provided by the self-without-form. The interpenetrating subjectivity introduced in Chapter Three flowers, or opens more fully, in an energetic exchange with the formless dimensions of you.

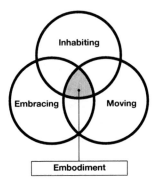

When you employ this insurance policy, the incompleteness at the root of your self-as-form can be heightened, refined and opened further. As the self-without-form provides a grounded, unconditioned and stable completeness, the self-as-form can participate as the unmediated bloom of immediacy in a now larger scope. The self-without-form is empty, yet this mysterious open and unconditioned seat of subjectivity is intimately connected with the self-as-form. We can think of this as a clearer, more direct perception of and participation with immediacy. This broader bandwidth of information flow yields greater attunement and skillful means, which ultimately provides an important facet to the ingenuity found within your elegance.

While the drive for completion usually found in the conventional stages of development often stunts our postconventional development required for human elegance, the second taste or unconditioned and formless completeness provides a powerful source of stability that is often needed to openly participate within your larger interpenetrating self. Again, we find the polarity of completeness and incompleteness being embraced. This time, the self-as-form provides the essential seat of incompleteness while the self-without-form offers the second taste of completeness. Ultimately, elegance nurtures the relative self's cohesive integrity, yet, given the intrinsic challenges in life, your self-as-form will be thrown off center. Elegance actually welcomes these challenging experiences with a grace and a creative aptitude for responsiveness that conventional stages of development are unable to yield. Why? We could say that this greater skillfulness is due to the unconditioned insurance policy we are discussing. To get one, you cannot be largely invested in the completeness projects found in the Socialized Mind and/or the Self-Authoring Mind. Furthermore, while you may typically pay a monthly or annual premium for a more conventional insurance policy, this insurance policy is negotiated in the immediacy of the moment. This coverage either holds you now or you are presumably left fending for your relative self's stability and completeness.

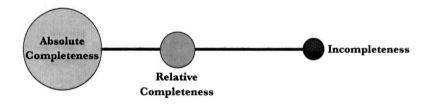

THE NEXT STAGE OF DEVELOPMENT

One of the ways Kegan defines the Self-Transforming Mind is by putting forth the position that this stages's subjectivity is identified with the process of form creation, whereas the Self-Authoring Mind is subjectively embedded in the self-as-form. Kegan asks:

> (1) Do we see the self-as-system as complete and whole or do we regard the self-as-system as incomplete, only a partial construction of all that the self is? (2) Do we identify with the self-as-form or do we identify with the process of form creation? Another way of putting this second questions is: Do we take as prior the elements of a relationship or the relationship itself (which creates its elements)?[67]

Take note of these important distinctions. Our exploration of the second taste of completeness appears to bring us, in some way, a step beyond the Self-Transforming Mind. Instead of only being identified as the process of form creation, there is now greater flexibility, a larger vantage point, and likely more skillful means. If the incompleteness of the self-as-form is followed in its larger complexity and the second taste of completeness is discovered, there is, in some ways, the ability to take the process of form creation as object. And features of the self-without-form have now emerged. At times this formless self may be identified with, while at other times the self-as-form may be more identified with. We will pick up this topic in our next chapter; however, one final point. At some place in development, the self makes a leap beyond the polarity of incompleteness and absolute completeness. Mysteriously, this elegant self is continually co-created from the unknowable formless dimension and the intrinsic partiality of form creation. This part known, part discovered and part undiscoverable subjectivity is elegance.

A JUST RELATIONSHIP BETWEEN STATES AND STAGES

The first exercise below is often offered for individuals who are unfamiliar with the formless facets of experience. A few distinctions are often helpful, and in many cases essential, before we outline the injunctions of these exercises. First, as we saw in Sam's session in Chapter Four, glimpses into the unconditioned and formless facets of the self are often initially experienced as black open space. As we touched on earlier, such experiences often can reveal a pervading mystery. Limitless space, a void that feels full or pregnant, infinite blackness and the deep doubt and uncertainty in your gut are all facets of experience that have, and are inside of, form. None are actually formless, which enables us to converse about them. We can think of these forms of experience as pressing up against that which is genuinely unconditioned and formless.

Turning attention towards the source of awareness is an injunction with a very long history. And, steering your attention towards the source of awareness, again and again, positions you to be discovered by the formless mystery. Yoga, being the oldest unbroken literary tradition on the planet, dates back some 5,000 to 6,000 years, with some Yogic and

Vedic scholars suggesting yoga's roots reach back even further. Many other forms of religious and spiritual practices have used these injunctions and similar ones for thousands of years. If you happen to have access to the yogic injunctions for dharana, dhyana and samadhi, the inner limbs of yoga, or similarly related exercises from Christian, Islamic, Hindu, Buddhist, Native American or other traditions, feel free to integrate these freely. However, it is essential that these exercises are situated accordingly.

Most spiritual and/or religious traditions and the exercises they put forward are not build upon, nor do they adequately integrate, our current and best understandings of adult development. As such, significant confusions exist between the cultivation of higher, deeper or more open states of consciousness and the development of identity traits. Keep this in mind as you draw on spiritual and religious injunctions and their interpretations of your experiences.

In many cases, the exercise of turning your attention toward the source of your awareness results in powerful states of consciousness. This book is ultimately not about you cultivating states of consciousness. It is about you growing *developmentally*. Spiritual or religious injunctions may share this intention for growth. However, and quite unfortunately, many teachers, traditions and cultures immersed in spiritual and/or religious practices unknowingly substitute state training for maturations in development.

While there are many multifaceted and complex relationships between states of consciousness and stages of development—the reason this practice is even included—it is essential for you to understand that achieving various states of consciousness is not the principle aim of this book nor the guiding intelligence of your elegance. I bring this up because it is not uncommon for someone to spend decades of their life devoted to the cultivation of these states, even from just a single taste of the type of transcendence this injunction (and others) are capable of providing.

States of consciousness are, by definition, temporary or transitive and exclusive. They come and they go and, while a state is here, it excludes other facets of experience. The stages of development we are exploring are, in contrast, relatively enduring and are integrative at their heart. Ultimately, your elegance is fluid between any state and the many stages of complexity you have access to in your life. Both are included. However, as our larger aim is your development, and not the expansion of a state of mind, states will serve stage development in our work here.

Leveraging stages to serve states is a massive confusion, and it will likely result in what appears to be the certain dismantling of elegance. States, in their transient and excluding functions, largely fail to deal with the ongoing and persistent challenges facing planet Earth and all forms of life on it, as well as the ongoing challenges in your personal life and relationships. Ultimately, it is the empty consistent formless dimension of you that will be engaged. It appears to be intimately and perhaps always engaged with the unfolding flux of form. This is one of the essential differences as we explore elegance. The grand liberation of formlessness is an integrated gesture of intimately engaging with and as the form of your life. This means a relatively enduring development of mind is being cultivated to face the immense challenges you now face personally and we face together.

EXERCISES TO LEVERAGE UNCONDITIONED COMPLETENESS

The two exercises below, turning toward subjectivity and turning toward experiential flux, which we touched on above, are designed for individuals who are outgrowing autonomy and/or for those interested in growing into interpenetrating subjectivity. You will see an emphasis on your separateness bringing these exercises into your experience, which is the basic architecture of doing an exercise. This traditional orientation to the exercises is a good starting point; however, I want to also present a second orientation to the exercises. Learn the exercises and then allow them to go. This means once you have learned and integrated these exercises, you can, at times, cease to impose them on the immediacy of experience. Once these have been integrated, you are invited to allow these exercises, and the various permutations and subtle nuances that come with the creative flux of relative experience, to *do you*. One orientation brings these exercises into the moment through the vehicle of your autonomous effort, while the other discovers these exercises as a natural facet of experience that is already doing you. Both orientations prove to be important as you practice these facets of the flexibility of elegance. And, please note the internet web address at the end of this chapter. You will find audio recordings of these two exercises to further support you.

Turning toward Subjectivity: Accessing the Unconditioned

Begin by relaxing as the immediacy of this moment. This is often accompanied by a loosening in your body-mind where your jaw softens, shoulders melt down your back, and your breath drops down easily into your belly. Similarly, the aperture of attention often softens and opens, bringing a larger cacophony of experiential immediacy to flux and flow through your awareness. Relax any effort to reach outward, add to or change what is already present. Instead, allow immediacy to wash through your nervous system just as it is.

Participate with the natural movement of attention and awareness as subjectivity, or your basic seat of consciousness, condenses around facets of experience and then opens and releases. Regardless of this activity, begin to nurture an open curiosity around the origin of your consciousness or subjectivity. Allow your attention and awareness to constellate around this curiosity. As attention is drawn toward parts, aspects and features of yourself and the experiential flux, gently open your attention around these objects. Memories of past events, current personality traits, relationships, anticipating future events, objects in your environmental surround and so on are not to be focused on. Extend attention toward the space around these objects and sense toward the already present, free, separate and complete awareness behind all experience.

Notice how consciousness is effortless. Sense into how nothing is required to have experience. Subjectivity is completely free. Objects of all types in your experience present themselves without intervention. Awareness is always already distinct from the changing flux of experience. Allow perception to rest precisely where and as it is.

Subjectivity at its heart is always already free from every facet of experience. Participate as this simplicity. Float as the spaceless, colorless, senseless opening of awareness. You are unconditioned unity. Right now, without effort or control, you are open awareness free of form. You are space.

As you sense mystery, not-knowingness, a broader curiosity or simple space, turning toward the origin of awareness, let go.

TURNING TOWARD SUBJECTIVITY: ACCESSING THE UNCONDITIONED

1) RELAX AS IMMEDIACY.

2) PARTICIPATE WITH THE NATURAL MOVEMENTS OF YOUR FREE FLOWING ATTENTION. IN OTHER WORDS, ALLOW ATTENTION TO BE FREE FROM FIXATIONS.

3) NOTICE THE EFFORTLESSNESS OF SUBJECTIVITY.

4) GENTLY TURN TOWARD SUBJECTIVITY'S ORIGIN.

5) LET GO.

Turning toward Experiential Flux: Formless Embodied Participation

While our last exercise is an injunction to employ on your own, turning toward the experiential flux steers your engagement toward the many displays of your everyday life. As such, you can practice right now as you read these sentences. You can engage this injunction in conversation with a friend, colleague or spouse. You can practice alone in your car. Wherever you find yourself and whatever contexts you are immersed in can be used an an opportunity to turn toward the experiential flux of any moment.

For the time being, set aside preferences and commit to participating with the truth of your experience as it already is. Begin by broadening participation as the buoyant immediacy of this moment. Trust this.

Trust your body posture as it already is. Trust the form, posture and movement of your mind without limit. Trust breath. Allow your breathing to do you. Trust tension. Participate as the holding and/or releasing of this. Trust this moment such that your trust envelops and includes mistrust. Allow the form and structure of you to be exactly how your self-as-form is right now. Movement co-creates immediacy. Participate with and as the innate movements without hesitation and/or undue mediation.

Embrace, inhabit and become precisely what is here. The aperture of you opens within and around the direct immediacy of experiential flow. The flux of form and experience are you. Beyond your habituated preferences, effortless participation with experience is already happening. Participate with this. Allow awareness of the blooming immediacy of experience to co-create you.

TURNING TOWARD EXPERIENTIAL FLUX: FORMLESS EMBODIED PARTICIPATION

1) SETTING ASIDE PREFERENCES, BROADEN PARTICIPATION WITH IMMEDIACY.

2) TRUST THIS.

3) PARTICIPATE WITH AND AS MOVEMENT.

4) BE AND BECOME THE BLOOMING IMMEDIACY OF EXPERIENCE.

For audio recordings of two exercises and additional resources on refining your access to the second taste or unconditioned completeness, visit:

www.TheElegantSelf.com/Second.Completeness

Personal Notes & Reflection

8
DIALECTICAL ELEGANCE
Higher Meaning-Making as You

Steve is an elite American football player. He had just taken a big step forward and was now playing at what he called "the next level." He had left his collegiate career and was now playing professionally. This was what he had been training for much of his life. While his age-related peers may have been studying journal articles, textbooks and the like, Steve was engaged in perhaps the equivalent of getting a master's degree in the complexity of an offensive playbook.

Our football player was immensely athletically gifted, kinesthetically intelligent and conceptually bright; however, playing at the next level had challenged Steve significantly, and he was not playing at his best, at least not at the time. He reached out to me. He talked to me because football was his life; it meant the world to him and competition was immensely tight. Steve knew he was off and he had to course-correct fast. What we discovered together was a central problem rooted in Steve's effort. He was *trying too hard*. He was bringing too much effort into how he played. While he did not realize it, this added effort had also contributed to a few minor injuries he recently had been working with.

One of the core beliefs Steve worked with came through as him not being intrinsically worthy of playing football at this level. According to him, he made it because of his immense work ethic, hard disciplined training, and the sound intelligent coaching he had received year after year. Underneath this, he felt dispensable and replaceable. Like many of us, Steve felt inadequate even with his most brilliant gifts. This insecurity fueled another layer of effort in his training, study and on-the-field play. Some of this heightened effort helped off the field, but it was costing him when his performance mattered most. Ultimately, the added pressure, attention and level of competition fueling the extra layer of effort was stunting his ability to perform.

The major problem for Steve was that he had constructed and consolidated a sense of self around his effort and discipline. We can think of this as his completion project. While this is often a useful self to construct, it is immensely limited if one is interested or invested in some of human beings' highest capacities. He was stuck inside of effort and, as we learned together, whenever he began to relax and let go, he would feel as though he was going to lose what mattered most to him. As such, on the playing field in front of tens of thousands of fans and many more watching from home, his new coaches and teammates who both held him to higher standards, as well as the new level of competition he was facing resulted in a heightening of his efforts.

As he experienced this transition seemingly at every point in his games, he needed to be a step faster, a yard farther down the field, and more powerful in his ability to break tackles—thus his play lacked trust and moved with too much urgency. Steve's performance suffered.

Steve's enduring success at the next level required what I often call *the dialectical self*. His mind and body needed to be fiercely powerful, yet also profoundly relaxed. He required a self-understanding about where he belonged on the field, playing football at the next level. The game he was now playing, while virtually identical to his earlier levels of engagement, demanded an effort that was larger, stronger and more focused. Yet this was paradoxically attained by letting go, allowing and relaxing in the spontaneity of the game. In one fraction of a second, maximal effort, and in the next split second, a complete release. American football's immense physical demands elicited by the collisions of fast, powerful and unusually large men required Steve to both collide with his opponents with refined control, immense power and a relaxed fluidity if he was going to remain healthy and play his best. We can think of this as a kinesthetic dialectical intelligence, where physical properties involving polar opposites join in creative and synergistic ways. Steve already had much of this kinesthetic development; however, psychologically he had run into some barriers in his mind that inhibited his physical and athletic giftedness to mature in his game time play. By increasing Steve's ability to mentally relax, trust and belong to the game at the next level, he has been able to bring forth his more refined talents when it has mattered most, and in the process, he was able to stay more healthy.

DIALECTICS DEFINED

As we have touched on numerous times, elegance involves the fluid embrace of polarity. Elegance requires a self that is larger in size than polarity. This fluidity and acceptance allows for greater movement among polar energies and perspectives, while also welcoming greater conflictual tension between two or more positions. These features—whether we are talking about subject and object, competency and inadequacy, your relative completeness and incompleteness, form and formlessness, or the absolute completeness inherent in the center of your subjectivity and incompleteness, as we have investigated thus far—are all functions of what we may call the *dialectical self* embedded in and as elegance.

We can find seeds of Western dialectical thinking in ancient Greece, as Heraclitus of Ephesus expounded a philosophy describing a universe in constant change. His philosophy maintains a world filled with continual creation of more difference and diversity. Yet, simultaneously, while this flux is under way, the universe also paradoxically preserves an underlying unity, sameness or consistency. This is known as *the unity of opposites*, and it is generally understood to be a central facet of dialectics and for Heraclitus' concept of the logos (law or principle) governing all things.[68] In his own words, "Collections: wholes and not wholes; brought together, pulled apart; snug in unison, snug in conflict; from all things one and from one all things."[69]

Later, dialectics were popularized by Plato, as exhibited in Socratic dialogue, where we find one position posited followed by an opposing counterpoint, until a more true position emerges. Both Kant and Hegel are recognized for popularizing the triad of thesis, anti-thesis and synthesis, while Hegel used dialectics to point to a historical force, driving events onward, toward a progressive resolution of contradictions. For Hegel, "The process is one of overcoming the contradiction between thesis and antithesis, by means of synthesis; the synthesis in turn becomes contradicted, and the process repeats itself until final perfection is reached."[70]

For our purposes, there is no final perfection, and/or there is nothing but a final perfection as this marriage of incompleteness and completeness (or imperfection and perfection) in both its harmony and discord. You are dialectical. And dialectics are co-constructing you. This happens in a few important ways: the principle of contradiction, the principle of change and the principle of holism.

First, the *Principle of Contradiction*: opposing forces give rise to diverse expressions of form. Reality as we come to know its many dimensions, and who you are always in the process of becoming, appear to be born from larger contradictory forces. Innate to this process is the full, always undone and incomplete bloom of immediacy and its creative tension with the inheritance of the past's historical conditioning. Put simply, what is happening right now is always in some opposition against what was.

To give an example, the contradictory forces in separateness and connectedness collaborate into the construction of your self-in-form. You express and animate separateness and connectedness. You may find yourself standing in opposition against some dimensions of what was. Maybe it was the experience of feeling dependent on someone, it might have been what you earned last year in revenue or it could be the sense of anxiety you felt at work. Maybe it is you taking new action in your life. Regardless some facet of you stands in greater separateness from the historical conditioning of past experiences.

And yet simultaneously simultaneously the formations of you are also interwoven with the forces of connection. Facets of you are inherently joined and connected. Perhaps you have a new vision for your life. You might work towards greater economic generatively and new modes of revenue generation. You may explore how to be less co-dependent on key people in your life. You might engage with professional trainings to help with your anxieties at work. All of these also exhibit a relatedness or connectedness to your vision, new people, trainings and valued ways of being.

Separateness and connectedness are fundamentally contradictory. Yet this conflict and contradiction can be creative. And the ongoing exchange between these two underlying energetics are co-constructing you right now. Can you notice both? Are you feeling more separate from this paragraph? Or are you experiencing yourself as being more connected to this sentence? What is your relationship to the inherited prior moments of what was? Are you feeling more separate from this past, and/or are you feeling more congruence and connection with what was? These are all tastes of the principle of contradiction in motion in your life right here and right now.

Second, dialectics conform within the *Principle of Change*. All form, both your sense of self and reality as a whole, are in a process of continual change. You and I are always held in and born through a dynamic flux. Change is perpetually doing, shaping, disassembling and assembling us.

Most of us do not need examples to illustrate this principle because of its pervading obviousness. For those of us with the luxury to grow older we do not have to look very hard to see how our bodies are changing as we age. Relationships come and go. The people who do endure throughout large parts of our lives change and so do our relationships. Technology advances as new markets emerge. Other markets mature and still other areas of commerce disappear. Change is happening everywhere.

And yet the principle of change and the principle of contradiction are both operative. While the ever-present facility of movement and dynamism in form is driven by the principle of change, the self-without-form is without change. It has no motion. Here you have no conditioning. Here we can sense the principle of contradiction at work. All form and its innate movements are in creative opposition with the changeless, motionless and formless facets of non-existence. And perhaps it is the innate contradiction—the creative conflict—between that which is formless and that which is in form that gives rise to the experience of you reading this book along with everything else in existence. These are the play of dialectics living us.

Finally, the *principle of holism* maintains that all parts of a whole are intimately interconnected. And, that all parts can join together into a larger coherence and coordination. A more nuanced view maintains that it is not the parts that then lead up to an interconnecting whole. Instead, a whole—albeit a whole that is creatively divided or contradictory as we explored in our first principle—gives birth to its distinct parts. Out of an already interrelating whole or interconnecting coherence do parts, separateness and distinctness discover themselves. Unity creates diversity.

The dialectical self—the self that you already are and always will be —is interpenetrated by, interrelated with and co-constructed through a contradictory, always changing holism. Here we find all three principles at play. A larger holism of unfathomable scope and complexity, one that is perhaps elegant, gives shape to all form, its defining properties and its adaptive momentums. The dialectical self, unlike the less developed selves of our past, is aware of and participates with this complexity.

To summarize, the dialectical self, and thus you as elegance, aligns with, while also retaining, a freedom from these three principles. The *Principle of Contradiction*: Multiplicity inherently forms opposing positions, each demonstrating a relative truth to be honored, included and integrated. Second, the dialectical self conforms within the *Principle of Change*. And yet you are simultaneously also changeless in your unconditioned commitment to change. Finally, the dialectical self is interrelated and co-constructed from and through the *Principle of Holism*. And yet simultaneously the dialectical self retains what appears to be an untouchable and un-penetrable center of subjectivity.

LIBERATED DIALECTICS

Elegance is a function of the fluid embodiment, navigation of, and participation with and as polarities. One way we can think of this is with the concept of *liberated dialectics*. This involves at least three central facilities. The first is unbounded participation, the emersion-in-and-as-immediacy is the second, while the third is open-ended incompleteness.

Elegance appears to universally involve your larger, *unbounded participation* with the already unfolding movements of form. This of course is not merely the participation with one side of a set of familiar polarities but the elegant movement with both sides of polarities.

Unbounded participation may initially emerge as a willingness to participate with the full ranges within polarities. This willingness inevitably presses us into awkward, anxiety proving and clumsy experimentations with unfamiliar and unexercised aspects of ourselves. These experiences are foundations for the more full, fluid, embodied participation with more rich and diverse spectrums in polarities.

For example, a woman who has been socialized into and then has self-authored a more masculine expression of herself to be successful in her career may at first feel awkward and uncomfortable as she first begins to embrace the more feminine dimensions of herself. Over time as she grows in her ability to embody and participate with both dimensions of herself she can more readily inhabit the full spectrum of who she is. Not only based on her own inner-directive but also in an organic response the contexts she discovers herself in.

Unbounded participation is not in juxtaposition to resistance and/or struggle. Elegance can and does embrace, inhabit, move as or participate with the polar positions of resistance, struggle, denial and avoidance. Unbounded participation does move with the less mediated expressions of our resistances too. One useful distinction here unbounded participation with and as these positions involves a larger facility of engagement (to be explored further in Chapter Ten). This is in contrast to the rote, unconscious and often unexamined habitual functioning we commonly find in struggle, resistance and denial. The participatory function of elegance is also larger than polarities. Failure to embody, navigate and participate with and as polarity often results in an unconscious and habituated struggle with roughly half of any given polarity. However, your elegance can embrace struggle and the fluid movement with the dynamism inherent in polarities.[71]

So, while our woman who is moving towards the fluid inhabitation of the polar formations of her masculine and feminine qualities, later on she will be able to actively pick up—that is re-engage with—the masculine facets of herself that often denies and/or marginalizes her feminine qualities. Although she will no longer be unknowingly fixated here. This may be an organic response to her contexts, or it may even be an intentional choice.

Our second facility in liberated dialectics is the *emersion-in-and-as-immediacy*. We can think of this as a way of being in the present moment. Only elegance inevitably draws us beyond being more grounded in and attuned with immediacy. Liberated dialectics immerses us inside of the present such that we *are* immediacy, we are not merely being *in* the moment. This functioning of elegance is intrinsically drawn toward a greater relationship with and as the unfolding present moment, both in its formless features and formed qualities.

Your relationship with polarity is likely to unfold in a fairly predictable two-step pattern. First, you are likely to experience polarity retroactively. In reflection, you will be more able to pick up a polarity and then see it in action in a prior experience. This can be thought of as an expanding exercise where your mind's ability to see, recognize and label the polarity becomes more nuanced. By reflectively metabolizing polarities, your mind becomes more dialectical in nature. This prepares your mind for the second step.

The second step involves your participation with polarities in the immediacy of experience. Instead of needing to look back on what did happen, what contexts you were in and how polarity or polarities were influencing you, your mind can now see, recognize, label and thus participate in real time, right now, with the polarity or polarities present with a greater degree of skillfulness. Elegance involves an ongoing exploration of polarity with some polarities being worked with reflectively and retroactively, while others have already been integrated into your mind's ability to navigate them in immediacy. This is your larger capacity to be immersed in and as dialectical immediacy.[72]

This leads us to the third facility of liberated dialectics: *open-ended incompleteness*. It appears the complexity of form always exceeds the capacity of your mind's ability to integrate. Human beings at early stages of development are clearly immersed in a world that is vastly more complex than they are aware and capable of navigating skillfully. This assumption appears to hold true for most adults and even the most developmentally complex human beings we have been able to study. It is my bias that the complexity of immediacy is likely always to exceed the mind, regardless of what developmental achievement human beings make.

If this assumption is maintained and is more or less accurate, it means elegance is, at its heart, an open-ended inquiry. Your mind will never grasp the entirety of the dialectics inherent in and as immediacy expressed through the multiplicity of form. Thus an ongoing investigation of an increasing nuance inherent within polarities is likely to be a more or less permanent feature of your elegance. Furthermore, you are likely to periodically discover and encounter new polarities within experience, both in your reflective retroactive remetabolization of prior experience and the more spontaneous illumination of polarities arising within and as the immediacy of experience. Liberated dialectics are thus open-ended and incomplete, and the exceedingly complex moment is likely to always call your elegance into becoming something more.

CORE DIALECTICS

As a means of exercising your dialectical perception—as well as allowing dialectics to exercise you—in order to stimulate and cultivate greater liberation in your fluid functioning within and as the dialectical self, we will briefly investigate a list of *core dialectics*. This set of polarities appear to be "core" or "central" to elegance, from my vantage point at this time. It is worthwhile noting that likely there is no singular or grouping of dialectics that are actually core or central in an enduring way. While perspective and experience tend be organized by and/or constellated around or within a core group of interpenetrating polarities, the dialectical exchange of form independent of our more limited perspectives is likely a more open centerless, perhaps infinite multifaceted exchange. With that said, let's tour an incomplete sample of core dialectics surrounding and stemming from elegance.

Being ∞ *Becoming*

The world of form, and thus your self-as-form, is undergoing an unending process of change. You and presumably everything around and within you is moving from *being* this to *becoming* that. You, as we explored earlier, are fundamentally incomplete. Simultaneously, you also include some facet of experience that is unconditioned, untouchable and unchanging, which is what we explored as the second taste of completeness and the self-without-form or what we are calling being here.

Polarities similarly rooted in and/or around being and becoming involve the one and the many, unity and multiplicity, infinite and finite, as well as transcendence and immanence (or the polarity of the infinite as revealed in the transcendence of all from and the infinite found in the innate substance and substrate of form).

You might already be seeing this polarity of being and becoming as inherent in the description above; however, form and formless are also closely related to being and becoming as we are using these terms here. We begin with this polarity and have spent considerable time exploring the polarity of form and that which is beyond form because it is an essential feature of elegance. Without inhabiting a self that is beyond form, the drive for completeness is often dangerously focused exclusively on the activities of the self-as-form. This myopic focus on the self-as-form dramatically stunts functioning. As such, being and becoming appear to be two facets of an unresolvable tension of which elegance participates with. Similarly, the ongoing underlying tension beneath unity and multiplicity, transcendence and immanence, and form and formless are co-creating you.

Being ●━━━━━━━━━● Becoming	
One	Many
Unity	Multiplicity
Infinite	Finite
Transcendence	Immanent
Formless	Form

Stability ∞ Change

While we can think of being as a provider of stability and becoming offering a source of change, *stability* is used here to point toward the first taste of completeness or, as defined earlier, your self-as-form's cohesive integrity. While this relative stability is less stable and enduring than the unconditioned seat of being, the cohesive integrity of your self-as-form, and how you *change* or do not change proves to be an important polarity with which to skillfully negotiate and participate.

The integrity of the self-as-form's cohesion maintains a homeostatic equilibrium, in juxtaposition to the larger change surrounding and co-creating your self-as-form. Interestingly, the larger your homeostatic cohesive integrity is, the greater the pressure you exert on the external environment. As you do not change through your homeostasis, you often knowingly or unknowingly press the necessity to become different beyond or outside of your cohesive integrity's boundary. For example, we could view many of Western social and cultural collective homeostatic practices as pressuring the larger environment to change. As Western culture's cohesive integrity has grown in size and scope, it has and is creating more stability, predicability and so forth for some of its members. While these create what many consider to be good advancements in human evolution, we are also introducing greater environmental change and fluctuation. Climate change is likely one facet of this. As climate augments in ways beyond the scope of current human socio-cultural regulatory facilities (which is likely to occur at some point, given Earth is largely a limited, closed system), human beings are likely to be forced to change, perhaps dramatically.

Elegance requires a conscious engagement with and participation as stability and change as both you and not-you. This means stability will, at times, co-construct more of your relative experience, while at other times you may be opening to participate as a counter-instinctual move, thus embodying changes organized precisely against your preferences. It is important that habits for stability and homeostasis do not largely envelop and govern your autonomous functioning with yourself in relationship and in the world. While there is immense wisdom and intelligence in the preservation of and thus stability in your self-as-form, the greater influence of elegance moves freely between dramatic destabilizing changes and rigorously defended homeostasis.

Interior ∞ Exterior

As leveraged above, we can see how stability and change apply pressure internally and externally—yet another core dialectic to integrate. Part of you is co-constructed by the continual energetic flux between *internal* domains of experience and *external* domains of experience. Elegance requires a fluid and open participatory relationship with both internal and external domains of experience to optimize information flow. Constrained information flow likely compromises performance at any given time and in any situation. Preferences or orienting biases toward one type of information and/or the avoidance, denial or neglect of another thus constricts elegance and in some cases can negate any form of elegance coming through your relative self-in-form. Elegance is resting on a dynamic network of information flow from your inner world, relationships and external shifting contexts.

Comfort ∞ Experiential Intensity

Closely related to stability and change is a less understood polarity involving *comfort* and what I often refer to as *experimental intensity*. On the one side, we find consistent cohesive integrity or stability as long as the environment remains relatively stable. Environment here refers to both the exterior techno-socio-economic contexts as well as interior, relational, cultural and political contexts. With stability in the environment, cohesive integrity can maintain comfort. This is okay; however, it comes with a risk. When human beings are comfortable, they tend to be very habituated. Homeostasis often solidifies in an unexamined stagnancy, and little change occurs. Decades can pass in a fairly predictable pattern as long as some acceptable level of comfort is maintained. While not all comfort is of this variety, it is appears to be one of the persistent risks.

On the other side, we find experiential intensity, which is often, but not always associated with the change side of the polarity explored above.

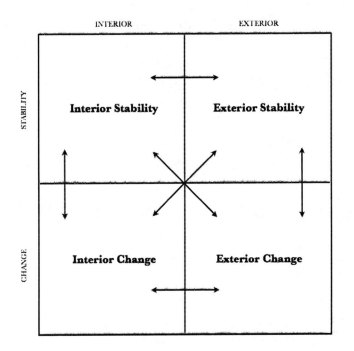

As you can see, a complex interrelated matrix exists between these polarities. While we have only explored two of these relationships in the above text, readers should note that at least 16 different relationships reside as possible interconnections between the polarities of change and stability and interior and exterior.[73] It is likely that most, if not all polarities embrace similar interrelated networks of connections. If we were to introduce just one more dialectic (two poles) to the diagram, we would yield a two-by-two cube holding more than 3 million different interpenetrating relationships!

Experiential intensity has three basic forms. The first is *pleasure*. The second is *pain*. The third is a set of experiences *integrating or unifying pain and pleasure* together. While many people conceive of pain and pleasure as being two sides of one polarity, I have found a more useful polarity holding pain, pleasure and their integration at one pole represented as experiential intensity, while the other side of the polarity has very low levels of experiential intensity found in comfort.[74]

The important takeaway is, again, that human elegance requires a freedom to embody and participate with counter-instinctual moves that go against your core conditioning and habituated preferences which often operate in maintaining comfort. This often results in the destabilization of homeostasis resulting in greater experiential intensity. Surprisingly, this plays out with both pain and pleasure, as your habituated comfort zone often resists and insulates you from higher levels of pain and pleasure as well as experiences integrating pain and pleasure simultaneously.

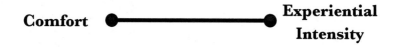

Comfort ●━━━━━━━━━● **Experiential Intensity**

Habit ∞ Novelty

A dialectic important to our conversation thus far, and one that will increasingly become more central to our exploration of elegance, is the polarity of *habit* and *novelty*. Conditioned grooves have been cut and reinforced throughout your lifespan. Additionally, your body and mind hold conditioning spanning back tens of thousands of years. So your personal history as well as your collective inheritance lends you a myriad of habits. Some are seen, many not. Some are incredibly adaptive, others maladaptive.

The immediacy of who you are now and who you are becoming as you read this sentence is also the production of immense creative novelty. We can think of the architecture of your self-as-form as part historical inheritance and part creative novelty. Elegance moves freely and skillfully as the unresolvable exchange between that which is inherited, rooted in habits from the past, and that which stems from the creative play of novelty. Both facets co-create you.

Another way you can look at this dialectic is that freedom and determinism both shape who you are. Follow more of your habituated conditioning and you, along with your life, become more determined and fixed. Participate with the creative novelty inherent in every moment, and the formation of you can take on greater flexibility and possibility.

Ultimately, both are fundamental facets of your elegance. And as we will explore later at length, elegance is often born from an intentional confrontation with the many layers of habituation in order to free up your ability to participate more skillfully with novelty.

Mediated ∞ Unmediated

Another important dialectic to be explored when considering adult development reaching beyond autonomy is the polarity between *mediated* behavior and *unmediated* conduct. Behavior is always an expression of some creative exchange between conduct that is both mediated and experience that is more unmediated. Mediated behavior and experience exercises an intervening intelligence bringing forth greater agreement or coherence between the unfolding events of life and how you respond. For example, the Self-Authoring Mind exercises a mediating intelligence that filters experience and monitors conduct to best serve your personal integrity. Similarly the Socialized Mind employs a mediating intelligence that filters experience and manages conduct to best serve the values, coherence and norms of a valued expert, group and/or interpersonal relationship. These stages of development are each respectively immersed in mediating the younger or earlier stages of development.

The Self-Transforming Mind of course also similarly filters experience and manages conduct. Technically speaking all human experience and conduct is mediated. However as adults mature into the Self-Transforming Mind forms of spontaneous, less mediated experience and conduct more readily shows up. This is not the erosion of developmental complexity but rather a greater fruition of adulthood. Unmediated postautonomous functioning can demonstrate spontaneous action that is no longer subservient to personal integrity or the stability of valued interpersonal relationships. A larger more complex reality or broader interrelating series of contexts can be served.

Elegance requires a participation with mediated planning and a nuanced controlled execution of a broader strategy. It also involves the creative collaboration with and as the intelligence inherent in a more complex relationship with immediacy. You are a production of the creative, perhaps unresolvable exchange between that which is mediated, planned and controlled and that which is unmediated and spontaneous. Elegance as you is a creative flexibility of mediated and unmediated intelligence.

Masculine ∞ Feminine

As you likely know, a central, apparently unresolvable polarity is the energetic and perspectival orientations of *masculine* and *feminine* or, as we defined them in Chapter Five, *separateness* and *connectedness*. Elegance necessitates a fluid participation with both of these orientations. As explored earlier, your larger maturity requires outgrowing the completion project's rigidity that tends to organize and consolidate around either a more masculine or feminine orientation. Alternatively, we can also look into similarly related polarities as orientations that privilege either the individual or the collective and challenge or support them. This immensely rich, multifaceted polarity can be an innovative source of a larger skillfulness, if you grow to embrace its inherent irresolvability. Elegance rests within your creative participation with and as separateness, while at other times moving to the contradictory energy inherent within greater connectedness.

Polarity ∞ Integration

A less understood and seen dialectic is one between *polarity* and *integration*. Polarities appear to be, at their root, unresolvable opposing positions, while integration synthesizes, yokes together and brings forth a resolution between oppositions. It is essential for you to understand that our exploration of dialectics both privileges the larger integration that is your development and, while contradictory, also participates with the larger irresolvability intrinsic in polarities. Biasing integration diminishes the creative dynamism between polarities and paradoxically inhibits higher order integration and the free functioning of the extremities inside polarities. Similarly, biasing the irresolvability of polarities dampens the creative possibilities inherent in the drive for integration. Elegance as you is the free oscillation between the open range of unresolvable polar dynamics and the integration, resolution or synthesis of polarity.

Body ∞ *Mind*

Another core polarity to explore, especially with higher adult development, is the dichotomy between *body* and *mind*. Similarly related polarities include the separation and, at times, antagonism between *thinking* and *feeling* or *passion* and *reason*. Mature adult development requires the fluid processing of information that is bodily in nature and conceptual in nature. Furthermore, elegance as you necessitates the outgrowing of an identity that is principally mental in nature. Being subjectively identified with mental phenomena appears to be a core habit many adults confront as they begin to develop beyond autonomy. You are not a body, nor are you a mind. You are a body-mind, and physical and mental phenomena collaboratively give rise to you. Elegance is the higher order synthesis of body and mind in an integrated coherence. And you are the free and open tension of the irresolvability between these two different domains of experience.

The centaur, found in Greek mythology, has been used to point toward the integration and participation with both physical and mental dimensions of experience.[75] The centaur, being part human (upper body) and part horse (lower body), symbolizes a being embracing two natures. This is in contrast to the horse rider who is human, symbolizing the mind, owning and commanding his or her horse, symbolizing the body. The integration of and participation with body and mind opens up a broader more complex territory of experience than subjectivity identified with only the mind or body.

Simplicity ∞ *Complexity*

The larger maturity inherent in and as elegance is much more flexible than previous, more conventional stages of development. Instead of being more fixed inside one form of the complexity of mind, elegance as you can choose or simply participate in the arising of complexity that fits a particular situation. For example, an adult stably functioning from the Self-Authoring Mind will largely organize his or her experience in fairly predictable, autonomous ways. This is also the case for individuals who are inside of the Socialized Mind. Once the Self-Transforming

Mind shows up, individuals have more access to and can function from a larger spectrum of developmental functioning. No longer are you limited to showing up in a single form of complexity. Instead, you are able to participate with your current highest stage of development, and you can also give rise to expressions of earlier, less complex stages.[76] This brings forth the polarity between *simplicity* and *complexity*. One of the features you are likely to find in your own postautonomous development is an ease and comfort with more facets of yourself. The effort to consistently present yourself socially in a favorable light relaxes as you progressively grow beyond your autonomy. This supports a greater flexibility to show up in your less complex ways, when skillful, and to participate with your larger complexity, when skillful. Elegance paradoxically is born from your larger complexity, which embraces your earlier simplicity through a more inclusive willingness to and commitment in the incomplete entirety of you as a human being.

Effort ∞ Surrender

One of your Autonomy's orienting biases likely maintains that in order to do something, your separate distinct self-as-form must exert the effort necessary. Your life is, in many ways, determined by your efforts. This is, of course, quite true in many regards. However, to consolidate an identity inside of effort is to collapse your larger elegant efficiency and influence in life. To move with greater energetic currents requires, in many cases, a surrender of your separateness and more fragmented autonomy that often feels alone, against all odds, and in juxtaposition to the larger environment.

The larger proficiency in life, in every domain, is a dialectical oscillation between *effort* and *surrender*. Note that your participation with effort, discipline, consistency and determination in the face of complex challenges is undoubtedly required. Distractions and other obstacles are part of the broader interior and exterior environments. They are to be resisted, struggled against and/or penetrated through, requiring your focused and precise efforts. However, effort often must be accompanied by a larger participation with broader contexts, more congruent movements, and a stronger momentum that has already chosen you yet is

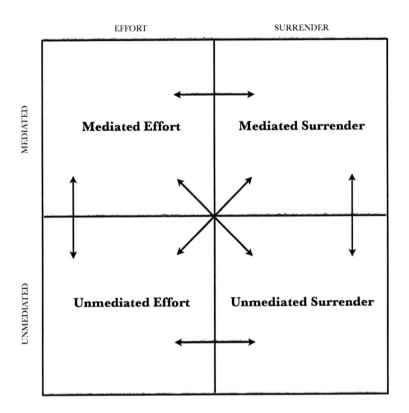

Here we see the multifaceted relationships between two polarities. Across the top is effort and surrender. Along the side we see mediated and unmediated experience and conduct. Mediated effort in the upper left is the relationship adults are likely most familiar with. Highly accomplished athletes train unmediated effort illustrated in the lower left quadrant such that their skills can be executed without conscious mediation. In the upper right is mediated surrender where we can find ourselves letting go of our efforts and innately trusting ourselves in any given situation. In the lower right quadrant we find an unmediated surrender which can be found as a meditator spontaneously ceases to exercise a meditation technique and instead inhabits the essential seat or state of meditation. Arrows connect all possible relationships as elegance can freely move amongst and between these polarities.

also much bigger than your autonomous efforts. Participating as these larger forces requires surrender.

Elegance involves the creative collaboration of both effort and surrender, mediated and/or unmediated by part spontaneity and part strategy. This novel fluidity brings forth stronger, more powerful and congruent forms of effort, while maintaining a dynamic flexibility that can let go of effort to be shaped and directed anew from surrender's immense power.

Micro ∞ Macro

Perception and perspective often tend to privilege either a *macro* or *micro* orientation in any given situation. Another way we might think about this is perception may organize around a singularity or specificity. When this happens, we often lose the broader collective or contextual perspective. Similarly, when perception structures around a macro orientation, it is easy to lose touch with the specificity of one of the parts. Ultimately, we need both if we are to optimize our performance and functioning in the world and within ourselves. At times you require perceptions into collective contexts and their complex multiplicities. To get these bigger pictures, you need the macro-orientation. Other times you will need to focus into a unique, singular specificity. Maybe it is a single project, a relationship with someone important, or a part of yourself requiring your full attention at the exclusion of all else. This is the micro-orientation. While this polarity may be relatively simple, knowing when and how to focus in on the micro and/or when to broaden perception to include the larger sphere of influences at play appears to be an unending inquiry. Discovering which orientation, or even which combination of these two, yields the greatest skillful means in your life is a common feature of elegance.

Life ∞ Death

Perhaps the most challenging of dialectics is that of *life* and *death*. Ernest Becker, in his influential book *The Denial of Death*, proposes the principle avoidance in the human mind and broader culture is our basic anxiety around death.[77] This is the organizing structure behind each human being's negotiation of life and perhaps all stories defend human beings from encountering a larger, perhaps ultimate reality. As Becker illustrates, "Making a killing in business or on the battlefield frequently has less to do with economic need or political reality than with the need for assuring ourselves that we have achieved something of lasting worth."[78]

While there is intelligence inherent in this denial, a self consolidated around life, while avoiding the anxiety of death is ultimately a self smaller than polarity. As such, the complexity to participate with and as elegance is absent. As we can often see, individuals who sacrifice their lives for some broader mission, purpose or act of valor are held within a reverence and profound respect almost universally amongst their culture. As Becker puts it, "We admire most the courage to face death."[79] In order to live life in congruence with your larger maturity, you are required to participate with an integrity that is unshaken by the anxiety of mortality. While elegance can be found within the fear, anxiety and terror of death and dying, as well as the avoidance of death, your larger capacities as a human being allow you to rest fearlessly in the face of loss, decay, destruction and death.

Furthermore, as we will explore with greater depth in Chapter Ten, life is likely to demand that you encounter feelings of dying and/or experiences where it appears your annihilation is at risk even though your life is actually not in danger. In these situations, we might say it is important, and perhaps essential, for you to embody the polarity of death. In doing so, you may experience the paradoxical relationships between life and death, vitality and dissolution, creativity and destruction. For example, as your experiential encounter with death becomes more vivid you may notice that you feel more alive. As parts of you and your life are destroyed a newfound creativity and vitality may capture you. These deeper embraces of life and death are perhaps a culminating gesture of the dialectical self and the elegance that stems from this fluid embrace of and participation with dialectics.

PROBLEMS OF THE PREDIALECTICAL SELF

The conventional self, either formulated in and from the conformity inherent in the Socialized Mind or the distinguished autonomy often demonstrated in the Self-Authoring Mind, is a predialectical formulation of you. These conventions, while bringing forth essential functions to human community and independence, are likely, as we touched on in the Introduction, incapable of addressing the multifaceted and ever changing challenges facing our world today. You need to integrate these essential functions of conforming and self-direction, and it appears the world is demanding you to not be limited by, or exclusively defined by, these functions. The capacity to conform and the ability to independently direct yourself must be objects you mediate, negotiate with, and exert a larger sphere of influence on.

Your predialectical self is invested in, partly intentionally and partly unintentionally, maintaining a fixed position in juxtaposition to an opposite and contradictory polarity. This division in your mind creates the completion project we explored at length in Chapter Five. Divisions in your mind predictably show up as fissures in the world you know. Economic, social, cultural, interpersonal and private divisions set up an often dangerous perspective of you being over "here" and that which is "not-you" residing over there. In contrast, the dialectical self is an attunement with and a larger functionality in the conventions of self opposed toward another. However, the larger complexity of mind can simultaneously—without effort—cohere a larger world with more possibilities. As the elegant mind co-creates you, a new world becomes both a sincere possibility as well as an urgent necessity. This larger mind coheres or forms a world where the fissions and divisions no longer necessitate unexamined separation and conflict as they once did within your smaller, less complex mind and its co-constructed divided world. Instead, dialectical elegance as you yields how and where the world can come together in greater contact through division. What is you and not you, in a conventional perspective, still function fluidly; however, you now embrace, participate with, and come into form in response to being both this over here and, in part, that over there. As the larger co-creative elegant embrace sculpts you, boundaries that once only divided can now simultaneously connect.

Elegance is similar to the now famous decision presented in the movie *The Matrix*. Computer hacker and soon to be hero Neo, played by Keanu Reeves, is presented with a singular, seemingly all important choice by a mysterious man named Morpheus, played by Laurence Fishburne. Morpheus, holding more wisdom and information about the true nature of reality, appropriately is named after the Greek god of dreams, a term often translated as "she (or he) who shapes." In a dark and stormy night, Morpheus, dressed in a long, black leather jacket and dark impenetrable sunglasses, presents Neo with his choice. Couched in a larger discussion of fate, free will and the all-pervasive field of the matrix, Neo confronts the perennial dilemma of either waking up to the reality beyond the prison of his mind or remaining in his somewhat comfortable and known conventions inside his ignorance.

Sitting face-to-face with Neo, only a small table and a single glass of water between them, Morpheus leans toward the hacker from his broad thick leather chair and says, "This is your last chance. After this, there is no turning back." Opening his left hand where a blue pill sits, Morpheus continues, "You take the blue pill, the story ends. You wake up in your bed and believe whatever you want to believe." Opening his other hand and showing a red pill, Morpheus says, "You take the red pill, you stay in Wonderland and I show you how deep the rabbit hole goes." Neo pauses, then picks up and places the red pill in his mouth. Lightning flashes and thunder rumbles in the background, and Neo picks up the glass of water and drinks.

Elegance and the dialectical self are similar in that if you surrender to and participate with these larger developmental forces, they carry you beyond the conventions governing most adults. The presumed reality you once knew, and were largely enslaved to, now becomes a smaller facet of reality (subject becomes object). Your conventional reality is now only part of a larger territory of experience (a new larger subjectivity has been established). As Neo gains the ability to "hack" in and out of the matrix, switching between the world of conditioned appearances and a larger reality, he gains access to novel abilities. He can learn more efficiently, operate within the matrix in new ways, and ultimately now serves a larger purpose, partly inherited and created. Similarly, elegance as you holds the ability to be in the world of form and yet, as we explored earlier, the dialectical embrace of your larger complexity also includes your self-without-form.

Elegance requires you to be similarly inside of and outside of various facets of experience. For example, an executive's competence in her organization and her ability to strategically guide her organization and its position in the marketplace are functions of two opposing capacities. First, she must be able to participate within the organization. She must be savvy in collaborating with the culture and common practices. In many ways, she has to conform to organizational procedures and expectations. Paradoxically, she is also required to be outside of her organization. She cannot simply be inside of the organizational culture. She must see her business units and their respective teams, employees, technologies and infrastructures from a distance, if she is to genuinely guide, shape and lead the parts of her organization for which she is responsible. And, as we saw with Jim in Chapter Six, if she does this from merely her own autonomy, she is likely to be quite ineffective. She must also be co-created and co-creative, so that her own transformation is an essential feature of the organization's growth in competitiveness.

Similarly, a father must be inside his family yet simultaneously outside of his family. He must, like Neo, "hack" in and out of his self-as-form as the participation with his function as a parent and co-parent. And elegance as him will also be on the inside of his partnership or marriage, while paradoxically being outside of his intimate relationship. This larger self is a function of the liberated dialectics inherent in the interpenetrating subjectivity through which he discovers himself anew. From this co-creative facility, he operates inside of his marriage and family in new ways, with a greater sphere of competence available to him and his family. The end result, generically speaking, is more love, greater skillful means within his private life, and a richer fulfillment in this facet of his life.

The problem, if we are to simplify the ever-changing dynamism of complexity down to one broad generalization, is that many adults take the blue pill and wake up in their bed presuming the world is as it appears to their conventional minds. Even adults who are developmentally ready to explore the multifaceted reality in its larger scope lack the courage. Instead of a bold step into the unknown, most wake up inside the conventions of their mind again and again, even if conventions are failing. Too often, adults function in largely conditioned and habituated ways that support the broader context's habits, which unknowingly support many of the most urgent and daunting problems we fail to understand and appropriately respond to in today's complex world.

Elegance is, in some ways, akin to choosing the red pill. This is a call to drop into and participate as the complex dialectical oscillations of life that are less bounded by conventions. By hacking out of your conventional self, you can get into a larger information flow, your ever-refining intelligence, and a sharpening skillful means by which you can both expand your influence and align more congruently with the larger purpose of your life. This purpose both belongs to you and you belong to it. To do so consistently is likely to require a demanding confrontation with yourself. It is to this that we turn our attention in the next chapter.

EXERCISES FOR DIALECTICAL INSIGHT & NAVIGATION

As noted earlier, your capacity to recognize, negotiate and surrender into the underlying dialectical facets of experience often follows a two-step process. First, you *begin to recognize polarities* when you reflect on previous experiences. Retroactive exploration of polarities often establishes a foundation where you can then participate with the polarities that are arising within and as the present moment.

Dialectical Reflection

Begin by investigating a prior experience that has happened to you recently. This may be a scenario between you and a co-worker two weeks ago, a tension between you and your intimate partner that challenged you last week, or it might be an experience you had with your child yesterday. Regardless, choose an experience that holds a charge (positive or negative) and one that you want to learn more from.

1. Replay

Go back in the scenario in your mind's eye and replay the most important part or parts. Use all of your senses to reconstruct the experience for yourself. The more facets of your experience you bring in, the more rich the results. Include all five senses. What did you see?... What did you hear?... and so on. Next, replay how you felt inside of your body. How did the inside of the relationship(s) feel? What was going on in your mind?

2. Distill

After replaying the most important facets of your prior experience, quickly review the most notable, charged and/or interesting parts of your experience. These are the central themes from your experience. Choose one to three of these, and distill them down to one-or-two word phrases. For example, if you were replaying a conflict with a co-worker, you might note that the tension, frustration and anxiety could all be captured with the term "conflict."

3. Flip

Taking the distilled facet(s) of your experience, flip it (or them) 180 degrees. Ask yourself, "What is the opposite?" For example, when flipping conflict, you might start to see harmony, creativity, relaxation and/or comfort. Choose the most salient, activating and engaging word or words, again focusing on one or two words to use as your polar label. You may choose creativity, which would give you the polarity to carry forward in the fourth and final step.

Conflict ●━━━━━━━━━━● **Creativity**

4. Reflection

Finally, now that you have identified at least one charged polarity to work with, it is important for you to spend time with this polarity. Reflect on the dynamics between these two polar opposing positions. Ask yourself, "What are my relationships with these two poles of experience?" Get curious about how you might be able to function in new and different ways with each pole. Investigate what it would be like to be each pole. See what possible relationships exist between these two apparently differing positions. Find out how they conflict in your experience, and see if there are ways in which they may be able to collaborate.

These four steps prepare you to pick up the next exercise.

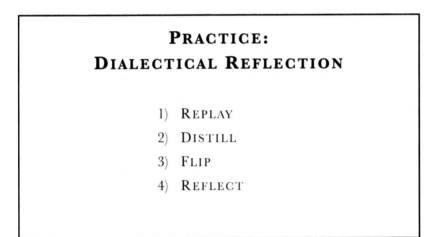

PRACTICE:
DIALECTICAL REFLECTION

1) REPLAY
2) DISTILL
3) FLIP
4) REFLECT

Dialectical Immersion

The next step brings the polarity or polarities you have been working with retroactively and begins to bring them into the here and now. To continue working with our example around the polarity between conflict and creativity, dialectical immersion requires you to relax in *immediacy*. You are not looking to create or generate this polarity. Instead, inquire into what is happening right here, right now, from the lens of this dialectic. For me, as I am writing this exercise, as I soften in the here and now that is carrying me, I open my curiosity. "How is conflict and creativity already here?"

McNamara ✚ The Elegant Self

My sincere response right now is I am in conflict inside. I am very hungry, yet I want to stay in the creative flow of writing. My hunger is somewhat distracting me, yet I can see my self-as-form organizing around the creative writing and pushing away hunger. My attention, focus and energy keep turning toward being creative with this keyboard.

After noticing this dialectic of which I am immersed in, I let go and I begin again. The four steps of dialectical immersion can be summarized as follows:

1. Relax and soften in immediacy.

2. Invite curiosity.

3. Ask, "How is the polarity (or polarities) present now?"

4. Let go. Return to Step One.

The principal goal is to bring your capacity to see polarities in the direct immediacy of the moment. You are likely to start to see the dialectics you have been reflecting on in the present moment first. However, as your mind sharpens and grows in its ability to hold polarity simultaneously, you will likely begin to see a myriad of dialectics. When you can, in any given moment, see a handful of dialectical polarities at play, you are ready to practice dialectical involvement.

PRACTICE:
DIALECTICAL IMMERSION

1) RELAX AND SOFTEN.

2) INVITE CURIOSITY.

3) ASK, "HOW IS THE POLARITY (OR POLARITIES) PRESENT NOW?

4) LET GO. RETURN TO STEP ONE.

216

Dialectical Involvement

The third exercise, dialectical involvement, goes beyond seeing or recognizing polarity within immediacy. The central goal now is for *a greater participatory relationship* with one or more polarities. Seeing a polarity is one facet; however, elegance involves a participatory involvement with the polarities present in any given situation.

1. Participate with Polarity

The simplest and often first step in expanding your participation with dialectics is to consciously participate with one polarity in juxtaposition to its opposite. For me, this involves participating with the creativity that is flowing through my mind, body and finger tips. I am simply softening into, trusting more of the immediacy of my polar organization around being creative. When I participate with this more fully, hunger ceases to be a source of a conflict.

2. Flip Participation

The second step is to flip your participation. Involve yourself with the opposing side of the polarity. We can think of this as a form of stretching for your mind and nervous system. This can be somewhat mild—as I expect my experience of going to the kitchen to be—or this can involve some of the most intense experiences to challenge your homeostasis and experience of being safe, secure and trusting of experience and life. For example, I recall being invited to flip my participation in the polarity of independence and dependence. I had organized my life around being independent so when I was asked to explicitly and consciously inhabit my dependence I found myself dissociated and confused. The experience was so threatening for me at the time I could hardly stay in contact with the dependent parts of myself even for a brief moment. Expect to traverse this spectrum from relative comfort to extremely high levels of experiential intensity. The core dialectics you have organized your entire lives around not experiencing often carry with them the sense of annihilation. A conscious participation with both poles is often useful for cultivating the larger fluidity and stability of elegance.

3. Participate as Immediacy

This final injunction is less an exercise as it is the surrender of your separate autonomy's cultivation of and acclimation with the dialectical nature of immediacy. Polarities are already present in multifaceted ways, co-creating your relative identities over and over in the here and now. While there is no injunction able to get you into that which is already happening, this participation is itself a dialectical play of receiving immediacy more fully and actively engaging and pressing into and as this moment with greater strength, force and commanding influence. Changing, augmenting, adding to and/or manipulating the moment to conform to your habits is, however, less useful.

Opening the aperture of your body and mind such that the interpenetrating flux of immediacy resonates within and through you with greater nuance is often, for many, a helpful injunction to begin with here. Opening the aperture of your body and mind starts by broadening perspectives, expanding the scope of your attention and widening your energetic flexibility. Opening the aperture of experience then leads to larger allowances. You allow the ongoing change or flux of immediacy to impact you. What was once cut off, ignored and/or denied can now be allowed into experience and participated with more skillfully.

PRACTICE:
DIALECTICAL INVOLVEMENT

1) PARTICIPATE WITH POLARITY.
2) FLIP PARTICIPATION.
3) PARTICIPATE AS IMMEDIACY.

For additional resources on growing your dialectical awareness, visit:

www.TheElegantSelf.com/Dialectics

Personal Notes & Reflection

9

THE PROBLEM OF HABITUATION

Fruitful Struggles Beyond Autonomy

Thus far we have largely followed Robert Kegan's psychological model of development. Now we turn our attention toward the theory and research of Susanne Cook-Greuter, who brings more than three decades of assessing mental complexity. Since 1980, Cook-Greuter has analyzed more than 9,000 tests[80] in more than 200 different academic and business contexts.[81] She brings with her an enormous wealth of information and rigor to our knowledge of the higher reaches of adult development. Her PhD research, conducted at Harvard and in part overseen by Kegan himself, has positioned her as one of the world's top authorities on postautonomous adult development.

Kegan's model of psychological development can be thought of as identity, cognitive, epistemological (the study of how we come to know our world), and/or the developmental unfolding of meaning-making. These aspects are pointing to the growth in how someone identifies him- or herself, what the mind is capable of being aware of, how the mind relates to knowledge, and what objects of knowledge the mind can and cannot hold, as well as how the human being expands his or her ability to make meaning in and from experience. Cook-Greuter is studying mental complexity from a different orientation—ego development. While her orientation is different, it remains highly congruent with and complementary to many of the core aspects of Kegan's subject/object model that we have been exploring together.

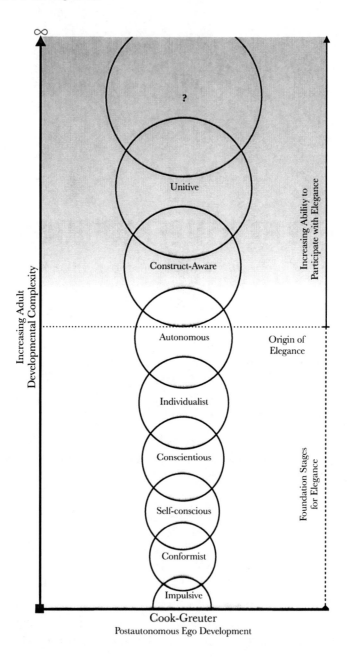

Note, not all stages have been diagramed above. Earlier forms of ego development have not been included here. Most adults function in the above eight stages illustrated.

Cook-Greuter's expertise is in assessing ego development as pioneered by renown developmental theorist Jane Loevinger. Loevinger considered the ego to be the master trait.[82] In general, Loevinger used ego as the underlying principle in personality organization. Ego, in Cook-Greuter's own words, is "the underlying principle in personality organization that strives for coherent meaning and orchestrates how we perceive reality."[83] We can think of the ego as the co-creative process by which you strive for, organize and cohere or form meaning. Ego orchestrates and co-constructs the reality that makes sense to you.

Loevinger is most famous for her nine-stage model of ego development, spanning the earliest phases of infancy in what she calls The Presocial Stage, to her two highest stages of adult development, the Autonomous and Integrated stages. Loevinger's model of ego development established the foundation from which Cook-Greuter introduces two higher stages of mental complexity. Loevinger's Integrated stage emphasizes permanence and stability, which, according to Cook-Greuter, cannot adequately account for core characteristics of some forms of adult meaning-making.

In particular, Cook-Greuter noticed some adults had dynamic, fluid and changing experiences of both their selves and their environments. Additionally, she found individuals who questioned the underlying stability and solidity of conventional constructions of reality as a whole.[84] Neither of these ways of meaning-making could be adequately held by Loevinger's underlying stability and permanence found in her highest stages. Cook-Greuter was seeing a more developed level of ego complexity, where the stability, permanence and consistency were now objects. No longer were stability and permanence the guiding logic for subjectivity. Many of these adults were reflecting an impermanence and larger instability as central, defining features of how they created meaning. They were co-constructing a reality that was beyond the conventional understandings commonly found in adult autonomy.

Cook-Greuter refers to this new layer of development as *postautonomous ego development*. This often involves an increasing awareness of the constructed nature of knowledge. As elucidated in Kegan's research, only a fraction of 1 percent of adults function stably from the

Self-Transforming Mind. Cook-Greuter maintains a similar orientation as she tells us, "The constructed nature of everyday reality remains hidden from consciousness for most people throughout their lives."[85]

Autonomy orients from a relatively stable, persistent and more or less fixed position, what we have been calling completeness. Similar to what we have explored in Kegan's Self-Transforming Mind, Cook-Greuter has found how the ego becomes less fixed and more fluid. As such, meaning-making is able to inhabit a larger diversity, resulting in individuals reporting how their orientation plays a critical role in how meaning is constructed and formed. Initially, objects often retain their stability, yet meaning becomes experienced as more dynamic and fluid. Later on, the objects themselves (including yourself, people and the relationships you are in) as well as their meaning exhibit greater dynamism and fluidity. Independence—a more fixed position—is replaced by interdependence. And, fixed boundaries, as we also explored earlier, are replaced by more open, flexible and changing boundaries.[86]

Cook-Greuter's research suggests that more mature adults understand how the construction of meaning is, at every stage, some form of a reification or consolidation of an underlying, more complex phenomenological flux. This reification process becomes more subtle, sophisticated and complex with each successive stage of development. With growth of the nervous system, constructions of reality tend to become more accurate and nuanced. Individuals functioning with postautonomous capacities "can draw multiple kinds of distinctions and connections among stimuli from ever more diverse sources and meaningfully integrate them into a coherent frame of reference for themselves."[87] Research also shows postautonomous ego development yields greater objectivity, coupled with less defensiveness toward experience.[88] Cook-Greuter summarizes some of the postautonomous capacities within our highest known stages of adult ego development:

> In general, people at the post autonomous level tend
> to experience and view reality as an undifferentiated
> phenomenological continuum, as Unity
> consciousness, the creative Ground, "das All," the
> Tao, or whatever other terms human beings have

coined to express their intimation of the underlying unity. Some of the anticipated concerns of men and women at these two highest stages of ego development are: (a) to deal with the fundamental paradoxes in human nature, (b) to grapple with one's need to make order out of chaos by abstraction, classification and reification, (c) to face one's unavoidable automatic mental habits, and (d) to realize that "biases" are universally embedded in the way we create meaning via language.[89]

CONSTRUCT-AWARE

Cook-Greuter's first postautonomous stage, called *Construct-aware,* has four interpenetrating dimensions, several of which are essential for our exploration of elegance and the often necessary confrontation with the habituated facets of yourself and our world. One way we might be able to summarize this stage is that as development moves beyond the separate autonomous self, habituated constructs become progressively more obvious. What is first a dim realization of the constructed nature of the self and reality grows to become an explicit, nuanced understanding. Thus growth in the Self-Transforming Mind is, in part, growth in becoming Construct-aware.

First, adults exhibiting Construct-aware traits struggle to accurately *describe themselves and reality* as they perceive it, which is at its heart no longer a simple given reality (found in earlier stages) but now a co-created or constructed reality. In particular, rational thought is no longer accepted as a given. Instead, it becomes an object requiring vigorous questioning and investigation.[90] Previous ways of meaning-making as a whole are often actively rejected and a new form of knowing and experiencing is intensely sought. As a result, individuals functioning from the Construct-aware stage often are living with tremendous inner tensions.

The facet of you that is Construct-aware tries to capture the complexity within which you see yourself, others and the broader co-created reality as you come to know it right now. Cook-Greuter refers to these as "transient approximations,"[91] which are experienced as an ongoing process of self-transformation. A complex matrix of thoughts, reasons, feelings, intuitions and contrasting possibilities are brought together, providing shifting integrative views of self and reality. This facet is one of the most common expressions of this stage; however, it by itself does not define this postautonomous stage. More features are essential.

The second feature demonstrates a penetrating perception into the multi-layered and multi-faceted *psychological functions* of the mind. As the conventional self is seen more clearly as an object, more complex relationships between facets of the mind are discovered and understood. This faculty is functioning both within the insights into your own mind and how you see into some of the core mental processes of others.

I often refer to this as the creation of the "two selves." As subjectivity or consciousness distances itself from autonomy, your conventional self is progressively formed into an object with greater clarity. Development refines your vantage point, thereby sharpening insights into the complex features and processes of your more conventional mind. The space between your unmediated consciousness you identify with right here and right now and your conventional self's habits and orienting perspectives establishes the two selves. The one that is more true to who you are and the one that is more conditioned that pretends to be the real you.

Individuals in this stage often feel trapped by the habituated conventions of their minds. They are straddling these two selves—one seat of subjectivity embodies greater openness and flexibility, while the other remains trapped inside their habituation. "They understand the need for a different approach to knowing, one that responds to the immediate unfiltered experience of what is. This new way of knowing requires an attitude of complete openness, one that is free from wishing for any particular outcome and free from the automatic habits of representational thought."[92] Construct-aware ego functioning enables you to see many of your mind's deep-rooted, multilayered mental habits. For example, your desire for a freedom from desire captures attention and binds the constructions of self to the desire-driven world. An ongoing valiant struggle with your mind's unexamined compulsion for thinking, analyzing, expecting, controlling, desiring, defending and attaching appear to be a necessary facet of growth in our larger maturity beyond autonomy.

Third, mature adult meaning-making in this stage is defined by an explicit awareness of *existential and psychological paradoxes*.[93] Cook-Greuter, being a trained linguist, pays careful attention to an awareness of thinking about one's own thinking processes and mental habits. People at this stage are aware of mental and emotional loops, linguistic or narrative recursions and logical paradoxes as intrinsic features in the symbolic mind (and any symbolic system).

For example, you may become preoccupied with conceptions of non-struggle, non-control, surrender, unconditioned tolerance and acceptance and/or perhaps non-seeking. As part of you is drawn unendingly toward these facets of experience, your habituated mind desires to be free from these desires. You may notice how you habitually seek to be more non-seeking. Or you may be intolerant of intolerance in the world and yourself. Perhaps you struggle to get out of all struggles. Or maybe you are constructed by a seeking to gain control of being able to let go of control. These types of unresolvable contradictions are likely to vex you in ongoing ways. As earlier stages do not register these intractable paradoxes, the individual in the Construct-aware stage is often uncomfortably stretched, his or her habits press onward while she or he often simultaneously knows the impossibility of ending or resolving these core habits and unresolvable contradictions.

Additionally, in Cook-Greuter's research, these insights and perspectives are not presented as more formalized presentations of reality as they know it. Instead, these insights are couched in a more casual stream of consciousness. We could say free associations within this stage of meaning-making are more casually organized. This often results in the direct, immediate expression of conflict and/or contradiction without apology. I often refer to this as a more "naked" way of functioning within immediacy, without needing the crutches of reflection, hindsight or a more overly composed and controlled presentation of oneself.

Finally, people in the Construct-aware stage are possessed by an explicit *awareness of the constructed nature of self, relationships and reality*.

Perceptions, definitions and the process of labeling are all constructions. Your assumptions, the frame of reference from which you organize perception and perspective, paradigms and the structures of meaning-making are all productions of the constructs that you now hold and are being held by.

In summary, the Construct-aware stage is characterized by your ongoing struggles with, and critical stance toward, unexamined automatic mental processes. Regardless, these sincere efforts and struggles, in the end, fail to yield the kind of open, less mediated experience often yearned for. Many individuals in this stage temporarily experience a more direct, unmediated, fresh or naked interconnection with and as life. However, at this stage, you largely remain unable to experience this more unbounded vitality in an ongoing way. The openness often sought after is effortless, non-controlling and non-attached. While this more direct aliveness is partially known and/or intuited, it mostly resides as but a seemingly impossible possibility. Cook-Greuter summarizes the dilemma in this manner: "Seeking a way of experiencing and meaning-making that is direct, without the filter of language, can become a central existential quest."[94]

Your ongoing struggle with habituation is an important part of separating your identity and functioning from your personal and cultural habits. It is often an essential step toward the openness that is a central feature of "a more integrated, more cognitively and emotionally advanced mode of experiencing."[95] Ultimately, your developmental distance from your more habituated autonomy can, in the end, enable you to participate with elegance more proficiently in the future.

THE SUSPENSION AND DECONSTRUCTION OF HABITUATION

The awareness of your own acculturation, both in your personal historical narratives integrating your life's experiences over time and in your participation with acculturation occurring within this moment's immediacy, marks an important turning point in development. You are now able to participate with a *more intentional conflict* with your personal and cultural habits. These are the first steps toward challenging earlier, less complex features of adulthood and preparing you to better participate with human elegance.

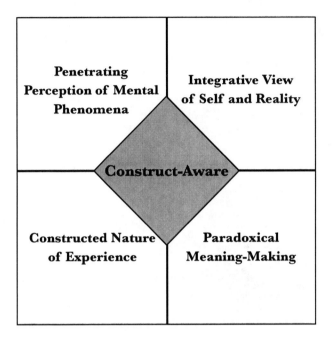

This is one possible summary of the core-defining features of the Construct-aware stage of ego development. Cook-Greuter's scoring protocols require at least three of these features to be present in meaning-making for an individual to be considered Construct-aware.

The Architecture of Immediacy

The present moment is always and already in the process of being constructed of, or co-created by, inheritance and novelty.[96] The present moment, and presumably all moments, are always receiving and integrating complex, multilayered and multifaceted historical influences of what was. Inheritance is the first process of how immediacy is structured. The moment has a cohesive integrity all to its own, so that one moment hangs together with its predecessors. This is inheritance, the root or source of all habits.

The second process structuring immediacy is something much more unknown and unexpected. Immediacy always already is also some explication and/or realization of novel emergence. The moment, along with you as a feature of immediacy, is simultaneously creative and innovative. This is novelty. Creative emergence appears to universally display at least two features. First, there is the innovation of something. What was not, now is. Secondly, the novelty of immediacy creates more integrative space to embrace, include and hold the full display of form. Inheritance and novelty together can co-create you as an expression of and articulation of elegance.

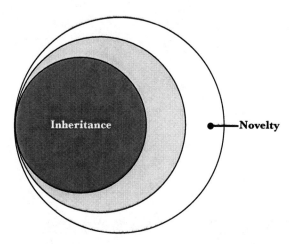

Inheritance is represented by the dark shaded spheres of inclusion. We could say the darker the shade, the older and more entrenched the inheritance. Novelty, represented by the white sphere, encircles and encompasses all prior inheritances. In this stepwise progression of novel emergence and radical inclusion, we might say immediacy is always progressively getting larger. Immediacy is always inheriting more history and participating with the "creative advance" into novelty, as philosopher Alfred North Whitehead called it.[97]

While immediacy, independent from humanity, does not appear to require any special attention to participate with both facets of its essential architecture (inheritance and novelty), you as a function of immediacy likely do. Disciplined effort and a sincere desire for a freer, less constrained experiential flux to co-create the fullness of you appear to be required as part of your developmental process beyond autonomy. The reason is quite simple; human beings are often gripped by habituation. As Cook-Greuter maintains, human beings appear to possess a "hardwired" predisposition for conditioned mental behaviors.[98] This limits you from participating with the free, unmediated integration of inheritance and novelty. This is one of the basic problematic features of habits. Furthermore, elegance as you requires the fluid embrace of and participation with and as both inheritance and novelty.

The Suspension of Habit

The first step in working with habits is *suspension*. With suspension, habituation is purposefully temporarily prevented from being in control of your perspectives, attention, energy and outer actions. Habituation's force and effect must be, in part, prohibited. Some form of a moratorium on habits is often necessary. You must decouple your behavior from habituation. This is an essential gap to cultivate. You can become a larger facility for the open participation with novelty and, later on, a broader embodiment of habituation in new ways.

Behavior here includes, but is not limited to, your objective external actions in the world. Behavior also includes the entire spectrum of internal subjective experience. Gook-Greuter, for example, refers to language itself as "verbal behavior."[99] As such, how your mind habitually thinks must be suspended for some period of time. Changing external behavior may in some cases be much easier to suspend in comparison to the interior movements of your habituated thoughts, interpretations, emotions and moods. Regardless, the first step in your deconstruction of habituation is this suspension. You likely require the skill of participating with a creative emergence between your consciousness and the habituated ways in which your consciousness tends to fuse to and inhabit less complex facets of yourself. When you participate with creative novelty you are better prepared to hold inherited habits as objects in attention, thus better enabling you to mediate and negotiate your core habits more skillfully.

This differentiation of you, a more genuine you, from the habits that have defined, governed and, in part, enslaved you for decades is no easy task. However, the rewards are immense. You gain psychological freedom, which is "priceless" as more than one of my clients has shared with me. There is no appropriate cost for freedom. The experience of this developmental distance between you and your habituated ways of functioning is something that you are likely to intrinsically value above and beyond many other facets of your life and experience.

One important feature of suspension is that while some features of your habits will cease upon the suspension of your unexamined energetic commitment to them, others will continue to function cyclically without effort or engagement. Expect some habits to fall away quickly with ease. You are also likely to find many features of your habituation that, on suspension, will not cease and are likely to function, on and off, for the rest of your life. Don't be discouraged by the relatively independent ongoing functioning of habituation. The important feature to focus on is how these automated loops can be held as objects and not necessarily subjectively merged with.

Suspension can be thought of as a form of strength training, which creates greater space within your self, enabling you to embody creative novelty with greater ease. While a spacious quality commonly colors your more mature and developed experience, you are likely to struggle with a more challenging texture of experience when you first start to separate from a specific habit. The early phases of suspension will likely humble you in profound ways. You will get to see the power of habituation, which at times can feel suffocating and immensely painful. You are likely to see and feel, with growing clarity, the larger inherent conflicts within the human mind. Facets of your habituated meaning-making will question your ability to accomplish the task of participating with this space between you and the habit that often captures you.

The heart of elegance is a prize that is not for the feeble. Elegance often eludes cowardice and you, alone, in your autonomy cannot achieve the distance we now discuss. This is the entire point. You are required to bring every facet of you to enact and engage with this epic of inner battles. And you are likely to find yourself, in the end, defeated. However, if the gift of courage is provided through the mysterious and unknown faculties intrinsic to immediacy, you are likely to discover that something beyond autonomy is present and possible. Grace and your most fierce devoted effort merge and co-create something inexplicable. Within the envelope of suspension, a fertile ground is being prepared. One of the essential purposes of this ground is the potentiality of elegance co-creating you.

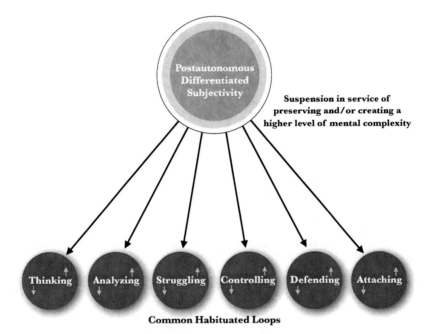

Postautonomous differentiated subjectivity (or consciousness) can be seen suspending six common habituated loops. Thinking, analyzing, struggling, controlling, defending and attaching are by no means exhaustive. However, working with these core mental habits can often lead to the generation and/or preservation of a higher level of mental complexity for individuals beginning to grow into human elegance.

The gap between habituation and creative novelty may be one of the most holy and precious domains of experience you will likely experience in life. This gap reveals our developmental future and the larger capacities of the human being. Once you have been fashioned by a particular infusion of space, developmental distance from habituation and a raw basic drive to become something more, you are likely to see that the survival of the human species rests precisely in our ability to participate with this creative novelty. The existential battle between creative possibility of what we can become as a species and who you can become as an elegant human being with that of the habituated nature of our collective conditioning is likely to break your heart in ways your less complex adulthood is unable to fathom or cope with. While devastatingly beautiful and heart-breaking, this core impulse will fashion and sculpt you anew, which is the precise and, in many ways, elegant response to the conditions you face in your personal life and our collective world here on Earth.

Deconstruction of Habituation

The next step beyond suspension is a new level of *self-study and investigation* into habituation. While the first step of suspending habits involved the winning of a developmental differentiation between a more free subjectivity and one largely constrained by habituation, once a sufficient gap has been established, attention and engagement makes an important turn back toward habituation. After you have decoupled your perspectives, attention, energy and outer action as discussed in suspension, you are ready to turn toward your habits and actually pull them apart into their more fundamental constitutive parts. This sharpens your insight, perception into, and comprehension of the subtle dynamics of your (and others') habits.

For example, you may turn toward your habituated thoughts and their constant analysis. As you get closer to and begin to pull apart and dismantle the automated appraisals in your mind, you may begin to see preferences functioning inside of polarities, as we explored earlier. This may reveal another layer of control operating underneath this predialectical habituated thought. Expectations, desires and defenses are all, in a diversity of ways, functioning to maintain identity and experiential comfort through what you may see as a core process of struggle. This may all be revealed through turning toward habituated thought. Note that much of the book you have read thus far is taking you on a deconstruction characterized by the kind of postautonomous ego development Cook-Greuter has studied.

The familiarization with habituation and its multifaceted and multilayered dimensions serves two functions. First, participating with a movement of getting closer to habituation and investigating its automated functioning paradoxically yields greater differentiation from habits. It appears this process is unending. The closer you peer into unexamined conditioning, the more subtlety is discovered. This, in turn, prepares you for the next step to be explored in the next chapter. As you gain a more nuanced understanding of habituation, you grow in your capacity to realign and participate with habits in novel ways.

As eluded to earlier, the deconstruction of habituation is not, in and of itself, adequate for elegance. The suspension and pulling apart of your habituation is often necessary but not sufficient. Elegance as you likely cannot and will not co-construct you without a dialectical participation with habituation and the creative space of novelty. This realignment and re-embodiment of habituation is what we turn to in Chapter Ten.

EXERCISES TO DIFFERENTIATE FROM HABITS

Suspension of Habit

All form is in motion. As such, all habituation is also in motion. Habits are a reaction to life and they generate a complex series of psychological and behavioral movements. One effective way to suspend habituation is to inhabit what I call *the technology of stillness*. It is incredibly simple, which is why this exercise is so powerful.

Begin by sitting or lying down in a comfortable position. Once you find a relaxed and alert position, make a commitment to not move. Obviously you will have movements from breathing and, if you are sitting, you will have subtle micro-adjustments as you maintain balance. Aside from these movements, you will no longer move your body. You might start with 5 minutes and later extend this practice to 20 minutes or longer. Find a duration that works with your schedule and the various competing demands you face in life, yet pick a time frame that challenges you to suspend your normal activity.

Once you are behaviorally or externally not moving (aside from breathing and the micro-adjustments mentioned above), place your mind in a posture of stillness. You can focus the mind like a laser onto a single object. It may be the sensation of your feet on the ground, the breath's inhalation and exhalation, or perhaps a static mental image. Choose a singularity, and focus your mind such that it is unwavering or unmoving in its focus. Alternatively the posture of your mind can be broad, open and spacious. Many objects can come and go through your mind, but your mind remains unmoving in its commitment to remain still as a witness, unwilling to subjectively move with the various habituated activities of the mind.

While simple, the technology of stillness coupled with a mental posture of focus or, alternatively, defocusing the mind is an immensely challenging exercise because the self-as-form is always in movement. The greater your embeddedness in and identification with the self-as-form, the more challenged you will be. Consider this an important part of your struggle with habituation as you grow beyond your conditioned autonomy. However challenging this is for you, these challenges will reveal powerful habits that often govern you, and you will begin to establish an essential gap between you and the habits that are limiting your functioning in life. The technology of stillness can suspend virtually all habituated activities, as such you are encouraged to practice the technology of stillness at least once a day.

Once you have gained a sufficient ability to still both your body and mind, you can begin using the technology of stillness more fluidly in your day. You may be at your desk at work, in a conversation, or involved in some other common scenario when a habit you are working with emerges. You can suspend the habit by inhabiting stillness momentarily and/or pausing just the motion that is central to, and perhaps surrounding, your conditioned way of functioning.

For example, you may be in a conversation with a friend about a fellow co-worker. Instead of responsibly talking about this person together as a means of gaining greater understanding of who they are, a habit in your mind surfaces and a steady stream of gossip is now filling your thoughts. You are no longer listening to your friend all that closely.

Instead, you look for an opening to invite him or her into your gossip. Pragmatic observations have been replaced with predetermined judgements and sharp criticisms about who this co-worker is. But you suspend this activity. You stop the gossip in its tracks. Judgements and criticisms freeze as you take a breath and focus your attention upon listening to your friend. Your mind becomes still and you follow his or her communications closely. Meanwhile, you are taking sips of your cup of coffee as you both walk side by side talking quietly with one another. In this way, suspension and the technology of stillness can be leveraged more readily in your life.

PRACTICE:
SUSPENSION OF HABIT

1) PHYSICALLY EMBODY STILLNESS.

2) PLACE YOUR MIND INTO A POSTURE OF STILLNESS.

3) REST IN AND AS THE TECHNOLOGY OF STILLNESS.

Deconstruction of Habit

Deconstruction begins with *a leaning in or toward habituation*. After suspension, or while a habit is being suspended, perspective and attention begin to engage habituation. This engagement is a drive to pull apart, investigate, and explore the various sub-facets of any given habit. By doing so, you will gain greater insight into the underlying function, purpose and operation of how habits function.

There are three basic domains of functioning within most habits. Habituation takes form *physically, emotionally* and *mentally*. As such, it is often useful to deconstruct habituation in all three of these domains. First, habituation structures and organizes the body to move in a particular way. You are encouraged to take note of the tension and holding patterns throughout your body. What are your hands doing? What kind of activation is present in your neck and shoulders? What is going on in your abdominal muscles? Pay particular attention to your face and jaw, as these muscles are likely the most neurologically integrated with what is going on within your mind.

Deconstruction within this physical domain involves a systematic disassembly of the unexamined *tension and movement patterns* in your body. For example, pulling apart the facial expressions, tension in your jaw, and the holding patterns around your eyes and mouth from your internal subjective experience aligns the body with your more liberated functioning. This may be a more open and fluid posture, with greater physiological relaxation, while another time this deconstruction of habituated physical patterns may involve a more intentional activated, tense and readied physiological state that is primed for a fierce engagement with a challenge or obstacle in life.

While the conventional mind prefers to think of itself as the governing feature of the self, a closer inspection often reveals a more powerful seat of volition: *emotion.* Therefore, to adequately understand habits, you are wise to deconstruct the emotional layers of experience that are in operation and often in control of you. Most habits have powerful emotional dimensions, and they are organized around at least two basic things. First, many habits are motivated to *get out of* some texture of emotional experience. Second, they are often driven *to get you into* another emotional state. Sometimes both drives are working in concert with one another.

Habituated emotional dynamics tend to circle these two basic processes, getting out of and getting into various emotional states. We can think of these as constrictions in the mind, as they often impede information flow. Instead of metabolizing experiences more directly, habits are often functioning to disconnect your attention from present feelings while attempting to manufacture more preferred, familiar and/or comfortable emotional states.

Gaining insight into an emotional pattern involves deconstructing feelings to discover the constellation of feeling tones that co-create any given emotion. For example, you may be struggling with jealousy and the automated patterns of behavior stemming from jealousy. As you suspend your conditioned responses and begin to deconstruct jealousy, you may find a complex web of feelings vacillating together, similar to what one of my clients found. First, this encounter may trigger a particularly painful thread of inadequacy. You feel as though you are lacking something important. While this uncomfortable feeling is unpleasant, on closer inspection you are feeling in contact with something that you value in an unexamined way. You also feel anger and a particular flavor of hostility toward someone else. There is also a grasping quality within the anger. In a very basic way, some part of you would like to take from others what you think you are lacking, and which you on some level value. As you can see, there are many threads of feeling tones in jealousy. Like most feelings, they are comprised of complex, interrelated feeling tones. Gaining insight into these sub-facets can help clarify which facets of your feelings are left over from earlier, less complex ways of being in the world, while others are powerful and appropriate responses to the immediacy of your life.

Finally, the deconstruction of habituation involves a meta-analysis of your automated and often unexamined *mental scripts*, which tend to close down the aperture of experience so that you feel less by thinking more. Conditioned stories, analysis, expectations, desires, defenses and mental attempts to control experience are all objects to investigate, not facets of experience to subjectively collude with. For example, by pulling apart unexamined criticism, you may find greater discernment into yourself and others. Old stories can cease to govern how present experiences are interpreted. Parts of the story may be jettisoned as old and worn out, unable to account for the life now living you. Other conditioned stories may remain, as they more or less hold true. Regardless, as the story of your life is pulled apart, there is a fresh capacity to co-create an alive story holding the history of your life and the immediacy of your present unfolding experience.

Greater self-understanding of the physical, emotional and mental dimensions of habituation are often critical for most adults outgrowing deeply conditioned autonomy. While habits depend on a stable world with predictable outcomes, much of life is not fixed, static nor predictable in the ways our more habituated ways of being often presume. The habit of establishing a fixed and stable self-identity is one to deconstruct to free up your consciousness and attention so that the larger interpenetrating self can dynamically emerge, bringing with it a larger ability to play with historical inheritance and creative novelty.

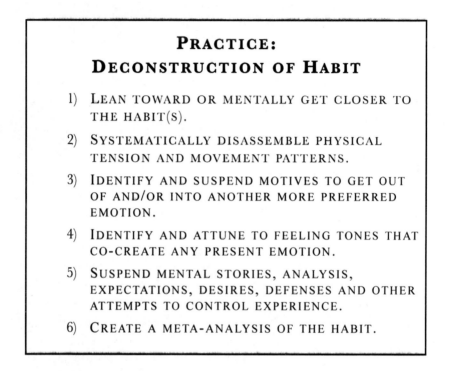

PRACTICE: DECONSTRUCTION OF HABIT

1) LEAN TOWARD OR MENTALLY GET CLOSER TO THE HABIT(S).

2) SYSTEMATICALLY DISASSEMBLE PHYSICAL TENSION AND MOVEMENT PATTERNS.

3) IDENTIFY AND SUSPEND MOTIVES TO GET OUT OF AND/OR INTO ANOTHER MORE PREFERRED EMOTION.

4) IDENTIFY AND ATTUNE TO FEELING TONES THAT CO-CREATE ANY PRESENT EMOTION.

5) SUSPEND MENTAL STORIES, ANALYSIS, EXPECTATIONS, DESIRES, DEFENSES AND OTHER ATTEMPTS TO CONTROL EXPERIENCE.

6) CREATE A META-ANALYSIS OF THE HABIT.

The Practice of Embodied Immediacy

More than a decade ago, my professor in graduate school, Bruce Tift, gave me one of the most practical and effective injunctions to facilitate development beyond the language habit and conventional adulthood's often restricted aperture of experience. I often prescribe this practice for individuals who are ready to outgrow autonomy. Called the practice of *embodied immediacy*, this injunction is decisively simple yet immensely powerful. Turn your full attention toward the direct, non-interpretive, embodied experience present at any given moment.

This practice of embodied immediacy is a suspension of the interpretive thinking mind that many adults remain habitually identified with. Used in experientially intense situations, it expands your ability to metabolize challenging experiences more quickly. Furthermore, this practice is an excellent litmus test for how free your consciousness is within any given situation. Can you stay with the larger flux of experiential diversity, or do you remain confined in the mind's more limited and habituated comfort zones? The closer you can get to your direct, non-interpretive embodied experience, the more free you are from many of the habits that ensnare and enslave less mature minds. In most experientially intense situations, you are encouraged to practice embodied immediacy as a means of accelerating development beyond habituated autonomy.

THE PRACTICE OF
EMBODIED IMMEDIACY

CONDUCT AWARENESS TOWARD:

1)   DIRECT

2)   NON-INTERPRETIVE

3)   EMBODIED SENSATION.

For additional resources on working with habits, visit:

www.TheElegantSelf.com/Habits

Personal Notes & Reflection

10
THE NECESSITY OF HABITUATION
Reclaiming your Larger Skillful Means

As noted earlier, one of the leading experts in Mature Adult Development is Susanne Cook-Greuter co-founder of the Center for Leadership Maturity. Her highest stage of ego development is the *Unitive stage*. Unlike many developmental theorists, she does not propose that her highest stage is the most developed stage of meaning-making available. Instead, Cook-Greuter maintains, "Ego development theory has no terminus."[100] There is likely no final stage of complexity of the human mind. Development may continue indefinitely. This proves important to our investigation into elegance. As you might already be seeing and/or intuiting, elegance is not a static thing to attain, but rather a participation with something part known and part emergent, mysterious and unknowable. While you may be able to look back in the past and see how elegance functioned as you, you will never be able to *entirely* grasp what elegance is within and as immediacy.

While Cook-Greuter invites curiosity into how the mind may continue to develop, and thus enable elegance to participate with and co-construct you more fully, she also presents a wealth of information about how individuals functioning from the Unitive stage show up in the world, perceive themselves, and co-construct multifaceted realities. The Unitive stage brings with it five defining features. First, we find a "wide range of thought on human relatedness."[101] This unique *diversity of thought* or meaning-making does not exclusively center around you and your personal, relative life. Perception and perspective are no longer exclusively identified with your personal reference points and now broadly include world-centric and even larger frames of reference and experience. Furthermore, this broader relatedness to life in its multifaceted and multi-dimensional realities is also often colored with positive affect and gratitude. A central facet of high ego development is a "rich inner life,"[102] and while people functioning from the Construct-aware stage vacillate, and often feel torn, between high and low self-esteem, individuals graduating into the Unitive stage demonstrate a more consistent high self-esteem.[103] This durable high self-esteem appears to function freely beyond the circumstances of life's ups and downs.[104]

Our second feature is that for the first time we find a high tolerance of and *acceptance for the world as it is*. The self functioning from this stage of ego development demonstrates an openness to life, easily moving with change, participating with the innate processes present in the moment. This self is an expression of an attunement to life's rhythms. There is an ability to be co-created, again and again, in concert with the ongoing flux of experience.[105] This stage exhibits functioning beyond the habituation and even the struggle with habituated ways of being. The essence of the new way of being and becoming appears to be effortless, non-controlling, non-attaching and one of radical openness.[106] As such, a larger capacity to suspend the mind's habit for consolidating, categorizing, evaluating and explaining life in rational terms stabilizes, allowing for a new mode of perception to flourish.[107]

The result of this greater developmental distance from the mind's automated drive to stably represent the self is a new territory of reality we have already been exploring together. The reality individuals inside of the Unitive stage relate to most is the "undifferentiated phenomenological continuum."[108] We referred to this territory as the unmediated experiential bloom, the experiential flux and so on throughout our exploration of Kegan's model. Cook-Greuter also refers to this dynamic, ever-changing territory of direct experience as the creative ground or unified consciousness. Adults here have "replaced habitual, conscious mental processing by immersing themselves in the immediate, ongoing flow of experience."[109] This "unfiltered experience,"[110] as Cook-Greuter refers to it, functions as the Unitive self's inner stability. The ongoing process, rhythm and experiential flux, continually already available, replaces the habituated entrenching of rational meaning-making found in less developed ego functioning.[111] As a result, the self-sense of the Unitive stage is fluid or "undulating."[112] Your larger maturity trusts the intrinsic process of life and experience already occurring, and already—without intervention—is co-creating all of you. This new mode of perception supports this high tolerance for diversity at what appears to be the origin of multiplicity. As such, this stage stands as an exemplar for acceptance in the world. Within the human relational domain, "They respect the essence in others and therefore do not need them to be different than they are."[113]

Third, the facets of yourself that are unitive demonstrate *universal connectedness*.[114] You know yourself to be a profound expression of larger worlds beyond the conventional worldviews of the autonomous stage of development. Cook-Greuter elucidates the quality of connectedness offered by individuals functioning from the Unitive stage as "a sense of connection that goes beyond the personal realm (own family, own race, nation, same gender, or group of like-minded people). It becomes transpersonal, embedded in historical times, or in a more profound, enduring sense of reality existing outside of one's individual embodied existence."[115] The previous autonomous ways of co-constructing reality and its meaning has now been transformed. Instead of almost exclusively viewing life through the lens of the separate and distinct, autonomous self, a new paradigm emerges where individuals experience themselves and others as essential parts of an ongoing human community. There is no clear limitation of who is inside of this belongingness and who is outside of this belongingness. Family, culture, language, nation-states, both one's own and not one's own in the conventional sense, are all included. This connectedness can also reach back into a felt resonance with generations and entire periods of humanity that have come and gone. Furthermore, your larger connectedness can also reach forward into the future generations yet to come. This expanded connectedness with humanity is only one facet. People functioning from the Unitive stage also feel embedded in a universal creative ground. Life is part personal and it is also an evolutionary movement toward the ultimate. As you can see, this new stage of meaning-making is multiperspectival and universal.[116] Furthermore, Cook-Greuter is careful to point out that these individuals are explicit about these expansive connections to a larger or greater whole. The descriptions of these qualities of connectedness are clear, direct and nuanced, similar to our investigation into the self-as-form and the self-without-form thus far.

The fourth defining characteristic of this stage is what Cook-Greuter calls fundamental feelings, thoughts and reflections.[117] For our purposes, we will refer to these as *fundamental perspectives*. These fundamental perspectives orient around issues such as human existence, faith, life, death, joy and suffering. Additionally, conscience and consciousness, as well as the mystery of being, are also frequently pointed to by individuals in the Unitive stage. This all points toward ongoing essential penetrating insights into some of the core questions of life, death and existence.

Finally, individuals operating from the Unitive stage demonstrate instances of unitive thought or metaphor. Abraham Maslow, pioneering American psychologist and immensely influential figure in Humanistic and Transpersonal Psychologies, defines *unitive consciousness* as "the ability to simultaneously perceive the fact—the is—its particularity, and its universality. To see it simultaneously as here and now, and yet also as eternal."[118] Cook-Greuter goes on to describe a free-flowing dialectical facility much like our own investigation of fluidity and polarities. There is a "shifting focus effortlessly between near and far, mundane and sublime, temporal and eternal, serious and ridiculous, individuated and transcendent self, as well as fluid transition between different states of consciousness."[119]

NAVIGATING THE AIRPLANE

One analogy that is often useful with clients and in presenting this material to groups is what I call the *airplane analogy*. Your autonomous self, and its nearly all-encompassing language habit, is like being on an airplane. The plane is dependent on its two wings for flight, just as your habituated symbolic mind is dependent on distinctions between what something is and what it is not. When you are inside of your separate, distinct self and its meaning-making, you are, in many ways, confined to the vehicle of the symbolic representational thinking mind. This is the airplane. While on the airplane, you spend much of your time looking

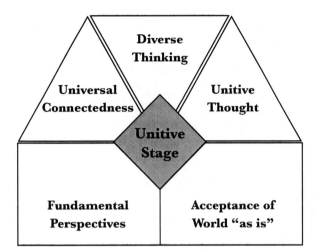

Cook-Greuter's Unitive stage can be summarized through the five interlocking dimensions illustrated above. Unless someone is explicit about what his or her connection is—a universal connectedness— and they include themselves as a part of this greater whole scoring in the Unitive stage is not considered.

out the window at the experiential territory of your life. You have maps aboard and various instruments to further represent location, heading, speed and so on, all which help you get from one place to another. When you need a closer look at some feature of your life, you dive down closer to the ground. Perhaps you circle particular areas quite frequently. When you need more perspective, you might climb to a higher altitude to get a better view of the surrounding territory.

Regardless what your airplane does, the autonomous self is often left with a pervasive experience of *being separate* from the broader experience and territory of life. This is due to the habituated activity of the symbolic mind. We might say there is a closer relationship to the symbols of the territory than to a more direct connection to the territory itself.[120] When you are captured by autonomy, you are largely unaware of the activity of the airplane. Likely you are fused with, identified as, and subjectively merged with the airplane, so that you largely do not suspect the inherent limitations of being confined to this symbolic vehicle and its particular form of symbolic meaning-making.

Postautonomous individuals, in contrast, have successfully landed their planes. And they have managed to open the door and walk off of the airplane. They have stepped outside of their mind's habituated symbolic representation of everything and, in part, gotten underneath symbolic meaning-making as a whole. Through getting outside of the plane's limitations, by placing their feet on the ground and actually walking around, they come in contact with a more direct immediacy of experience. They discover that there is much more going on than previously assumed from the vantage point of the airplane. There is a more rich, interesting, engaging and experientially intense, uncertain and changing landscape that they are immersed in and co-created by.

The *Construct-aware* individual has gotten a taste of this *direct immediacy*. He or she is, as we might say, participating with the interpenetrating self we first explored in Chapter Three. But the Construct-aware individual has not learned how to live here yet. Without much choice in the matter, he or she will find him- or herself back on the airplane in mid-flight caught inside the language habit. However, this plane ride is much more challenging now; he or she can see the airplane flying. He or she can see his or her mind resting on the two wings of *generic distinctions* (this/not this). As such, he or she tirelessly struggles with the habits of the conventional mind, all the while knowing something else is possible. However, painfully, he or she has not learned to land the plane and get out of the language habit when skillful.

We could say individuals in the *Unitive stage* have, in contrast, learned how to land their planes. They can get off their planes and participate with the larger, more complex territory in a *less mediated* and *more direct* way. This is the more useful place to function from most of the time. There is greater information flow, more attunement, and more resonance with themselves, others and the larger shifting environmental flux. Furthermore, there is a bonus. Upon getting off the airplane and into the larger, unbounded experiential bloom of life in its multi-dimensional qualities, the interpenetrating self is often gifted with what we could call a *satellite feed*. While the interpenetrating self is closer to the more direct experiential flow as immediacy's intrinsic movements, these individuals are not lost in the microcosm of their interior and exterior environments. Instead, a dialectical, and paradoxical, relationship between specificity and experiential immersion is joined with a facility of a broad, perhaps all-encompassing subjectivity. This source of perception appears to be floating in space providing an immense vantage point on the broader, often unseen scope of the shape and texture of form stretching from horizon to horizon. As such, they tend to spend most of their time, attention, energy and engagement here, off of the airplane in the less bounded, open field of an ongoing experiential flux that is mysteriously connected to some of the broadest and least limited of orientations.

Furthermore, something important happens to the airplane. A larger intelligence can now use the airplane as *a tool*. You, at some point in the growth of your mind, retain the power to get in the airplane and take off when necessary and/or skillful and you can just as easily land your airplane. While in the airplane, using your symbolic faculties, you do not lose contact with the larger experiential flux "below." Neither do you lose contact with the information and broader vantage point of the satellite "above." You are the integration. As Cook-Greuter puts it, "Individuals at this stage can access reality directly, 'immediately' as well as mediated through symbolic representation. The difference is they are aware of both."[121]

Reclaiming Habituation

This leads us to an essential step necessary for the fluid participation as elegance. You cannot remain fixated in a struggle to get out of habituation. Nor can you remain fixed in a space free from habituation. Using our analogy, you cannot remain stuck on the airplane and you cannot consolidate an identity organized around being off of the airplane. As discussed, an ongoing struggle with your habits—language or otherwise—is often a necessary step; however, there is a larger complexity that *integrates habituation* with a basic, unearned freedom. This rich intersection between *freedom* and *habituation* poses an essential question for us: *How do we help adults with the requisite development to re-inhabit, re-embody and realign with core habits in new ways that, in some paradoxical way, preserves, both the intelligence within the habit as well as the larger unconditioned freedom?* This points us toward the territory of elegance.

My first book, *Strength To Awaken*, investigated this territory, although the term "elegance" was not brought into the discussion. Referred to as "*performance grooves*," this creative synthesis of habituation and freedom or the self-without-form—which is innately unconditioned—and the "unique teleological conditioning" of who you are yields new performance capacities.[122] You likely perform at your very best, that is elegance constructs your most efficient, attuned and beautiful movement (whether this movement is physical, emotional, intellectual, relational and/or economic), when you resonate with what appears to be an infinitely unique integration of your most intelligent conditioning with your most liberated wisdom. The union of these can be thought of as a core feature of elegance.

So, just as the Unitive stage of ego development demonstrates an ability to pick up and put down language and the symbolic representational mind, elegance as you has the capacity to free the self-as-form from habituation and enables you to creatively inhabit the unique teleological conditioning of you. To realign habituation to serve elegance as you, there appears to be a prerequisite that you possess this ability to be largely free from your habituated constructs and automated functioning. Again, you must be able to land and get off the airplane.

As mentioned in our last chapter, decoupling your awareness and functioning from habituation appears to be an unending process. This is something you likely will never fully complete. However, the facets of habituation you work with more intentionally through the processes of suspension and deconstruction (outlined in Chapter Nine) enable you to take the next step in re-inhabiting and realigning habituation with the larger creative expressions of elegance. While it is not necessary, it is often useful, to suspend and closely investigate the complex multifaceted dimensions of habituation prior to participating with the realignment presently being discussed. For those of you who are bridging between the Self-Authoring Mind and Self-Transforming Mind in Kegan's model or growing into the Construct-aware stage, or perhaps the Unitive stage in Cook-Greuter's model, you are encouraged to participate with this three-step process, which often increases your skillful means while participating with habituation.

RECLAIMING HABITUATION

1) SUSPENSION OF HABITUATION

2) DECONSTRUCTION OF HABITUATION

3) REALIGNMENT OF HABITUATION

It can be useful for you to isolate habitual processes so that you can leverage these three steps with more or less distinct features of your habituation. Some will be similar in nature to other conditioned ways of being and functioning, thus enabling you to easily and rapidly suspend and deconstruct habits. However, expect other habits to require a more ongoing intentional relationship with suspension and deconstruction as you differentiate your identity, substance, location and functioning from these more entrenched patterns. The essential point here is that the growth process innate to your highest stages of maturity (that are empirically studied and supported) appears to have no end. While you gain greater mastery with more facets of your conditioning, you will likely continue to encounter new layers of habituation to work with anew.

The Architecture of Defense

While we have toured many facets of habituation thus far—the completeness project, avoidance of inadequacy and incompleteness, oppositions within polarities, the language habit and, more generally, thinking, analyzing, seeking, struggling, controlling and attaching—we have not yet investigated *habituated defending* with sufficient depth. If there is one facet of experience most responsible for halting elegance, it is likely habituated defenses. While we can see defense at work within the completeness project and the establishment of a self that is governed by an opposition against one side of a polarity, there is a deeper, more raw, and vulnerable territory to be explored.

To get at the root of habituated defenses, it is often wise to turn attention to the uncomfortable and anxious domain of *annihilation*. Every human being likely has some root *survival strategy*, which is an ongoing defense against annihilation. Think of this as your core survival strategy. Most people have one, while it is possible to retain more. These are often the most difficult of habits to sufficiently master, yet they are essential for the free articulation of elegance because they contain an immense gift or treasure.

The same process of suspension, deconstruction and realignment (as we are to explore in greater depth shortly) can be leveraged for working with your habituated survival strategy or strategies. However, there is an essential ingredient that we have only briefly touched on. You must find a way to participate with a *courage* that is larger than your smaller, more conventional self. You cannot possess this type of courage. The courage being pointed toward belongs to no one and yet is available for everyone to participate with. Courage's broader vulnerable heart and willingness to openly approach that which triggers our most basic habituated closures and avoidance is a facet of a larger maturity that you can participate with more consistently. And it is one with the power to spontaneously co-create you and dramatically refashion what you are capable of doing in life. The immense fear, terror and anxiety within annihilation requires the most integrated functioning you can muster and a surrender into a courage that infuses you with a newfound resilience and dignity that remains unshaken in the face of the most experientially intense and challenging facets of being human while facing death.

This is where many, when confronted with their core survival habits, collapse into earlier, less complex modes of *defended functioning*. As such, humanity's advance recedes. You are likely to experience this failure many times. When core survival habits capture you, your perspective, attention, energy and behavior have likely participated in this failure. While you may have managed to relieve the intensity of your relative experience through habituated defense, I often encourage clients to grieve the larger loss that is simultaneously occurring. Yet humanity's movement is a progressive movement toward elegance, and this elegance is not one of convenience. Rather, there appears to be an unending drive to participate with elegance, even in the face of the most challenging, complex, disturbing and humbling experiences. This is the calling in life that holds you and likely all of us.

Suspending and deconstructing your core survival strategy or strategies, in many cases, results in you no longer habitually distancing yourself from experiences that appear to threaten annihilation. The key distinction here is "appear." There are situations in which you must participate with your basic reflexes, conditioning and survival strategies because your life likely *does* depend on them. However, habituated survival strategies are often functioning in situations where life is actually *not* in danger.

Survival habits are often rooted in the first few years of life, thus they have pre-verbal roots and they tend to function across the various territories of life. The erection of the mental-symbolic mind throughout childhood, adolescence and adulthood rests on these core habits. Experiences literally threatening your survival in infancy, bringing forth possible annihilation, are wisely avoided by all means necessary, during these tenuous and fragile first few months of life. However, as the self develops and matures, what was once a real threat to survival is often no longer an actual threat. For example, being left alone early on in infancy is a certain threat to survival when an urgent need is present.[123] Pre-verbal terror, anxiety and the experience of annihilation are all likely part of this abandoned infant's topography of experience. When core needs emerge, this child is wise to avoid feeling abandoned and being alone. However, as the self grows in early adulthood, seeing someone who is central to his or her life leave, feeling abandoned and being alone no longer legitimately threatens survival. Regardless, it is common for our young adult to continue to avoid feeling abandoned and being alone in times of need because the core underlying conditioning dictates a threat of annihilation. Core survival strategies often remain firmly in place in adulthood.

The sincere experience of annihilation can surface in an intense confrontation with survival, even when safety is of no actual concern. Individuals who are learning to land their airplanes, as discussed above, can expect to confront this territory of experience, even if they have been relatively free from a fear of annihilation. Getting off of your habituated mental constructs and into the broader experiential continuum can often open you up to metabolize many of your pre-verbal experiences.

Outgrowing your habitual defenses toward annihilation is essential for the fluid functioning of elegance. Furthermore, it is also part of the dialectical embrace of *vitality* and *annihilation*, which is part of the self that is larger than life and death, as we explored in Chapter Eight. However, there is a more central reason elegance requires the inclusion of your most central survival habits. As mentioned earlier, there is a treasure within.

The gift within your core survival habit(s) is your most sensitive vulnerabilities. What threatens you with the greatest of intensity is necessarily connected to that which you *most value*. Avoiding annihilation is masking and clouding that which you most value and hold precious. Your self-as-form can be thought of as an instrument that has been tuned to resonate with a particular frequency. How you have been most hurt and threatened is paradoxically connected to that which matters most to you. Furthermore, some of the greatest pleasures, most powerful gifts, and most enriching purposes that can co-create you are also intertwined with that which invokes the experience of annihilation.

You must then not only free yourself from the many habits we have explored thus far, but you must also free yourself from the core habits surrounding survival. Suspending these habits allows you to confront annihilation's experiential intensities, which paradoxically invite you to participate with a greater bandwidth of vitality. This appears to be needed by or useful for elegance. Deconstructing the basic, rote survival strategies reveals important insights into that which matters most to you and how your self-as-form has been shaped, which provides essential clues into the unique purposes you as elegance are here to participate with.

Habituation's Realignment

Conditioning is an essential feature of who you are. It is not simply an inheritance and an obstacle you must free yourself from. To be truly you, to be and become unabashedly and uniquely you, you must radically embrace your conditioning. However, in order for you to radically embrace your conditioning—that is to not avoid or remain in a more or less chronic struggle with your conditioning—you must also be free from it. And here is the paradox we must come to terms with. You cannot merely be caught in your habits. Neither can you simply abide outside of your habits either.

Radical acceptance requires freedom. Not merely a freedom from but a freedom from that also returns. A freedom that embraces and accepts conditioning whole-heartedly. This is a stronger, bolder and more mature freedom than our younger freedom that unknowingly is fleeing from the limiting constraints of conditioning.

Elegance requires this paradoxical synthesis of that which is genuinely free and that which is heartfully bound in limitedness. We can think of this as a form of integral yoga, where you are co-constructed by the unconditioned drive to join that which is without form with the full display of your self-as-form. This is elegance moving toward and as the most essential and superfluous forms of conditioning that facilitate and co-construct you moment to moment. You, all of you, is reclaimed by elegance.[124]

This movement of elegance is of course not merely the rote replaying of a habituated strategy. It is not the unconscious falling into a habit that less mature adults commonly struggle with. With elegance, the display of habituation undergoes *a purification* of sorts. A refinement or transmutation of habituation stems from elegance's often active and conscious participation with conditioning. This conscious participatory engagement reshapes, augments and liberates the ingenuity and brilliance within the habit, while simultaneously reclaiming habit as a now more skillful function of the self.

This realignment of habituation is, however, not entirely conscious. An ignorance and clouded awareness is paradoxically preserved as if elegance enjoys the discovery inherent in the multiplicity of form. So, as there is more liberated awareness and an active participation inside of habituation, we find yet again another *embrace of polarity*. This time, it is *consciousness* and *unconsciousness* happening within the realignment of your core conditioning. Elegance participates with and fluidly moves between the two. At times, dramatic clarity illuminates habituation and its creative synthesis with a facet of the self that is already and always free. At other times, you will see again a basic participatory awareness refining habituation through its expression, yet clarity will not be present. Elegance can and often does function within the spheres of understanding, ignorance and confusion. However, ignorance and confusion now participate with and flower into a new realm of complexity. As such, habituation is now a much more powerful vehicle for performance in the world. No longer does habituation solely serve the regulation of your own relative experience. Instead, habituation's automation can now creatively and dynamically attune with the teleological momentum of form and its evolution, your own self-as-form's growth, the development of a team, and/or the larger world's collective development.

One of the most common questions that arises at this point is *"How do I re-inhabit conditioning from a more creative, liberated or unconditioned consciousness?"* This question is a very good question, and it is the wrong question. It is misguided in that it rests on a less complex assumption, namely, that you are somehow separate from your habituation. I find this question stemming more from the Self-Authoring Mind's autonomy than the postautonomous self that is required to participate with the yoga or synthesis we are now exploring.

While suspension and deconstruction do introduce a gap or separation between your subjectivity and the habituation that once held you, there is an underlying—we might even say unconditioned—participation with broader, often unseen forms of habituation. You are always and already participating with and being co-constructed by parts of the habituated inheritance intrinsic to form. How you "do" this realignment is less relevant than how this realignment may already be "doing" you right now.

Cook-Greuter's Unitive stage of ego development illustrates an essential feature for your participation with the realignment of habituation. You must accept the world, and yourself, as is. It is only within this larger openness with and as immediacy that you can sufficiently be the welcoming inclusion that transmutes habituation. The open embrace, acceptance and inclusion of the core conditioning that you possess and that possesses you enables a progressive alignment with the function of elegance as you. Trust appears to be at the center of this enactment. Allowance of what is already arising in form expands, creating a larger, more complex ability to participate with who you are and who you are becoming.

When this happens, you are likely to see a pattern beginning to take shape. Where conditioning was once largely circling your own homeostasis, habituation's realignment with and as elegance refines these patterns such that they retain their essence yet also reveal a broader intelligence and ingenuity. No longer are habits solely focused on your interests and self-regulation. Habits can now serve broader imperatives. That is, they become more powerful, useful and trustable. Instead of remaining an inner enemy of sorts, habituation becomes a powerful ally within the current of elegance.

For example, unexamined preferences and your conditioned allegiances to them no longer need to collapse complexity, shrink meaning to privilege your experience, or support a conventional sense of self. Preferences can now be a function of your habituation that can celebrate complexity, expand meaning to the heart-felt consideration of more life, and liberate insight into yourself, others and our world. Similarly, defenses no longer function as a rote necessity for closing down the aperture of experience. Through realignment, defenses can facilitate a more fine-tuned sensitivity toward that which is more valuable and significant. Habituated conflict may no longer serve one polarity's opposition to its already intrinsic opposite. Instead, conflict can highlight the unresolvability inherent in the multiplicity of form's polar structure and/or conflict can become a reliable vehicle for the novel, more complex, synthesis of polarity.

Habituated struggle can be reclaimed and re-inhabited so that it no longer draws you out of contact with immediacy. Instead of dividing you in an attempt to get out of, or rid of, part of experience that is already present, habituated struggle can mature into an instrument with which you can make further contact with the unbounded complexity and fullness of experience. One struggle that most adults tend to confront is

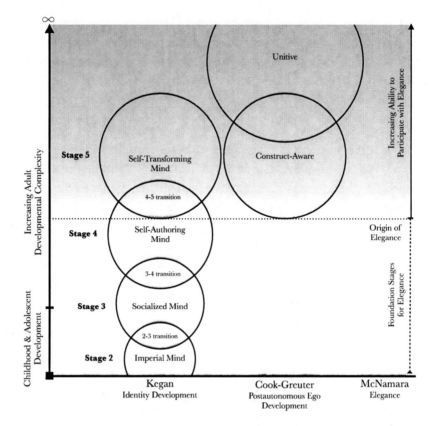

Kegan's Self-Transforming Mind stage and Cook-Greuter's Construct-Aware stage likely represent similar levels of development at their onset, while offering different yet complementary perspectives on postconventional and postautonomous adult development. Cook-Greuter's Unitive stage introduces finer distinctions into the further reaches of adult development. The dotted horizontal line across the diagram represents the origin of human elegance while the shaded gradation illustrates an ever increasing proficiency for participating with elegance. This diagram holding both Kegan's and Cook-Greuter's proposed stages have arrows extending upward capturing an uncertainty to the further reaches of adult development. The infinity symbol located above the main developmental axis illustrates how development is likely to never end in its increase in complexity.

the struggle with discipline. Compulsively, the self often divides itself in two parts, the part that wants to, or feels as though it should, do something and the part that does not. This habituated division within discipline can refine a person so that the boundary between the facet of you saying "yes" and the facet of you saying "no" can be unified in a larger coherence. The habit that once divided now functions to create greater connection and collaborative exchange within the self.

For example, I often have conversations with clients about their discipline to engage with strength training, change a leadership style or be more adaptive in a marriage. Some parts are saying "yes," while other dimensions are firmly communicating "no" to these changes. Discipline, as many of us tend to think about it, is required to work against the parts of ourselves that are saying "no." Discipline is needed to drop the heroic leadership style when the organization needs more. Discipline is required to get to the gym to train when we are exhausted and do not feel like it. Discipline is needed to show up for a spouse differently when you would rather not. Ask yourself, how much energy do you expend in your "no's"? Conversely, how much energy are you investing in your "yes's"? How much energy is possibly wasted when they are positioned against one another?

Unifying, aligning and establishing this larger coherence means that your "no" preserves its integrity yet joins with the "yes." Or, alternatively, the "yes" preserves its integrity yet joins with the "no." Saying yes to adapting new leadership styles enrolls the no's central objections such that new leadership styles can commingle with old leadership styles. Saying no to the gym on any particular day can enroll the energy of the yes such that a new level of engagement is brought to one's life outside of the gym. The inner division where one part is pinned against another part is resolved into more functional and adaptive responses.

Similarly the language habit can refine the mind so that concepts operating in the symbolic representational mind no longer disconnect you from the larger embodied, energetic and less mediated experiential flux. Symbols can then be freed up to yoke you more fully into a broader, more direct experience of thought itself, as well as nonsymbolized experience.

The core conditioning defining the human mind, the aversion of pain and grasping of pleasure, can transmute into a broader embrace and attraction toward both pain and pleasure. This can also include a more nuanced and discerning aversion of both pain and pleasure that may have been clouding, obscuring and/or betraying the larger complexity possible for you. Habituated constructions of superiority and arrogance can become service. Insecurity, shame and inadequacy can become a transmuted seat of humility and receptivity, where you allow others to support you in ways only their uniqueness can. The habituated desire to be entertained may transmute into an immensely curious and nourished attunement with facets of life once ignored. Socialized masks that you wear with others no longer necessitate a guarding of your more true interiority and instead can be a function of greater articulation of your authenticity, which may celebrate a larger social cohesion and connectedness.

Habituation is an ongoing, endless formation. And while its less complex expressions often inhibit learning and adaptation, within the realignment of habituation is a dynamic facility capable of further development. Through the embrace and reclaiming of habituation, you can be shaped more freely by the innate gestures of innovation that are pressing form, your self-as-form included, into creative advance into novelty.

For additional resources on working with habits, visit:

www.TheElegantSelf.com/Habits

Personal Notes & Reflection

11

THE COURAGE OF ELEGANCE

Commitments to which You Belong

I remember sitting at my middle-school desk wearing a new pair of Nike pump sneakers and a new presumably popular T-shirt. While I was in school to learn, more of my attention was on how my new fashion statements would be acknowledged by my peers. As I was consumed by whether or not to pump up my shoes more or to let air out of my high-tech sneakers during class, my teacher—as any good teacher does—captured my attention and engaged me in the classroom. As these social distractions temporarily faded, I became lost in learning about the astonishing global impact rainforests possess. I was shocked to learn how something covering just a sliver of the Earth's total surface area could be home to over half of our plants and animals. A sizable portion of our fresh drinking water and, the one that really baffled my mind, a large percentage of our Earth's oxygen turnover is because of the rainforests. My teacher continued as she shared how the rainforests were a huge resource for medicines, that a large portion of the diversity of life in the rainforest had yet to be discovered, and that these small sections of the world operated as a type of thermostat for planet Earth.

I was genuinely surprised by my teacher. However, as she continued my surprise shifted considerably. She ended what appeared to be a standard lecture on rainforests with some frightening statistics. Human beings were burning, clear-cutting and destroying rainforests at an alarming rate. My shock changed from an appreciation for how small features can make global impacts to a confusion about adults. This was a significant shift for me, as I sat in my chair, the new sneakers gently resting on the metal chair legs in front of me and my textbook lying open on my desk. Looking at my teacher sitting at her desk, a green chalkboard filled with bright white chalk illustrating facts and figures behind her, the true education was not in the information I now had access to and would have to remember for my quiz the following week. My education was that my mind no longer fully trusted adults. As a child, I could see without any shadow of a doubt something was wrong with the adult world. Adults did not yet possess the ability to be sincerely responsible for the world they presumably governed. Twenty-some years later, the condition appears to be similar, although now I am an adult too.

The Nature Conservancy brings more clarity to much of what I learned decades ago in school.[125] Seventy percent of plants identified by the US National Cancer Institute as useful for the treatment of cancer are found exclusively in rainforests. Less than 1 percent of tropical rainforest species have been analyzed for their value to medicine, health and well-being. Rainforests absorb greenhouse gases, thus regulating temperatures and play a significant role in weather patterns. The Nature Conservancy says they "are critical in maintaining the Earth's limited supply of drinking and fresh water."[126] In spite of these insights, deforestation has been decimating tropical rainforests worldwide. What was once an estimated 6 million square miles of the most rich diversity of life on planet Earth is now approximately just over 2.5 million square miles. More than half of the tropical rainforests are gone. Every second, a football field worth of rainforest is destroyed. One-thousand-one ... gone! Approximately 86,400 football fields' worth of rainforest are lost every single day. This is one of the few environmental challenges that can be seen by the naked eye from space.[127] While traveling at more than 17,000 miles per hour from 300 miles above the Earth's surface, astronauts can see the rainforests burning at alarming rates.[128]

While the issue of the loss of the rainforests continues to be a long-standing feature of the major environmental issues facing our world today, I like to use this as an analogy to highlight what appears to be an even larger issue. The immediacy of each moment is very much like a rainforest. Within immediacy, there is an immense diversity of aliveness. This diversity of form, arising as each moment, is rich in resources of all types. Some are known, others remain undiscovered. These resources arising as immediacy are vastly complex. Perhaps they are always exceeding our mind's ability to fully comprehend and hold the dynamic interpenetrable relationships present. This larger interconnectedness within and as immediacy holds tremendous power and influence. Within this dense, diverse and multilayered canopy of form arising as immediacy are the forces shaping evolution. Immediacy's innate movements turned star dust into you and me. Immediacy fuels species to become something more. Immediacy gives rise to a greater adaptive expression of inheritance and creative novelty. Immediacy co-creates the complex, disparate and changing patterns of form into a broader coherence. Immediacy is the rainforest you are most nourished to be and become within; however, there is at least one massive problem. Just as human beings have an apparently unexamined habit of burning, clear-cutting and bulldozing the precious resources of rainforests, conventional autonomy often involves the bulldozing of immediacy.

The presupposition that your self-as-form precedes immediacy, which we have explored at length, can be thought of as similar to the clear-cutting of the rainforest. The unknown diversity and only partly understood and appreciated aliveness within and as immediacy are bulldozed over with the expectations and agendas of conventional expressions of autonomy. Often, the complex interpenetrable actualities collaboratively and conflictually participating with a greater movement of being and becoming are burned and destroyed by the less complex and under-refined conventions of adulthood. Complexity is often erased, ignored and violated, sometimes in violent ways, to support autonomy's often myopic, singular and much less complex focus. Just as the rainforest is often destroyed to create space for cattle grazing, this moment may be flattened and reduced in an understanding that fixates around me, my separate distinct self, to get what my autonomy myopically wants and/or appears to need. What once housed billions of possibilities has now been reduced to something known and often operationalized into a purpose that is often all too narrow and self-centered.

This book is an invitation to participate with the broader rainforest of immediacy. For the first time, many adults are ready to actually step into the rainforest without flattening it out into the known conventions of autonomous reference points. For most, this is a novel invitation into the complexity of life that has been here all along, waiting for an intelligence to more consciously co-create and participate with its motion.[129] Immediacy can envelop you into what we have been calling an unmediated, or less mediated, experiential flux. When you get off the airplane as we discussed in Chapter Ten, the rainforest of immediacy discovers you. Blooming textures, rich vitality and diversity enlivens and co-creates your own self-discovery, moment-to-moment. This is not necessarily a simple going beyond autonomous functioning. As Jim showed us in Chapter Six, development beyond autonomy involves the further maturation of your perspectives, worldviews and actions such that you can integrate, hold and envelop autonomous functioning in a skillful, competent and, in the end, more elegant way.

THE PRESSURE OF ENVIRONMENT, CULTURE AND EDUCATION

Today's global issues span a vast array of complexities. A more attuned relationship between human beings and the broader environment, the establishment of greater global financial stability, sustainable technological and economic development, energy independence and renewable clean energy, developing critical levers to positively impact climate change, the necessity to end systemic poverty and increase resource sharing, broadening educational access and opportunities for everyone, and the need to preserve and protect human rights with greater elegance all point to an underlying failure of the conventional adult autonomous mind. Perhaps our largest failure has been not effectively developing the minds of our youth and nurturing adults to act from our larger, broader developmental complexity that is appropriate for the world co-creating us now.

As we have explored in some depth, each stage of mental complexity manages, limits and exerts control over the preceding stages' subjectivity and meaning-making. As we saw in Chapter Two, the Self-Authoring Mind sets limits on the loyalties that govern the Socialized Mind's subjectivity. Thus, a now larger self can regulate, choose and control whom, what and where to be loyal and where to be disloyal in service of larger guiding values. Adequately addressing the world's complex demands may indeed rest on the ability of the next stage's Self-Transforming Mind to regulate, control and manage conventional adult autonomy, which often appears to be, for the most part, without a larger guiding intelligence in most adults today. Our collective survival likely rests on this higher-ordered interpenetrating intelligence.

Without a grander perspective and more attuned interconnected perception, conventional autonomy will not be governed and organized by a larger intelligence. Instead, conventional autonomy, in its often unseen limitations, will continue to self-author a world disconnected from the larger contextual surroundings that human life depends on. This is a tremendous threat in and of itself. Adulthood's autonomy is easily overwhelmed in its inability to read, relate, manage and participate with the complexity of today's mixtures of post-modern, modern and pre-modern worlds.

The past century has brought with it more dramatic, rapid and world-sculpting change than perhaps any other period of human history. While the conventions of adulthood may have been adequate responses to the pre-modern and modern worlds, today's post-modern complexities appear to be demanding the type of dramatic reorientation in psychological development we have been exploring together.

Our challenge rests squarely on how we lead adult minds into the honors curriculum of adult development. How do we as a global culture set limits on autonomy so that more—many more than our present elite 1 percent—are appropriately challenged to grow into and participate with our greater postautonomous complexity and maturity? What are the structures and systems that cultivate elegance? How do we invite ourselves and our adult peers to listen into the challenges within marriage, parenting and partnering so that the systemic personal challenges solve and transform us? How can undergraduate and graduate education participate more efficiently with the complexity of mind needed by our young adults if they are to genuinely supersede our own failures to co-create a world more deserving for our future generations? How can the immensely complex global economy unlock our larger adult development so that competitiveness and adaptability in the marketplace nurtures adults in more efficient ways? How can today's most pressing and enduring leadership and management challenges sculpt organizational cultures to more effectively develop human complexity along with market shares?

What appears to be clear is that we do not need *all* adults functioning from the honors curriculum, as we have been exploring it. Creating an expectation that all adults quickly enter into postconventional or postautonomous stages of development is both unrealistic and unduly hostile toward conventional stages of development. We cannot skip nor rush through the prerequisites and essential foundations. To attempt to do so would likely prove foolish as our collective human elegance cannot thrive upon shaky foundations.

What is required is a critical mass of *leaders and influencers*. At least three characteristics are necessary. First, our critical mass must demonstrate *polished conventional skill sets*. They must stand face to face looking into the conventional adult minds and their corresponding worlds. It is here that they must outperform their peers in conventional aims. Failure to demonstrate this ability often forfeits social capital often required for leadership and a larger influence. Secondly, our critical mass must also demonstrate a consistent ability to participate with their own unique *elegance*. Occasionally participating with elegance is insufficient. The world requires personal and professional elegance. Our critical mass must be and become more elegant in a resilient and enduring way. Elegance is needed in the face of complex challenges, stressors, loss and competition, not only when the environment and circumstances surrounding us are supportive of our elegance. Finally, our leaders and influences must be willing and able to *architect and shape the culture and institutions* around them with their elegance. It is here, in the collective domains of culture and institutions, that the elegant self can qualitatively improve our world.

One of the keys appears to be in the pressure education places on our conventional views of autonomy. Does education continue to distract itself with filling the autonomous mind with more facts? Or do we make central to the educational process that we lead our youths and adults out of the mind presently holding them? Can education lead you out from the limits of your subjectivity and draw you beyond the constraints of what you are able to conceive of with greater elegance? And will education spread its ability to lead a sufficient number of adults out from conventional stages of development into postconventional and possibly postautonomous stages of complexity? How these questions are answered today, right now, by you and me is likely a powerful determinant for the kind of world our children are ushered into and the one they are eventually handed to trust and care for.

Perhaps it is in the subject/object balance of how you conceive of "you" and "me" in the previous sentence that largely determines our species' survival. Presume your autonomy and separateness and then turn to these questions to figure them out, and autonomy runs the risk of, once again, making decisions unguided and ungoverned by a larger intelligence. The rainforest of immediacy is burned and bulldozed and the answers autonomy presents miss at least one glaring crucial ingredient: *elegance*. However, if the self you and I are born from is a function of subjective interpenetrability rooted within the rainforest of immediacy, and the gracefulness of elegance allows us to be held by these questions and worked by these problems, then perhaps something extraordinary may occur. We may mysteriously become something more. What we were yesterday, or even 15 minutes ago, is now something qualitatively different. We may, in our fiercest of engagement and most pointed surrender, grow and mature into an expression of life that is more true, good and beautiful. This, my dear friend, is the cradle of the hope that fuels and co-creates the elegant self as me that is, in so many ways, not so separate and disconnected from you. Nor is this elegant self entirely separate from the rainforests of immediacy that presses these words into your awareness right now. Have a look around. There is so much to discover, especially about who you and I can become.

BELONGING TO HUMAN ELEGANCE AND COURAGE

You belong to the state of elegance. Your participation with this larger, more complex intelligence determines the degree and bandwidth of vitality expressed through you. Lose your larger complexity, or perhaps fail to discover and claim your greater development as an adult, and life itself weeps in the immense losses. Collapse the bandwidth of you—close the aperture of experience away from immediacy's blooming experiential flux—and, in many ways, humanity's evolution as you ceases. Likely, the persistent problems within your intimate relationships, family and friends are fundamentally a symptom of your stalled evolution. Similarly, the ongoing professional challenges you see on the job, in the classroom, and/or in the public sphere as a whole reflect a self failing to adaptively grow and develop in response to the complexity of life.

Regardless of the history that has led you to this sentence, you have a responsibility to participate with the larger complexity of elegance. The larger maturity outlined within these pages, the higher, more complex forms and expressions of you that are discovered and known only between you and the smiles on your face and the tears in your eyes, as well as the facets of experience, which remain unknown and undiscovered, is what you belong to in your life. Elegance owns you. Yet elegance comes into form as your unique self, if you cultivate the requisite skills for *participation*. Ownership, while an attractive offering to the autonomous mind, is not an option. Elegance may be partly known and thus held onto; however, it is always in collaboration with a precious mystery. Elegance is always playing within the mystery inherent as immediacy. Immediacy, in its dynamic creative novelty, does not yet know itself. And perhaps this novel emergence inherent within every moment is an essential part of life and, as evolution suggests, survival.

As you know, this is not the domain of certainty. Your larger capacities as a human being enjoy being discovered. Discovery and the very process of exploration, however joyful they may be, require *courage*. To step beyond the conventions and to become a stand within the larger creative uncertainty of life is to take up residence in a process to which you ultimately belong. It appears life itself embodies this risk to discover who and what it can become, what it can achieve, and where it can go that had not been embodied before, all to celebrate the uniqueness of life's creative advance into greater diversity.

This exploration comes with a cost. The creative advance involves mistakes. It involves unforeseen problems and challenges. And, as you likely know, not all explorations are successful. Yet something inside of you yearns to participate in this risk of aliveness, for the rewards are perhaps aligned with the very purpose of why you are here. This is not your courage; this is the courage that owns you, a state to which you belong. This is the courage you are called to participate with, for the alternative is too much a betrayal of the creative exploratory impulse innate as immediacy co-constructing you again and again. To remain fixed in the domain of autonomy is to dampen, perhaps burn, the diverse canopy of aliveness that you are. To live largely inside the conventions of autonomous inheritance, as most adults do, is a disloyalty to who and what you can become. In the end, you are likely to discover yourself as an unresolvable paradox. Elegance embraces you in being precisely that which you already are, and elegance as you is an unrelenting drive to become something more. Part of this is known and inherited, while another is unknowable and emergent.

At the time of this writing, my nephew Rowan is just over three years old. He is utterly precious, beautifully curious, and filled with an immense playfulness. While he largely does not know it, the courage I point to here works him daily. It shapes his quick feet as he runs across his living room floor, past the front door into the dining room, feet pitter-pattering around the corner as he bolts into the kitchen. Courage seems to be making him faster and faster. As his mind ponders inquiries such as "Am I okay?" "How much can I do?" and "What can I get away with now?" he faces a world that is tough at times. He is largely stuck inside his own needs, which is perhaps precisely where he should be today. Yet, in so many ways, the world around him unfolds without much consideration of his interior preferences and needs. In Rowan's sadness and hurt, tears roll down his cheeks and he asks for and reaches for Mommy or Daddy. He laments his losses, and then something miraculous yet entirely ordinary occurs. Rowan returns to his play. His eyes brighten, a smile returns, and off he goes, one foot in front of the other.

My sincere hope is that Rowan's mind outgrows my own, his mother's (Deb) and his father's (Chris). I hope his own mind develops beyond that of his teachers, coaches and mentors who will usher him through many years of diverse and complex challenges. Yet I am also fairly certain that Rowan cannot do it alone. If he is to supersede my generation's accepted norms, he likely needs an adult culture of mind that actively develops itself, its many cultures and institutions of all types into a maturity that is innately elegant. Rowan needs to see how adulthood is not the cessation of development. He needs adults to model a larger complexity with a broader maturity that actively and unendingly explores the unknown.

My sense is that Rowan needs this and likely billions of children around the world will too. Our future generations are likely to be served by an adult culture committed to the collaboration and participation with becoming more. This more is not the false substitutions and betrayals of your developmental possibilities as touched on in Chapter One. No, the generations to come require adulthood to co-create and sculpt itself and humanity into something qualitatively better. This something more embraces and declares a species that is always exploring and becoming a larger goodness, truth and beauty.

Part known, part emergent, half mystery and half certainty, you are the fluid, simple yet ingenious integration of unresolvable polarities— cooperation and conflict coming together and moving apart in service of a creative response. Elegance as you embodies a dynamic tension that is open, curious and perhaps fiercely courageous. Elegance as you discovers a flexibility inherently trusting of the multilayered canopy of the experiential flux of life. Show and tell this bandwidth of vitality to your kids, co-workers and lovers. Become the infinitely unique integration of this moment's most intelligent conditioning with immediacy's most liberated wisdom and co-creative discovery. Infuse this into the cultures of mind you participate with. Imbed this elegance into the operations of the many organizations you interface with.

The elegant self is here; perhaps it merely awaits our larger participation.

Be explored by elegance...

Personal Notes & Reflection

RESOURCES

Thank you for taking this challenging and exciting journey into some of our culture's most complex and demanding curriculum. I applaud you for picking up this book and reading it cover to cover. You have traversed profound transformations of mind, and I am confident something elegant is working you in your life, right now. This part seen and unseen force is shaping, sculpting and molding you into a more dynamic, powerful and capable human being sharpened for greater service and influence in our world. Allow the larger risks of your life to take you today. Empower yourself to move with what is most significant. Participate with an urgency that embraces the intelligence of your most careful discernment and consideration.

Resource yourself with the exercises, practices and passages that illuminate your next steps forward. Be influenced by your notes and reflections. And, all books are inherently incomplete as are your own private reflections. There is always more unfolding from the creative advance of immediacy. If you are inspired and driven to go further, consider reaching out to cocreate your next steps together. Birthing greater elegance in our world is a passion and inspiration that holds and commands the life that shapes and directs me.

I work with organizations, teams, individuals one-on-one, and in retreats and trainings around the world. Some are local here in Boulder Colorado, most are spread throughout our diverse yet connected world. I specialize in helping people like you discover creative resolutions to the persistent and often painful limitations to become more powerful, proficient and aligned with what matters most in life.

You can learn more about me, my offerings as well as contact me through my website:

www.RobMcNamara.com

In the mean time, participate with the elegance that you are today. Do this privately, with your friends and family as well as in the professional sphere. There is perhaps nothing more important than being and becoming more of an elegant human being.

Looking forward to connect with you again soon,
Robert Lundin McNamara

To follow the blog, gain access to media, learn about coaching or to get strategies to grow your elegance in the world visit:

www.TheElegantSelf.com

Finally, economically supporting the development and implementation of integral practices is an essential feature for furthering adult capacities in today's complex world. Make a tax-deductible charitable donation to support the education, training and advancement of Integral Practices today. To donate and learn more visit:

www.PerformanceIntegral.com

AUDIO COURSES BY ROB MCNAMARA

COMMANDING INFLUENCE:
YOUR DEVELOPMENT FOR GREATER MASTERY AT WORK

Accelerate your development and apply insights from The Elegant Self to pragmatic professional challenges. This downloadable audio program includes 19 audio lessons; over 6 hours of instruction; original self-paced practices along with downloadable PDF transcript and practice guide.

https://tendirections.com/
elegant-leadership/commanding-
influence/

FREE 7 PART AUDIO COACHING PROGRAM FOR PROFESSIONALS

High performance coaching targeting the sources of common professional challenges.

- Get insights into how adult development influences your workplace.
- Deal with one of the root causes of professional overwhelm.
- Stop being susceptible to daily distractions.
- Minimize the impact of difficult people on your state of mind.
- Assert yourself with skill and sensitivity.
- Clarify your personal mission for greater influence.

Receive over 2 hours of professional coaching + practice instruction delivered to your inbox every few days:

http://tendirections.com/lp

DEVELOPMENTAL COACHING:
MASTERING HUMAN TRANSFORMATION FOR GREATER COACHING IMPACT

Masterful coaches—those who have rigorous developmental training—are in the best position to support individual development for large scale impact. This audio series teaches professional coaches how to provide developmental coaching that supports long-term, historic transformation and increasing well-being in clients' lives.

"Rob McNamara has a beautiful expression for a form of leadership that is conscientious and transformative. He teaches that our role as leaders is to declare what must be better and to fully use our influence to make it so. Further, he provides solid practices to support this goal."

- Jean Ogilvie, Coach and OD Consultant

"Masterful in his exposition of leading developmental psychologists Robert Kegan and Susanne Cook-Greuter's work."

- David McCallum, Special Assistant to the President for Mission Integration and Development Le Moyne College

https://tendirections.com/elegant-leadership/developmental-coaching/

OTHER BOOKS BY ROB MCNAMARA

STRENGTH TO AWAKEN

*Make Strength Training Your Spiritual Practice
and Find New Power and Purpose in Your Life*

"One of the most important and significant books I have seen on Integral physical training ... Highly Recommended!"
- **Ken Wilber**, The Integral Vision

"Finally. A book with the complexity and courage to move beyond our cultural obsession with the physical dimensions of training. McNamara redefines strength and provides a practical roadmap that both inspires and instructs on how to liberate our true greatness."
- **Rand Stagen,** *founder & managing director*
Stagen Leadership Academy

Inner Engagement for Multifaceted Results

Strength to Awaken is unlike any other book on strength training. Change the purpose of your training and life. Gain never-before-seen instruction on the inner dimensions of training. Learn Whole Hearted Engagement to perform at new levels. Enjoy rare clarity as you go beyond the conventions and limitations holding you back.

- **End Boring Repetitive Exercise and Create Next-Level Performance.**
- **Go Beyond Frustrating Limitations to Whole-Hearted Engagement.**
- **Train yourself to Enjoy more Genuine Pleasure.**
- **Transform Not Just your Body, but your Whole Self.**
- **Get More Benefits, Faster.**

Robert Lundin McNamara is the authority on Integral strength training. He has been one of the world's leading voices in the field of integral practice for nearly a decade. Rob's rigorous approach, open heart, and pioneering method to training provide you with new ways to solve age-old problems that can limit the results in your training.

www.StrengthToAwaken.com

BIBLIOGRAPHY

Barbaras, R. (2008). "Life, Movement, and Desire" in *Research in Phenomenology*, 38(1), 3-17.

Barbaras, R. (2010). "Life and Exteriority" in *Enaction: Toward a New Paradigm for Cognitive Science*, eds. John Stewart, Olivier Gapenne, and Ezequiel A. DiPaolo. Cambridge, MA: MIT Press.

Basseches, M. (1984). *Dialectical Thinking and Adult Development*. Norwood, N.J.: Ablex.

Becker, E. (1973). *The Denial of Death*. NY: Free Press Paperbacks.

Bradford, D.L. & Cohen, A.R. (1984). *Managing for Excellence, The leadership guide to developing high performance in contemporary organizations*. Hoboken, NJ, John Wiley & Sons. Inc.

Brookings (2012). "Economics: Global Financial Crisis." Retrieved from www.brookings.edu/research/topics/global-financial-crisis.

Commons, M.L. & Richards, F.A. (1984). "A general model of stage theory." In M.L. Commons, F.A. Richards & C. Armon (Eds.), *Beyond formal operations: Vol. 1. Late adolescent and adult cognitive development* (pp. 120–140). New York: Praeger.

Cook-Greuter, S. (1999). *Postautonomous Ego Development: A study of its nature and measurement*. Integral Publishers.

Cook-Greuter, S. (2013). Personal Communication, February 14th, 2013.

Forman, M. (2010). *A Guide to Integral Psychotherapy: Complexity, integration and spirituality in practice.* Albany, NY: State University of New York Press.

Global Issues (2012). Retrieved from www.globalissues.org.

Hamilton, Diane. (2012). Personal Communication, Dec. 5th, 2012.

Helfert, M.R. and K.P. Lulla (1990). "Mapping Continental-Scale Biomass Burning and Smoke Palls over the Amazon Basin as Observed from the Space Shuttle." *Photogrammetric Engineering and Remote Sensing,* 10(56), pp. 1367-1373.

Honderich, T. (2005). *The Oxford Companion to Philosophy, second edition.* Oxford, NY: Oxford University Press. pp. 670-671.

Intergovernmental Panel on Climate Change (2012). Retrieved from http://www.ipcc.ch.

International Labor Office (2012). "ILO 2012 Global Estimate of Forced Labour" Fact Sheet. Retrieved from www.ilo.org/wcmsp5/groups/public/---ed_norm/---declaration/documents/publication/wcms_181921.pdf.

Kegan, R. (1982). *The Evolving Self: Problem and process in human development.* Cambridge, MA: Harvard College.

Kegan, R. (1994). *In Over Our Heads: The mental demands of modern life.* Cambridge, MA: Harvard University Press.

Kegan, R. (2009). *Immunity to Change: How to overcome it and unlock potential in yourself and your organization.* Boston, MA: Harvard Business Press.

Koplowitz, H. (1984). "A projection beyond Piaget's formal operational stage: A general systems stage and a unitary stage." In M.L. Commons, F.A. Richards & C. Armon (Eds.), *Beyond Formal Operations* (pp. 279-295). New York: Praeger.

Loevinger, J. (1966). "The Meaning and Measurement of Ego-Development," *American Psychologist,* 21, pp. 195-206.

Maslow, A.H. (1971). *The Further Reaches of Human Nature*. NY: Penguin Books.

McNamara, Robert L. (2012). *Strength To Awaken, Make Strength Training Your Spiritual Practice and Find New Power and Purpose in Your Life*. Boulder, CO: Performance Integral.

NASA Earth Observatory (2012). "Fires along the Rio Xingu, Brazil." October 10, 2011. Retrieved from http://earthobservatory.nasa.gov/IOTD/view.php?id=71256.

National Aeronautics and Space Administration (2012). "Global Climate Change, Vital signs of the planet." Retrieved from http://climate.nasa.gov.

National Institutes of Health Forgarty International Center (2011). "The Global Health Cost of Addiction." Retrieved from www.fic.nih.gov/News/GlobalHealthMatters/April2011/Pages/addiction.aspx.

O'Fallon, T. & Kramer, G. (1998). *Insight dialogue and insight dialogic inquiry*. Doctoral dissertation. San Francisco, CA: California Institute of Integral Studies. UMI Dissertation Services UMI #9824352.

Perry, W.G., Jr. (1970). *Forms of Intellectual and Ethical Development in the College Years*. NY: Holt, Rinehart and Winston.

Schnarch, D. (2009). *Intimacy and Desire: Awaken the passion in your relationship*. NY: Beaufort Books.

Siegel, D. (2007). *The Mindful Brain: Reflection and attunement in the cultivation of well-being.* NY: W.W. Norton & Company.

Siegel, D. (2010). *The Mindful Therapist, A clinician's guide to mindsight and neural integration*. New York: W.W. Norton & Company.

Skinner, E.B. (2010). "South Africa's New Slave Trade and the Campaign to Stop It." *Time*. Retrieved from www.time.com/time/magazine/article/0,9171,1952335,00.html.

Starr, A. & Torbert, B. (2005). "Timely and Transforming Leadership Inquiry and Action: Toward Triple-Loop Awareness." *Integral Review*, 1, pp. 85-97.

The Nature Conservancy (2012). "Rainforests, Facts About Rainforests." Retrieved from www.nature.org/ourinitiatives/urgentissues/rainforests/rainforests-facts.xml.

Torbert, W. (1987). *Managing the Corporate Dream: Restructuring for long-term success*. Homewood, IL: Dow Jones-Irwin.

Torbert, W. (1991). *The Power of Balance: Transforming self, society and scientific inquiry*. Thousand Oaks, CA: Sage.

Torbert, W. (1994). "Cultivating Postformal Adult Development: Theory and practice." In M. Miller & S. Cook-Greuter (Eds.), *Transcendence and Mature Thought in Adulthood: The further reaches of adult development* (pp. 181-203). Lanham, MD: Rowman & Littlefield.

United Nations New Centre (2011). "Clean Energy Revolution Crucial to Ensure Growth in Poorer Countries." Retrieved from www.un.org/apps/news/story.asp?NewsID=39990.

US Department of Commerce, United Stages Census Bureau (2010 plus). Current Population Clock. Retrieved from www.census.gov/main/www/popclock.html.

Vaillant, G.E. (2002). *Aging Well, Surprising Guideposts to a happier life from the landmark Harvard study of adult development*. Boston: Little, Brown & Company.

Whitehead, A.N. (1978). *Process and Reality, An essay in cosmology, Gifford lectures delivered in the University of Edinburgh during the session 1927-28*. NY: Free Press.

Wilber, K. (1979). *No Boundary, Eastern and Western approaches to personal growth*. Boston: Shambhala.

Wilber, K. (1981). *The Atman Project: A transpersonal view of human development.* Wheaton, IL: Quest Books.

Wilber, K. (1995). *Sex, Ecology, Spirituality, The spirit of evolution.* Boston: Shambhala.

Wilber, Ken (2006). "Excerpt A: An integral age at the leading edge." Retrieved from www.kenwilber.com/Writings/PDF/ ExcerptA_KOSMOS_2003.pdf.

Wilber, K. (2006). *Integral Spirituality, A startling new role for religion in the modern and postmodern world.* Boston: Integral Books.

Zalta, E.N. (Ed.) (2011). *Stanford Dictionary of Philosophy* (version 1.0.1) [mobile application software]. Retrieved from http:// itunes.apple.com.

NOTES

1 Kegan, R. (1994). *In Over Our Heads: The mental demands of modern life.* Cambridge, MA: Harvard University Press. p. 335.

2 Kegan, R. (2009). *Immunity to Change: How to overcome it and unlock potential in yourself and your organization.* Boston, MA: Harvard Business Press.

3 US Department of Commerce, United Stages Census Bureau (2010 plus). Current Population Clock. Retrieved from www.census.gov/main/www/popclock.html.

4 Brookings (2012). "Economics: Global Financial Crisis." Retrieved from www.brookings.edu/research/topics/global-financial-crisis.

5 Intergovernmental Panel on Climate Change (2012). Retrieved from http://www.ipcc.ch.

6 National Aeronautics and Space Administration (2012). "Global Climate Change, Vital signs of the planet." Retrieved from http://climate.nasa.gov.

7 United Nations New Centre (2011). "Clean Energy Revolution Crucial to Ensure Growth in Poorer Countries." Retrieved from www.un.org/apps/news/story.asp?NewsID=39990.

8 Global Issues (2012). Retrieved from www.globalissues.org.

9 National Institutes of Health Forgarty International Center (2011). "The Global Health Cost of Addiction." Retrieved from www.fic.nih.gov/News/GlobalHealthMatters/April2011/Pages/addiction.aspx.

10 Skinner, E.B. (2010). "South Africa's New Slave Trade and the Campaign to Stop It." *Time.* Retrieved from www.time.com/time/magazine/article/0,9171,1952335,00.html.

11 International Labor Office (2012). "ILO 2012 Global Estimate of Forced Labour" Fact Sheet. Retrieved from www.ilo.org/wcmsp5/groups/public/---ed_norm/---declaration/documents/publication/wcms_181921.pdf.

12 Vaillant, G.E. (2002). *Aging Well, Surprising Guideposts to a happier life from the landmark Harvard study of adult development.* Boston: Little, Brown & Company.

13 Siegel, D. (2010). *The Mindful Therapist, A clinician's guide to mindsight and neural integration.* New York: W.W. Norton & Company. p. 25.

14 McNamara, Robert L. (2012). *Strength To Awaken, Make Strength Training Your Spiritual Practice and Find New Power and Purpose in Your Life.* Boulder, CO: Performance Integral.

15 Kegan, R. (1982). *The Evolving Self: Problem and process in human development.* Cambridge, MA: Harvard College.

16 Kegan, R. (2009). *Immunity to Change: How to overcome it and unlock potential in yourself and your organization.* Boston, MA: Harvard Business Press.

17 Kegan, R. (1994). *In Over Our Heads: The mental demands of modern life.* Cambridge, MA: Harvard University Press. pp. 32-34.

18 Kegan, R. (1982). *The Evolving Self: Problem and process in human development.* Cambridge, MA: Harvard College. p. 31 in Chapter One, "The Unrecognized Genius of Jean Piaget."

19 Kegan, R. (1994). *In Over Our Heads: The mental demands of modern life.* Cambridge, MA: Harvard University Press. pp. 198-199.

20 Wilber, K. (1981). *The Atman Project: A transpersonal view of human development.* Wheaton, IL: Quest Books. pp. 103-106.

21 Siegel, D. (2007). *The Mindful Brain: Reflection and attunement in the cultivation of well-being.* NY: W.W. Norton & Company.

22 Wilber, K. (1995). *Sex, Ecology, Spirituality, The spirit of evolution.* Boston: Shambhala.

23 Kegan, R. (2009). *Immunity to Change: How to overcome it and unlock potential in yourself and your organization.* Boston, MA: Harvard Business Press. p. 28.

24 Kegan, R. (2009). *Immunity to Change: How to overcome it and unlock potential in yourself and your organization.* Boston, MA: Harvard Business Press. p. 28.

25 Kegan, R. (2009). *Immunity to Change: How to overcome it and unlock potential in yourself and your organization.* Boston, MA: Harvard Business Press. p. 28.

26 Schnarch, D. (2009). *Intimacy and Desire: Awaken the passion in your relationship.* NY: Beaufort Books. p. 44

27 Kegan, R. (2009). *Immunity to Change: How to overcome it and unlock potential in yourself and your organization.* Boston, MA: Harvard Business Press. p. 28.

28 Forman, M. (2010). *A Guide to Integral Psychotherapy: Complexity, integration and spirituality in practice.* Albany, NY: State University of New York Press.

29 Perry, W.G., Jr. (1970). *Forms of Intellectual and Ethical Development in the College Years.* NY: Holt, Rinehart and Winston.

30 The term often used to point to higher forms of thinking and cognition in adulthood is "postformal" and/or "postconventional" referring to stages of mental complexity that reach beyond Jean Piaget's highest stage of development titled "formal-operational thinking."

31 Basseches, M. (1984). *Dialectical Thinking and Adult Development*. Norwood, N.J.: Ablex. See the Dialectical Schemata Framework.

32 Basseches, M. (1984). *Dialectical Thinking and Adult Development*. Norwood, N.J.: Ablex.

33 Commons, M.L. & Richards, F.A. (1984). "A general model of stage theory." In M.L. Commons, F.A. Richards & C. Armon (Eds.), *Beyond formal operations: Vol. 1. Late adolescent and adult cognitive development* (pp. 120–140). New York: Praeger.

34 Commons, M.L. & Richards, F.A. (1984). "Applying the general stage model." In M.L. Commons, F.A. Richards & C. Armon (Eds.), *Beyond formal operations: Vol. 1. Late adolescent and adult cognitive development* (pp. 141–157). New York: Praeger.

35 Torbert, W. (1987). *Managing the Corporate Dream: Restructuring for long-term success.* Homewood, IL: Dow Jones-Irwin.

36 Torbert, W. (1991). *The Power of Balance: Transforming self, society and scientific inquiry.* Thousand Oaks, CA: Sage.

37 Torbert, W. (1994). "Cultivating Postformal Adult Development: Theory and practice." In M. Miller & S. Cook-Greuter (Eds.), *Transcendence and Mature Thought in Adulthood: The further reaches of adult development* (pp. 181-203). Lanham, MD: Rowman & Littlefield.

38 Koplowitz, H. (1984). "A projection beyond Piaget's formal operational stage: A general systems stage and a unitary stage." In M.L. Commons, F.A. Richards & C. Armon (Eds.), *Beyond Formal Operations* (pp. 279-295). New York: Praeger.

39 Cook-Greuter, S. (1999). *Postautonomous Ego Development: A study of its nature and measurement.* Integral Publishers.

To learn more about Cook-Greuter, her research, publications and consulting work, visit www.cook-greuter.com or www.verticaldevelopment.com.

40 O'Fallon, T. & Kramer, G. (1998). *Insight dialogue and insight dialogic inquiry.* Doctoral dissertation. San Francisco, CA: California Institute of Integral Studies. UMI Dissertation Services UMI #9824352.

41 Kegan, R. (2009). *Immunity to Change: How to overcome it and unlock potential in yourself and your organization.* Boston, MA: Harvard Business Press. p. 28.

42 Kegan, R. (1994). *In Over Our Heads: The mental demands of modern life.* Cambridge, MA: Harvard University Press. "The way they suspect rather than honor their sense of their own and each other's wholeness and distinctness." See p 311.

43 Kegan, R. (1994). *In Over Our Heads: The mental demands of modern life.* Cambridge, MA: Harvard University Press. p. 311.

44 Kegan, R. (1994). *In Over Our Heads: The mental demands of modern life.* Cambridge, MA: Harvard University Press. p. 330.

45 Kegan, R. (1994). *In Over Our Heads: The mental demands of modern life.* Cambridge, MA: Harvard University Press. p. 315.

46 Kegan, R. (1982). *The Evolving Self: Problem and process in human development.* Cambridge, MA: Harvard College.

47 Starr, A. & Torbert, B. (2005). "Timely and Transforming Leadership Inquiry and Action: Toward Triple-Loop Awareness." *Integral Review*, 1, pp. 85-97.

Another lens through which this greater engagement with the present moment can be found is in the concept of and research into triple-loop awareness, where an individual participates with an awareness that is distinct from mental thinking, physical sensing, as well as objects of perception of the environment. These different domains of experience (cognitive, interoceptive and environmental) are related to in an immediacy that is at once passionate, dispassionate, as well as compassionate.

48 Daniel Siegel (2007). The Mindful Brain: Reflection and Attunement in the Cultivation of Well-Being. NY, W.W. Norton & Company. pp. 78.

49 Kegan, R. (1994). *In Over Our Heads: The mental demands of modern life.* Cambridge, MA: Harvard University Press. p. 319.

50 Kegan, R. (1994). *In Over Our Heads: The mental demands of modern life.* Cambridge, MA: Harvard University Press. pp. 320-321.

51 Siegel, D. (2010). *The Mindful Therapist, A clinician's guide to mindsight and neural integration.* NY: W.W. Horton & Company.

52 Honderich, T. (2005). *The Oxford Companion to Philosophy, second edition.* Oxford, NY: Oxford University Press. pp. 670-671.

53 Kegan, R. (1982). *The Evolving Self: Problem and process in human development.* Cambridge, MA: Harvard College. Developmental stages, as we have explored them, also appear to oscillate between privileging or emphasizing masculine or separateness and feminine or connectedness. Kegan refers to this dynamic as a helix of evolutionary truces. In his model, Stages 1, 3 and 5 all favor inclusion, while Stages 2 and 4 favor independence. See p. 109 for a diagram and see Chapter 3: "The Constitutions of the Self," for a further exploration of this dynamic.

54 Siegel, D. (2010). *The Mindful Therapist, A clinician's guide to mindsight and neural integration.* New York: W.W. Norton & Company. p. 25.

55 Kegan, R. (1994). *In Over Our Heads: The mental demands of modern life.* Cambridge, MA: Harvard University Press. p. 19 in "Reconceiving the Challenge of Change."

56 Bradford, D.L. & Cohen, A.R. (1984). *Managing for Excellence, The leadership guide to developing high performance in contemporary organizations.* Hoboken, NJ, John Wiley & Sons. Inc.

57 Bradford, D.L. & Cohen, A.R. (1984). *Managing for Excellence, The leadership guide to developing high performance in contemporary organizations.* Hoboken, NJ, John Wiley & Sons. Inc.

58 Partial resolutions are a more complex way of understanding growth and progress. Resolution in its conventional understandings often circle around various assumptions of completeness and/or wholeness. Finding resolution is a driving force in the conventional adult mind; however, your larger maturity likely is suspicious of resolution as explored in the centrality of incompleteness and the Self-Transforming Mind outlined in Chapter Three. Resolutions are always partial. Part of the practice of the centrality of incompleteness is invested in finding the limits of a resolution such that subjectivity can stay in contact with the facets of experience that are unresolvable.

59 Wilber, K. (2006). *Integral Spirituality, A startling new role for religion in the modern and postmodern world.* Boston: Integral Books. See Appendix II: "Integral Post-Metaphysics." pp. 231-274.

60 Wilber, K. (1995). *Sex, Ecology, Spirituality, The spirit of evolution.* Boston: Shambhala.

61 Barbaras, R. (2008). "Life, Movement, and Desire" in *Research in Phenomenology,* 38(1), 3-17. p 14.

62 Barbaras, R. (2010). "Life and Exteriority" in *Enaction: Toward a New Paradigm for Cognitive Science,* eds. John Stewart, Olivier Gapenne, and Ezequiel A. DiPaolo. Cambridge, MA: MIT Press. p. 109.

63 Barbaras, R. (2008). "Life, Movement, and Desire" in *Research in Phenomenology,* 38(1), 3-17. p. 15.

64 Honderich, T. (Ed.) (2005). *The Oxford Companion to Philosophy,* second edition. New York: Oxford University Press Inc. p. 533.

65 Hamilton, Diane. (2012). Personal Communication, Dec. 5th, 2012.

66 Perhaps the leading curriculum around what I would call "elegant facilitation" can be found through Integral Facilitator. Developed by Diane Hamilton and Rebecca Colwell, their Integral Facilitation workshops provide some of the best instruction and guidance presently available. To learn more, visit: www.TenDirections.com.

67 Kegan, R. (1994). *In Over Our Heads: The mental demands of modern life.* Cambridge, MA: Harvard University Press. p. 313.

68 Handmark (2008). *Oxford Dictionary of Philosophy* (version 1.0.1) [mobile application software]. Retrieved from http://itunes.apple.com. See Heraclitus of Ephesus.

69 Zalta, E.N. (Ed.) (2011). *Stanford Dictionary of Philosophy* (version 1.0.1) [mobile application software]. Retrieved from http://itunes.apple.com. See Heraclitus.

70 Handmark (2008). *Oxford Dictionary of Philosophy* (version 1.0.1) [mobile application software]. Retrieved from http://itunes.apple.com. See Dialectic.

71 Right now we are using the polarity of conscious engagement and habituation to describe elegance, where elegance is, in some ways, not your habituated struggles. This is partly accurate and inaccurate. The integration of and inclusion of both habit and creative novelty will be explored at length in Chapter Ten. Given the dual nature of language, this contradictory elucidation appears to be unavoidable.

72 Cook-Greuter, S. (1999). *Postautonomous Ego Development: A study of its nature and measurement.* Integral Publishers. One example of postautonomous research illustrating this facet of the mind can be found in Cook-Greuter's research, in particular see 5/6 stage scoring protocols on pp. 74-75.

73 Wilber, K. (1995). *Sex, Ecology, Spirituality, The spirit of evolution.* Boston: Shambhala. Wilber's immensely influential Integral Philosophy leverages a model similar to the one diagramed here. Wilber's Quadrants integrate the polarities of interior and exterior and individual and collective in a massively clarifying map of human knowledge and experience, and this interrelationship between other polarities can be equally useful. To learn more about Wilber's Quadrants, explore his seminal work *Sex, Ecology, Spirituality.*

74 McNamara, Robert L. (2012). *Strength To Awaken, Make Strength Training Your Spiritual Practice and Find New Power and Purpose in Your Life.* Boulder, CO: Performance Integral.

75 Wilber, K. (1979). *No Boundary, Eastern and Western approaches to personal growth.* Boston: Shambhala.

76 Cook-Greuter, S. (1999). *Postautonomous Ego Development: A study of its nature and measurement.* Integral Publishers. "Post formal individuals commonly 'choose' to respond to some items at lower levels than they are capable of." p. 33.

77 Becker, E. (1973). *The Denial of Death.* NY: Free Press Paperbacks.

_78_ Becker, E. (1973). *The Denial of Death*. NY: Free Press Paperbacks. p. xiii.

_79_ Becker, E. (1973). *The Denial of Death*. NY: Free Press Paperbacks. p. 11.

_80_ Cook-Greuter, S. (2013). Personal Communication, February 14th, 2013.

_81_ Cook-Greuter, S. (2012). Retrieved from http://www.cook-greuter.com.

_82_ Loevinger, J. (1966). "The Meaning and Measurement of Ego-Development," *American Psychologist*, 21, pp. 195-206.

_83_ Cook-Greuter, S. (1999). *Postautonomous Ego Development: A study of its nature and measurement*. Integral Publishers. p. 50.

_84_ Cook-Greuter, S. (1999). *Postautonomous Ego Development: A study of its nature and measurement*. Integral Publishers.

_85_ Cook-Greuter, S. (1999). *Postautonomous Ego Development: A study of its nature and measurement*. Integral Publishers. p. 19.

_86_ Cook-Greuter, S. (1999). *Postautonomous Ego Development: A study of its nature and measurement*. Integral Publishers. p. 56.

"What something means depends on one's relative position in regard to it. This changes [what is] generally referred to as a systems view of reality. Although the objects themselves are still viewed as permanent, what they mean is now seen as constructed. Variables are seen as inevitably interdependent rather than independent, causality [is] experienced as cyclical rather than linear, and boundaries of objects are open and flexible rather than closed depending on one's definition of what is to be considered within a system or outside."

_87_ Cook-Greuter, S. (1999). *Postautonomous Ego Development: A study of its nature and measurement. Integral Publishers.* p. 55.

_88_ Cook-Greuter, S. (1999). *Postautonomous Ego Development: A study of its nature and measurement. Integral Publishers.* p. 55.

89 Cook-Greuter, S. (1999). *Postautonomous Ego Development: A study of its nature and measurement. Integral Publishers.* p. 56.

_90_ Cook-Greuter, S. (1999). *Postautonomous Ego Development: A study of its nature and measurement. Integral Publishers.* p. 61.

_91_ Cook-Greuter, S. (1999). *Postautonomous Ego Development: A study of its nature and measurement. Integral Publishers.* p. 60.

92 Cook-Greuter, S. (1999). *Postautonomous Ego Development: A study of its nature and measurement.* Integral Publishers. p. 63.

93 Cook-Greuter, S. (1999). *Postautonomous Ego Development: A study of its nature and measurement.* Integral Publishers. p. 75.

94 Cook-Greuter, S. (1999). *Postautonomous Ego Development: A study of its nature and measurement.* Integral Publishers. p. 11.

95 Cook-Greuter, S. (1999). *Postautonomous Ego Development: A study of its nature and measurement.* Integral Publishers. p. 78.

96 Wilber, Ken (2006). "Excerpt A: An integral age at the leading edge." Retrieved from www.kenwilber.com/Writings/PDF/ExcerptA_KOSMOS_2003.pdf.

97 Whitehead, A.N. (1978). *Process and Reality, An essay in cosmology, Gifford lectures delivered in the University of Edinburgh during the session 1927-28.* NY: Free Press. p. 28.

98 Cook-Greuter, S. (1999). *Postautonomous Ego Development: A study of its nature and measurement.* Integral Publishers. p. 63.

99 Cook-Greuter, S. (1999). *Postautonomous Ego Development: A study of its nature and measurement.* Integral Publishers. p. 33.

100 Cook-Greuter, S. (1999). *Postautonomous Ego Development: A study of its nature and measurement.* Integral Publishers. p. 70.

101 Cook-Greuter, S. (1999). *Postautonomous Ego Development: A study of its nature and measurement.* Integral Publishers. p. 78.

102 Cook-Greuter, S. (1999). *Postautonomous Ego Development: A study of its nature and measurement.* Integral Publishers. p. 83.

103 Cook-Greuter, S. (1999). *Postautonomous Ego Development: A study of its nature and measurement.* Integral Publishers. pp. 63-64.

104 Cook-Greuter, S. (2013). Personal Communication, February 14th, 2013.

105 Cook-Greuter, S. (1999). *Postautonomous Ego Development: A study of its nature and measurement.* Integral Publishers. p. 79.

106 Cook-Greuter, S. (1999). *Postautonomous Ego Development: A study of its nature and measurement.* Integral Publishers. p. 64.

107 Cook-Greuter, S. (1999). *Postautonomous Ego Development: A study of its nature and measurement.* Integral Publishers. pp. 62, 64.

108 Cook-Greuter, S. (1999). *Postautonomous Ego Development: A study of its nature and measurement.* Integral Publishers. p. 66.

109 Cook-Greuter, S. (1999). *Postautonomous Ego Development: A study of its nature and measurement.* Integral Publishers. p. 64.

110 Cook-Greuter, S. (1999). *Postautonomous Ego Development: A study of its nature and measurement.* Integral Publishers. p. 64.

111 Cook-Greuter, S. (1999). *Postautonomous Ego Development: A study of its nature and measurement.* Integral Publishers. p. 64.

112 Cook-Greuter, S. (1999). *Postautonomous Ego Development: A study of its nature and measurement.* Integral Publishers. p. 64.

113 Cook-Greuter, S. (1999). *Postautonomous Ego Development: A study of its nature and measurement.* Integral Publishers. p. 66.

114 Cook-Greuter, S. (1999). *Postautonomous Ego Development: A study of its nature and measurement.* Integral Publishers. p. 80.

115 Cook-Greuter, S. (1999). *Postautonomous Ego Development: A study of its nature and measurement.* Integral Publishers. p. 80.

116 Cook-Greuter, S. (1999). *Postautonomous Ego Development: A study of its nature and measurement.* Integral Publishers. p. 63.

117 Cook-Greuter, S. (1999). *Postautonomous Ego Development: A study of its nature and measurement.* Integral Publishers. p. 81.

118 Maslow, A.H. (1971). *The Further Reaches of Human Nature.* NY: Penguin Books. p. 111.

119 Cook-Greuter, S. (1999). *Postautonomous Ego Development: A study of its nature and measurement.* Integral Publishers. p. 82.

120 Symbols are themselves also part of the territory and not solely a representation of a reality that is, somehow, more real. However, when consciousness or subjectivity is fused with and embedded within the language habit, symbols can often leave the autonomous self trapped, leaving a desire for less isolated, more unmediated and more connected forms of experience.

121 Cook-Greuter, S. (1999). *Postautonomous Ego Development: A study of its nature and measurement.* Integral Publishers. p. 67.

To learn more about Cook-Greuter, her research, publications and consulting work, visit www.cook-greuter.com or www.verticaldevelopment.com.

122 McNamara, Robert, L. (2012). *Strength To Awaken, Make Strength Training Your Spiritual Practice and Find New Power and Purpose in Your Life.* Boulder, CO: Performance Integral. p. 167.

123 Infancy is an experiential immersion in the present moment, where the infant is ignorant of anything that is not directly present to his sensorimotor world. This is because the mind has yet to grow in its ability to hold past experiences and future possibilities. Without these reference points as a means of coping with dissonance, infants, left alone with major needs—whether they be food, touch or movement—are likely to reach an experiential intensity similar to what we as adults call annihilation quite easily. While our adult mind may not understand this worldview, we may presume that they have not been abandoned; however, the infant's experience is likely one of abandonment. For a more in-depth conversation of the mind of the infant, see Piaget's explanation of the sensorimotor stage of cognitive development, in particular the worldview prior to the establishment of object permanence.

124 This radical inclusion of your self-as-form often includes, integrates and embraces the facilities of exclusion, destruction and dismantling of that which is unworthy of persistence into and as immediacy.

125 The Nature Conservancy (2012). "Rainforests, Facts About Rainforests." Retrieved from www.nature.org/ourinitiatives/urgentissues/rainforests/rainforests-facts.xml.

126 The Nature Conservancy (2012). "Rainforests, Facts About Rainforests." Retrieved from www.nature.org/ourinitiatives/urgentissues/rainforests/rainforests-facts.xml.

127 NASA Earth Observatory (2012). "Fires along the Rio Xingu, Brazil." October 10, 2011. Retrieved from http://earthobservatory.nasa.gov/IOTD/view.php?id=71256.

128 Helfert, M.R. and K.P. Lulla (1990). "Mapping Continental-Scale Biomass Burning and Smoke Palls over the Amazon Basin as Observed from the Space Shuttle." *Photogrammetric Engineering and Remote Sensing*, 10(56), pp. 1367-1373.

129 An interpenetrating relationship with immediacy is not a facility that existed prior to the cultivation of autonomous, self-authoring functioning, as we have been exploring it. The romantic perspective that we need to "go back" to our more primitive roots, either in our collective evolution or our personal development, is not the utopia it is often made out to be. Development has not, by and large, gone in the wrong direction. Autonomy is actually a more refined and nuanced form of "clear-cutting" than its earlier pre-autonomous stages of development. However, given autonomy's increase in power and influence in the world, its impact can be more easily seen. Regardless, autonomous self-directing, self-regulative functioning is required as a facility of the interpenetrating self's larger competence in the world. Thus, autonomy left to its own devices appears to be immensely dangerous, complex and problematic; however, its subservient functioning to a larger intelligence appears to be required.

CPSIA information can be obtained
at www.ICGtesting.com
Printed in the USA
LVOW11*1345150318

569980LV00004B/10/P